PENGUIN BOOKS

GREAT BUYS FOR KIDS

Since 1972, Sue Goldstein has been the author of America's best-selling bargain shopping guidebooks, including *The Underground Shopper* and her most recent book, *Great Buys for People Over 50*. Value and getting your money's worth is her bargain "buyline." Called America's diva of discounts, she was born to shop at half-price out of necessity. Now she shops at half-price because she's smart. Since launching her publishing career, she has appeared on hundreds of talk shows—"Donahue," "Oprah," "Hour Magazine," "Good Morning America," "Real People," and "CBS News"—and has had countless newspaper and magazine articles written about her, which have appeared in everything from *Money* to *Newsweek*. She lives in a lakefront house outside Dallas with her two dogs and five cats. Her son, Josh, is a college student/photographer/TV grip and waiter in his spare time and is decorating his own apartment with the help of *Great Buys*.

SUE GOLDSTEIN

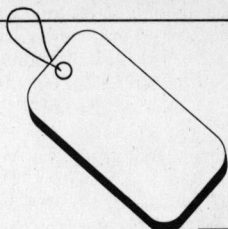

Great Buys

· FOR KIDS ·

PENGUIN BOOKS

PENGUIN BOOKS
Published by the Penguin Group
Viking Penguin, a division of Penguin Books USA Inc.,
375 Hudson Street, New York, New York 10014, U.S.A.
Penguin Books Ltd, 27 Wrights Lane,
London W8 5TZ, England
Penguin Books Australia Ltd, Ringwood,
Victoria, Australia
Penguin Books Canada Ltd, 10 Alcorn Avenue, Suite 300,
Toronto, Ontario, Canada M4V 3B2
Penguin Books (N.Z.) Ltd, 182–190 Wairau Road,
Auckland 10, New Zealand

Penguin Books Ltd, Registered Offices:
Harmondsworth, Middlesex, England

First published in Penguin Books 1992

1 3 5 7 9 10 8 6 4 2

Great Buys™ is a trademark of Money Business, Inc.

LIBRARY OF CONGRESS CATALOGING IN PUBLICATION DATA
Goldstein, Sue, 1941–
Great buys for kids / Sue Goldstein.
p.   cm.
ISBN 0 14 01.4781 0
1. Shopping—United States—Directories. 2. Children's
paraphernalia. I. Title.
TX336.G63   1992
380.1′45′0002573—dc20   91–43121

Printed in the United States of America

Set in Baskerville
Designed by Victoria Hartman

Here's looking at you, kid.
I love you, Josh.

Love is a boy by poets styled;
Then spare the rod, and spoil the child.

—Samuel Butler

Preface

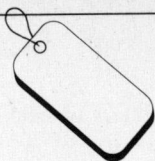

In the beginning, I wanted to be a mother. But first, I became a camp counselor. A teacher. A camp director. And then, a mother.

Josh was born in Phoenix, Arizona, on August 1, 1971, almost thirty years after I was born. And sixty years after my parents' birth. It seemed so perfect. The familiar continuation of the proverbial tree.

The baby bliss turned the corner. His teen years were a constant nightmare. I got a double dose of respect for parenting. Believe you me, there ought to be a law that requires every person considering bringing up a child to pass the course. It's no easy matter. And unfortunately, nobody can teach you how to do it right.

As he approaches his twentieth birthday, it seems to be easing up a bit. But it's still too early to tell, though it's never too late to recall the days when I shopped for him and he loved everything I bought.

Today, if he even accepts something I bought for him, I know enough of his demands to insure that it be all natural fiber, the pant legs be tapered to exact proportions, it not be trendy, and that it strictly make an understatement!

In the olden days, he loved his Oshkosh B'Goshes without reservation even if the straps kept falling off his shoulders. He never balked at his velveteen rompers or training wheels. He even ate fresh mushrooms and Gerber's baby food. And, too, he went everywhere with me to shop. Those were the good ole days.

Today's kids, like their mothers (and fathers, too), want it all. Only their parents want it for less.

So to that end, this book's for them. The best that money and time and information can buy. So who said, "You can't buy love"?

Welcome to the wonderful world of *Great Buys for Kids*!

Acknowledgments

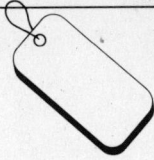

Another book. Another dollar. Another list of credits, where credit is due.

To my agent, Jane Dystel, who takes my ideas and runs with them.

To Lori Lipsky, my editor, who fortunately channeled those ideas into this, the second in the *Great Buys* series.

To my office helpers who corrected all my last-minute changes right up until Federal Express rang the doorbell. To Steve Walker, who worked the red pencil with much aplomb.

And to Cheryl Miller, who, like Truman, rose to the occasion when the assignment was issued and organized this mess! She even learned the computer in the process.

My sincerest thanks to all of the above and to the many unsung heroes who helped shape this fun-filled project.

And finally, to my dad, Bill Elkin, to whom *Great Buys for People Over 50* was dedicated and who, once again, needs to get the credit for fostering in me an amazing amount of energy and love when the subject of shopping comes up. He's the best any kid could have hoped for. And, lest I forget, Marion Altman, who has joined my dad in always looking for Great Buys wherever they go.

Contents

Introduction

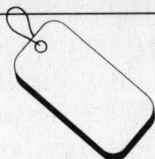

In 1910 my parents were born. Thirty-one years later, my breech birth was recorded. No doubt, pain is born in every generation and now my son, born thirty years after me, will face his future children with a No Pain, All Gain marketplace.

With the prevailing state of the economy, getting your money's worth within the serious time constraints of today's busy parents, the quality, the price, the convenience of ordering an item or service will be paramount.

When I was growing up in the 1950s, my parents were like all parents, wanting the best for their children. From piano lessons to camp, ribbons that matched my dress to the one good dress bought at Saks Fifth Avenue, on sale. Today's parents are concerned about lots more, including the big issue of education. In the '90s, it will be crucial for every kid's survival to know as much as he/she can. Technological advances will be commonplace to them. Though they may all want them, maybe even all know how to use them, will they be able to afford them? Can life be memorable without the microwave, the VCR, the computer, the CD player, the 4-wheel drive, or Nintendo?

The days of having one nice dress and wearing it to death are over. Kids are as conscious of fashion and labels as ever before. One dress will never do. And paying full price for the toy, the trip, or a think-tank seminar is *verboten*. Parents will have to know the rules of getting the best for less in order to be able to provide all the accoutrements. From children's cradles, to crayons, to college, pay attention, mom and dad, your kids will want, expect, deserve the very best. Now, it's up to you to know how, when, and most importantly *where* to get it, and hopefully get your money's worth.

Never in American history have there been so many opportunities to grab a bargain. Not that Americans haven't made smart purchases in the past. Buying Manhattan Island for $24 in beads and trinkets, securing the Louisiana Purchase from France, or acquiring Alaska from Russia all come to mind as pretty savvy buys. Americans have always appreciated a bargain. But those were real estate deals (and there aren't too many of those left!).

Fortunately, there are still deals left in clothing, furniture, electronics . . . all sorts of things with the ease of shopping-by-phone or bargaineering through the catalogs.

With the current state of the economy, today's pressed-for-time and shrinking budgets, coupled with the unprecendented changes occurring in retailing (like the elimination of the middleman), it's no wonder there are so many dedicated shoppers who have become "armchair bandits"!

Attention, shoppers (kids, parents, teachers, and other interested grown-ups), let us know how you fared.

For comments or your recommendations for future editions, see the section titled "Reader Feedback" (page xxv).

Happy shopping!

Notes to the Shopper

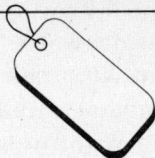

PAYMENT PLAN

It is recommended to shop by mail or phone with the use of a credit card. NEVER SEND CASH. If paying by personal check, merchants often will delay shipment until the check has cleared. Therefore, it pays to shop with your credit card for speed in delivery. AND if there is a problem, the credit card company will probably go to bat for you.

Some firms will accept COD (cash on delivery). Firms that accept COD payments usually qualify that with some type of restriction, such as a 25 percent deposit. When you order COD, know that this means CASH ($$$$) on delivery. If you expect to receive your order and pay by check, you will probably be disappointed. The seller will most likely require some form of "safe" payment.

CATALOGS

In each listing, where applicable, we've told you if there is a catalog, brochure, price list, etc., and if there is a fee charged. If it says "refundable" after the fee, that means the price will be deducted from your first order, or coupons for that dollar amount will be issued toward a purchase. The charges are usually small (if anything), only to cover postage and handling, and to discourage catalog lookers who aren't shoppers. A brochure is smaller than a catalog and often folds out. For our purposes, a brochure is eight pages or less. A flier is usually one or two pages. And a price list is just that.

PQ (PRICE QUOTES)

Price quotes are given by phone or by mail. If calling in for one, be sure to have the make, manufacturer's name, model number, description—whatever exact information will enable the merchant to give you an "apple-to-apple" price of what he charges. Be sure you know what the retail price is. It helps determine how great a buy you're getting. And, too, be sure to ask if the price quote includes delivery. If not, ask them to break out the delivery charges, if known. It's easy to shop by phone with your credit card. Most outlets will ship to your front door if an on-site visit is out of the question. A few won't, but we've listed them because of their popularity with both kids and their parents.

SASE

Any time you see SASE, you should send a self-addressed stamped business-size (number 10) envelope. Sometimes it is requested that you send two first-class stamps. Follow the instructions, please.

FAX

The facsimile machine facilitates your order by placing it within seconds. For those with a fax machine, it means instant gratification.

OTHER SYMBOLS USED

ISBN stands for International Standard Book Number—a number used as a form of reference for easy identification. You'll see it beside a book and publisher name. It makes for easier identification when ordering from the bookseller.

TDD refers to Telecommunications Device for the Deaf.

It appears beside the phone number for those calling from a TDD telephone.

LAST-MINUTE THOUGHTS

OUTLET and OFF-PRICE CHAINS. When referring to an outlet or an off-price chain, the corporate office was generally given as a place to call or write for location nearest you since some chains have hundreds of locations. It is advisable, however, to check your telephone directory and directory assistance for that information before calling the corporate number.

Furthermore, it is always recommended before making a trip to any of the stores to check ahead and verify all the information. And new locations are always popping up; there might even be one closer to home.

Outlet towns and outlet stores are a destination location all to themselves. Combining a family trip with shopping the outlet stores should be considered when vacation time rolls around.

Chain and outlet stores may also be amenable to orders by phone. Many outlets and discount chains, with a credit card, are all too happy to tell you what they've got and the price, and will add the customary shipping charges for the opportunity to make the sale. A few, however, know that in doing so, it will anger their full retail accounts and will insist you drive to their physical location to retrieve your bargain. It never hurts to ask!

ONE-OF-A-KIND

Some one-of-a-kind entries are mentioned because they are so unique, and a call for more information may lead to establishing a similar operation closer to home. In other instances, the entry was unique, hand-crafted, a time-saver, or just downright appealing, but not necessarily the lowest priced kid on the block.

800 NUMBERS

Note: We did not put a number 1 before dialing for bargains long-distance or before the toll-free 800 number. However, you must dial a 1. You will be disappointed to learn that many of the best money-saving furniture resources in North Carolina have been pressured into eliminating their 800 numbers because they were discounting. Well, we didn't say it was going to be easy. Still, even with the price of a phone call, you'll be saving hundreds, if not thousands.

PRICES

Remember, prices are quoted to give you a feel for the listing's pricing, reflecting the percentage, if applicable, off retail. Do not expect to see that exact item and dollar amount when you order the latest catalog or receive the most current price.

APOLOGIES FOR GOOFS

We admit it ahead of time. We know there are probably mistakes in the book. We hope there are only a few. In spite of what we think are Herculean efforts to tell it like it is with editors, proofreaders, and fact-checkers double-, even triple-checking every step of the way, we still find transposed numbers and misspelled words. And, too, there are probably a few retailers who, by the time you shop them, have closed their doors for good or fallen far from the madding crowd. Please forgive us. And let us know where we have strayed.

Tips for Ordering by Mail

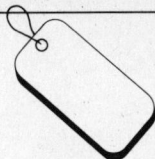

- *Never send cash*; order by check, money order, or credit card.
- Find out the company's policy on warranties, exchanges, and refunds.
- Keep a record of your order: name of company, address, telephone number, date of order, copy of advertisement.
- Know shipping charges.
- Orders (unless otherwise stated) must be shipped within 30 days of receipt of your order. If there is going to be a delay, the company must notify you.
- You are not required to pay for anything you did not order. Write "Refused" on the package and send it back (no postage needed).
- Complaints or questions regarding warranty policy, misrepresentation, or fraud? Contact:

  Postmaster or Chief Postal Inspector
  U.S. Postal Service
  Room 3517
  Washington, DC 20260
  202-245-5445

- Question or complaints about unordered merchandise or delay of your order? Contact:

Consumer Inquiries
Federal Trade Commission
Washington, DC 20580
202-523-3598

Complaints

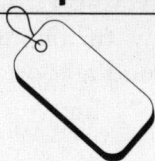

So you've got a problem. After attempts at resolution with the merchant in question and after you've correctly followed the procedures for complaints covered in the catalog, brochure, or by phone, you can seek outside counsel. If you've written or spoken to the company first and still aren't satisfied, you can turn to the following agencies. (It is a good idea to include all of your correspondence and photocopies of the documentation when seeking help.)

BETTER BUSINESS BUREAU (BBB): Always check with the local BBB *before* ordering from a mail-order company. This local BBB is in the area where the company resides, not *your* hometown. If you send a SASE to the Council of Better Business Bureaus, Inc., 1515 Wilson Blvd., Arlington, VA 21209, you will receive a directory of BBB offices. Though the BBBs are funded by the participating businesses, they do maintain files on firms, help resolve consumer complaints, and provide an overview on the firm's selling history. That way, if a firm has 100 unresolved complaints on file, chances are they're not a good bet.

CONSUMER ACTION PANELS (CAPs): These are third-party dispute resolution programs established by the industries they represent. For example, for a problem with a major appliance, you can write MACAP (Major Appliance Consumer Action Panel), 10 North Wacker Drive, Chicago, IL 60606 or call 800-621-0477. For help with other industries, consult a standard reference source in the public library called *Encyclopedia of Associations*.

DIRECT MARKETING ASSOCIATION (DMA): This is the trade association for mail-order merchants and direct-marketing companies. Its Mail Order Action Line (MOAL) helps resolve nondelivery problems with a mail or direct marketer. To get help, send a copy of your complaint letter and documentation to:

> Mail Order Action Line
> DMA
> 6 East 43rd St.
> New York, NY 10017

You may also get your name added to or removed from mailing lists through the DMS's Mail Preference Service. Write to the DMA at the address above to receive the "MPS" form.

FEDERAL TRADE COMMISSION (FTC): Though this law-enforcement agency does not act on individual complaints, every letter helps build a case. The Fair Credit Billing Act (FCVA) of 1975 offers mail-order shoppers who use credit cards some leverage if there's a problem of nondelivery. Disputes regarding the quality of goods or services are also covered but this coverage varies from state to state. It's best to contact your local consumer protection agency for clarification before proceeding to the federal level.

UNITED STATES POSTAL SERVICE (USPS): Probably the most effective of all the agencies; their track record of resolution is almost 85 percent. Send a copy of your final complaint letter and documentation to:

> Chief Postal Inspector
> U.S. Postal Service
> Washington, DC 20260

Contacting the local postmaster nearest the firm in question is often quicker.

Reader Feedback

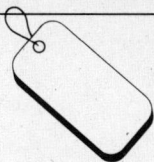

We'd like to hear from you! Comments, both good and bad, help shape our next edition and other books in the *Great Buys* series. Of course, we'd like to hear from you, our readers, and from merchants who would like to be listed.

If you've had a problem, and fail to resolve it with the merchant directly, don't hesitate to state your case to us, c/o

> GREAT BUYS
> 8117 Preston Rd., Suite 100
> Dallas, TX 75225

Be sure to include all the pertinent information and *copies* of any documentation relating to the transaction and what you would like done. Don't forget, too, to give your name, address, and your daytime phone number.

GREAT BUYS FOR KIDS

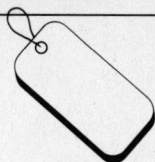

APPAREL

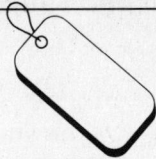

Children

AFTER THE STORK
1501 12th St. NW
Albuquerque, NM 87104
800-333-5347; 505-243-9100 (NM)
Catalog (full-color)

After the stork has paid his visit, there's still no rest for the weary. Now comes the fun, and the never-ending spending. It's nice to know that someone's out there producing durable, versatile, attractive clothes for kids at affordable prices. Buying children's wear in bulk allows them to pass the savings on to you. Coordinates for boys and girls come in cotton for comfort, rugged denim, knits, and fleece, and are practical for play or school. And there's not a Plain Jane (or Wayne) in sight. Bright, cheerful prints appeal to kids and parents alike. You'll find all the basics, top to bottom, from underwear to overalls. Value is their middle name when it comes to colorful cotton clothing from birth to age 14. Absolute satisfaction guaranteed. Call or write for free catalog.

BABY CLOTHES WHOLESALE
70 Ethel Rd. West
Piscataway, NJ 08854
908-572-9520
Catalog (full-color) $2.95; brochure free

Baby Clothes Wholesale offers a gargantuan selection of boys' and girls' clothing, size newborn to 7 years, at prices that are 50 percent off retail. Their 52-page, full-color catalog is just $2.95 and loaded with year-round values. If you choose not to spring for the catalog, send a SASE (business size—#10—envelope) and they'll send you the latest full-color brochure free, with information on the merchandise and the catalog.

CARTER'S CHILDRENSWEAR
Corporate Office: 1000 Bridgeport Ave.
Shelton, CT 06484
203-926-5000

If you thought Carter's just made liver pills, wrong! This is your prescription to revive even the most tired of children's wardrobes. Over 100 years old, this veteran of the kids' biz is famous for their full-line of sleepwear, playwear, underwear, and layette items. Sizes newborn to 14, they produce equal numbers of boys' and girls' clothing. Savings in the 20–30 percent range in first-quality items through their outlet stores, escalating to even greater discounts as the season wanes. Over 50 outlets in the U.S. from Alabama to Washington including Boaz, AL; Pacific Grove, CA; Rehoboth Beach, DE; Ft. Walton and Sun Rise, FL; Lake Park, GA; St. Charles, IL; Fremont and Michigan City, IN; Freeport and Kittery, ME; Chester and Ocean City, MD; Fall River and Sagamore, MA; Birch Run, Holland, Monroe, and Traverse City, MI; Branson and Osage Beach, MO;

Budd Lake, Flemington, and Matawan, NJ; Ballston Spa, Central Valley, Lake George, and Monticello, NY; Burlington, NC; Aurora, Brunswick, and Monroe, OH; Lincoln City, OR; Lancaster, Reading, Somerset, Tannersville, and Wyomissing, PA; Myrtle Beach, SC; Murfreesboro and Pigeon Forge, TN; New Braunfels, TX; Draper and Salt Lake City, UT; Brattleboro, VT; Lightfoot and Prince William, VA; Centralia and Tacoma, WA; Martinsburg, WV; Kenosha, WI.

THE CHILDREN'S PLACE
Corporate Office: 25 Riverside Dr.
Pinebrook, NJ 07058
201-227-8900

There's no place like the Children's Place for bargains with styles ranging from infant to size 14. Discounts of at least 20 percent on such brands as On-Track, French Coast, Raindrops, Rob Roy, Buster Brown, Jordache, Bear Tree, Blue Duck, and Fame. Stores have carpeted play areas and video screens for keeping kids occupied! 160 stores. Check directory for one nearest you.

CHOCOLATE SOUP
Corporate Office: 6515 Railroad St.
Raytown, MO 64133
816-356-8080

Scoop up a spoonful from this popular manufacturer of children's fashions. Stir the savings of 30 percent to 40 percent off comparable looks found in department and specialty stores. It's good 'til the last drop, especially if you want darling clothes, some appliquéd, some with brother-sister matching outfits, and all dressed to fit the bill. Other lines alongside Chocolate Soup include Boston Traders, Schwab, Calabash, and other famous brands discounted 20 percent. Fourteen stores. Call or write to see if there's one near you.

DANSKIN
Corporate Office: P.O. Box M-16
York, PA 17405
717-846-4874

Start paying peanuts for Danskin and Dance France bodywear, tights, and sportswear, Pennaco hosiery for girls and gals, and Givenchy, too, and shell out 30 percent–70 percent less than retail price. Get a leg up on the competition by kicking full prices out the door, in person or by phone: Foley, AL; Orlando, FL; W. Frankfort, IL; Story City, IA; Tupelo, MS; Nebraska City, NE; North Conway, NH; Niagara Falls, NY; York and Wyomissing, PA; Buffton and Hilton Head, SC; Crossville and Lakeland, TN; San Marcos, TX; Draper, VT.

EAGLE'S EYE
Corporate Office: 1001 Washington St.
Conshohocken, PA 19428
215-941-3700

All Eagle Eyes point to the direction of saving money. And this ladies' and children's wear manufacturer supplies overruns and irregular sportswear to their 14 outlets at 40–60 percent off retail. Visit or shop by phone in Boaz and Foley, AL; Rehoboth Beach, DE; Michigan City, IN; Kittery, ME; New Bedford, MA; Birch Run, MI; Stone Harbor, NJ; Burlington, NC; Conshohocken and Philadelphia, PA; Pigeon Forge, TN; Martinsburg, WV.

ESPRIT
Corporate Office: 499 Illinois St.
San Francisco, CA 94107
415-648-6900

Join the corps of dedicated outlet shoppers and save up to
40 percent on this popular California manufacturer's trendy
kids' and moms' sportswear and accessories. Visit Esprit in
person, or shop by phone from their outlet stores, located
in Boulder, CO; Palm Springs and San Francisco, CA; Dallas,
TX; and New Orleans, LA.

GAPKIDS/BABYGAP
Corporate Office: 1 Harrison St.
San Francisco, CA 94105

Closing the gap betwen generations who grew up with The
Gap has spawned a new age of Gap shoppers. Moms, pay
attention. This store's for kids. And babies, too. Made
expressly for The Gap stores, the prices are downright
affordable. Sale racks are downright cheap. From darling
overalls and jeans to tops and tees, you can practically tee
for two for the price of one. Call a Gap store for location
nearest you or send SASE to corporate office, attention Public
Relations.

GITANO KIDS FACTORY STORES
Corporate Office: 250 Carter Dr.
Edison, NJ 08817
201-248-1220

Hop aboard the Gitano train if you want to blow the whistle
on high prices. Stop first at their kids' factory outlets for
children's casual and active sportswear and accessories with
the names of Gitano, Gitano Kids, E.J. Gitano, Linea Gitano,
and Emporio Gitano at 20–50 percent off. Locations include

Boaz, AL; Birch Run, MI; Valley Stream, NY; Waynesboro and Williamsburg, VA. Then, it's off to the Gitano Warehouse Clearance Centers if you want more (including men's, women's, and children's) casual and active sportswear and accessories at 30–70 percent off. Some of the locations for their clearance centers include Monroeville, AL; Tampa, FL; Byron and Savannah, GA; Eddyville, KY; Wentzville, MO; Smithfield, NC; Reading, PA; and Lakeland, TN.

HANNA ANDERSSON
1010 NW Flanders St.
Portland, OR 97209
800-222-0544; 800-346-6040 (from Canada)
503-222-0544 (fax)
Catalog (full-color)

From colorful cardigans to pastel pinafores, having a Hanna in your closet is like having manna from heaven. This children's clothing line (some women's and maternity, too) is Swedish by birth and is bright, bold, beautiful, and a bargain. Their outlet stores, by the way, are in Portland, Oregon, and are the next best thing to heaven if you are in the area. And listen to this offer (bet you can't refuse): If you return your "Hannadowns" in good condition, they'll be donated to recognized charities and you'll receive a 20 percent credit of the purchase price, which can be applied to any item in the catalog. Ships worldwide via Parcel Post or UPS. Satisfaction guaranteed.

JACK & JILL CLOTHING
6401 E. Rogers Circle, Suite 12
Boca Raton, FL 33487
800-226-JANJ; 800-881-5455

Attention, baby boomers! Be your own boss! Jack & Jill Clothing provides an opportunity for profits by selling quality children's apparel at, or below, wholesale. That, in turn, enables you to sell for 25 percent below retail and still realize a substantial profit. You make a profit and your customer gets a great deal. Terrific opportunity for moms while getting children's clothing at bargain prices. Every piece of Jack & Jill clothing has the regular list price tagged on the garment so the customer will immediately see the savings. Clothing for school, play, or fashion. Top names at bottom prices. Proudly donates 10 percent of profits to Children's Defense Fund. Call for information-packed free brochure. Minimum order $250.

JOHNSTON FASHIONS FOR CHILDREN
Corporate Office: P.O. Box 310
220 N. Ballard
Wylie, TX 75098
214-442-2211

Designer duds have been Johnston's signature for upwardly mobile children for years. Stellar performers include Betti Terrel, Fischel, Mrs. Takis Kids, and Petite Gamine seen at retail prices at better specialty stores and boutiques around the country. Their outlet stores will save you 40–60 percent. Visit or shop by phone at Monroe, MI; New Braunfels, San Benito, Sulphur Springs, and Wylie, TX; Slidell, LA; Oshkosh, WI; Cabazon, CA.

JOLENE COMPANY
Corporate Office: 1050 W. 350 South, P.O. Box 1446
Provo, UT 84603
801-373-3206

This children's factory outlet store division houses the Jolene label which is a major little girls' dress manufacturer seen at chain and department stores nationwide. Their outlets also sell other brands such as Happy Kids and Tom Sawyer with discounts usually ranging from 20 percent to 70 percent for first-quality items, closeouts, overruns, and seconds. Outlets in Pocatello, ID; Provo and Salt Lake City, UT; Kenosha, WI; Vancouver, BC. Shop in person or by phone.

JUST FOR KIDS!
P.O. Box 29141
Shawnee, KS 66201-9141
800-654-6963
913-752-1095 (fax)
Catalog

This 56-page color catalog is Just for Kids! Great clothes. Great toys. Great fun is their buy-line. And for starters, don't rule out the ruler strap shoes for $12, the ruler barrette for $8, or the pencil jogging outfits for $22.50. Then try on the floral-appliquéd pant sets, the sweetheart jumpsuits, the sugar-and-spice denim coveralls, or the denim splash hi-tops. Superman, Teenage Mutant Ninja Turtles, and Barbie are sandwiched between the covers of this one-stop shopping cart. Dolls, toys, videos, room organizers, carry-alls, costumes for Halloween, bed and bath ensembles, professional outfits like firefighting and camouflage gear, art supplies, glitter pens and magic sticker art, sports equipment and outdoor accessories would make most kids jump for joy.

KARIN AND JOHN
525 South Raymond Ave.
Pasadena, CA 91105
800-626-9600
Catalog (full-color)

KARIN AND JOHN invite you to shop for quality children's clothing from their catalog. These are fashions with easy-to-live-with prices. You'll find an exciting collection of 100-percent cotton clothing for boys and girls (from newborn to

KARITAS
800-292-2272

This Denver-based organization is headed by President Bush's daughter-in-law Sharon Bush. It produces a clothing line and a stuffed bear sold by Gund, with all proceeds going toward funding organizations for homeless children.

size 6) with an emphasis on the kind of durability you'd expect from brands like Fix of Sweden and Mixi. In addition, they offer a selection of children's accessories. If not absolutely thrilled, simply return the purchase within 30 days for a quick and courteous refund. Mon.–Sat. 7:00 A.M. to 7:00 P.M. (PST). Ships within 24 hours of order. Gift certificates and gift wrapping available.

KIDS AT LARGE, INC.
Building 32, Endicott St., Dept. 900
Norwood, MA 02062
617-769-8575
617-255-0761 (fax)
Catalog

Having fits over finding clothes for hard-to-fit kids? Chubby children have always had it rough. Not any more. Kids at Large offers fun and fashionable clothing for the overweight and larger child, at last, for less. The only company in the U.S. that makes clothes exclusively for overweight children, this strictly-mail-order business features stylish, contemporary clothing for kids who long to look just as "trendy" as their slimmer counterparts. The catalog is chock-full of everything from acid-washed jeans and long-waisted dresses to funky neon shorts. G-r-e-a-t clothing for an equally g-r-e-a-t self-image. Shipping via UPS within 48 hours of placing order.

KIDS MART (THE LITTLE FOLK SHOP)
(division of Woolworth Company)
Corporate Office: P.O. Box 8020
City of Industry, CA 91748
818-965-4022

Get smart! Shop at Kids Mart, this off-price division of the Woolworth Company. No nickel and diming you to death, however. Get your money's worth with labels like Swat, Fame, Levi's, Britannia, Our Gang, Goodland, Health-Tex, Trimfit, Ocean Pacific, Candlestick, Sergio Valente, and Our Girl. Prices are an average of 30 percent below comparable retail, with some sale items reduced up to 80 percent. Sizes: infants and toddlers; boys 4 to 7 and 8 to 14; girls 4 to 6X and 7-14. Four hundred thirty stores nationwide.

KIDS 'Я' US
Corporate Office: 461 From Rd.
Paramus, NJ 07652
201-262-7800

A spin-off of the highly successful Toys 'Я' Us stores, they are in the circle of winning concepts. You can play your own wheel of fortune even if the arrow points to zero. Count the savings on some of the best for your kids. Shop 'til you drop a bundle here on stylish and discounted brands such as Oshkosh B'Gosh, Carter's, Buster Brown, and Jet Set (and these are bargains not to kid about!). Rapidly expanding, this chain is likely to be around when the kids are grown-ups. Almost 200 stores to date.

K.I.D.S. (KIDS IN DISTRESSED SITUATIONS)
Two Greentree Centre, Suite 225
P.O. Box 955
Marlton, NJ 08053

The fine art of giving is finely tuned with this organization, which gives to children in need. K.I.D.S. is a coalition of children's retailers and manufacturers like Buster Brown, Oshkosh B'Gosh, Carter's, J.C. Penney, and Kids 'Я' Us who donate clothing, toys, and other juvenile products to needy kids worldwide. Write for more information if you'd like to get involved.

MULTIPLES/INLOOK OUTLET
Corporate Office: 1240 Titan Dr.
Dallas, TX 75247
214-637-5300

Multiply the savings by shopping this manufacturer of mix-and-match modular interlock clothing. Women and girls can create entire wardrobes with one-stop shopping either by phone or at the Multiples outlet nearest you: Foley, AL; San Diego, CA; Commerce, GA; Michigan City, IN; Slidell, LA; Kittery, ME; Monroe, MI; Blowing Rock, NC; Myrtle Beach, SC; Dallas, New Braunfels, and LaMarque, TX; and Kenosha, WI.

POLLY FLINDERS FACTORY STORES
Corporate Office: 224 E. 8th St.
Cincinnati, OH 45202
513-721-7020

Good golly, Miss Polly. This Flinders is strictly for the girls. All sizes, all frills, all waiting for the first pageant call. Their outlet stores carry all first-quality overruns and cancellations, with savings up to 75 percent. Some irregulars, so shop carefully. Their hand-smocked dresses are a must for every girl. Underwear and sportswear, too! Call or write for outlet (33 stores in all) nearest you.

ONE AT A TIME
3313 Grandview
San Angelo, TX 76904
915-949-6788; 817-692-0895
Brochure

Take one day at a time but you won't be able to buy just one at a time. Jewelry designer Leslie Reeves creates intricate, one-of-a-kind jewelry for children and youth. The brochure gives only a sampling of her work so the possibilities are endless, and custom orders are welcome. Guatemalan "worry dolls," ceramic fruit and vegetables, ribbons, baskets, and chains woven into necklaces, so not to worry. She also designs hair clips, earrings, pins, and hatbands, as well as hand-painted T-shirts in southwestern motifs complete with coyotes, cacti, and chili. Items are available in stores, but you'll save 30–35 percent by ordering direct. When care instructions are followed, all items are guaranteed. Allow 2 weeks UPS delivery; $4 shipping and handling.

OSHKOSH B'GOSH
Olsen Mill Direct
800-537-4979
Catalog

Button up and fly right when the time comes to the all-American cover-up. Oshkosh B'Gosh is it. Golly gee, both guys and gals (from baby to school age) can get their overalls without leaving home via this free quarterly catalog that is mostly—you guessed it—Oshkosh B'Gosh. If you need to reach out and touch one, visit any of their outlet stores (call 414-231-8800 for location nearest you).

THE R. DUCK COMPANY
650 Ward Dr., Suite H
Santa Barbara, CA 93111
800-422-DUCK; 805-964-4343 (CA)
Catalog

Leakproof colored pants are everything they're "quacked" up to be. These are the original Rubber Duckie pull-on pants, now offered in the convenient Velcro-closing "Wrap Up" versions as well. Nylon binding leaves no telltale red marks on little legs. The "Wrap Up" comes in bright, snappy colors and, for more exotic skins, the "Jungle Wraps" are anything but tame! R. Duck Company also offers windbreaker/rain jackets, rain boots, rain pants, and rain capes (keeps baby dry even when it rains buckets). Everything your little one needs to face the "fowl" weather. Call or write for free catalog.

SEARS/KIDVANTAGE
Fierce competition in the children's apparel business prompted Sears to fight back with two programs sure to please parents' pocketbooks. Its KidVantage WearOut Warranty is a pretty liberal policy of replacing an item of clothing that is deemed to be "worn out." According to Sears, that means if an item is deemed by the customer to be worn out (for example, around the knees) before its time and the child is still wearing the *same size,* regardless of what brand it is, Sears will replace it with the same (or comparable value) item. No questions asked! Another program modeled after

the success and loyalty of airline frequent fliers is called KidVantage Frequent Purchase Program where the more you buy, the more you save. For example, spend $50 and you get a 10 percent discount. Spend $100, and the discount is 15 percent and applies to any item in the kids' store.

SMALL FRY
CHILDREN'S SAMPLE SHOP
330 Sunset
Denton, TX 76201
817-387-9915
PQ

There's nothing small about this kids' shop near big D. They'll get 'em covered at a whole lot less in brands from out-of-this-world manufacturers and designers. Boys and girls from infants to preteens will love 'em and never leave 'em until they've outgrown 'em. Shop by phone and save from 30 percent to 50 percent on items from their inventory that's stacked a mile high. Call for a price quote or write giving size and budgetary considerations and leave the shipping to them. Since 1969, this mini-mecca is considered one of the best-kept shopping secrets in America. Brands are cloaked in secrecy so as to not offend the boutiques and department stores of America.

STARBABY
Warehouse Row
1110 Market St.
Chattanooga, TN 37401
615-265-7552

Visit this California manufacturer's outlet for all-cotton children's clothing. Located in a restored warehouse in

STREETHEARTS INC.
Wichita, KS
800-735-3246

For every doll that finds a home here, $5 is donated to the Salvation Army programs that aid homeless children. That way, children who are more fortunate are sharing their good fortune with a child who's not.

downtown Chattanooga, along with other designer factory outlets like Ralph Lauren and I.B. Diffusion, you can expect this outlet chain to be a star performer as they spread their wings across the country. Locations of outlets to date include City of Commerce, Los Angeles, San Ysidro, and Vacaville, CA; Sarasota and Sunrise, FL; Raleigh-Durham, NC; Troutdale, OR; and San Marcos, TX. Permission in writing is requested before they will allow a credit card order to be fulfilled by phone. Just write to one of their outlets to authorize a purchase in advance. Save up to 50 percent on darling children's clothing.

SULTRA (CAMP BEVERLY HILLS)
Corporate Office: Sultra Corporation
462 Seventh Ave., 17th Floor
New York, NY 10018
212-967-5980

Can't afford to send your kids to Beverly Hills? Well, send them for Camp Beverly Hills clothes instead; it's cheaper than a trip down Rodeo Drive. Detour to Camp Beverly Hills outlet stores either in person or by phone and save up to 50 percent. All first-quality, and only in New York, in Saratoga and Central Valley at Woodbury Commons (914-928-2507).

WALT DISNEY CATALOG, INC.
One Disney Drive
P.O. Box 29144
Shawnee Mission, KS 66201-9144
800-237-5751 (orders)
913-752-1000 (customer service)
913-752-1095 (fax)
Catalog (full-color, free)

DISNEY/KIDS catalog is jam-packed with a dizzying array of clothing, playthings, and collectibles designed especially for children and available exclusively through the Disney Stores or catalog. Favorite characters come alive across the T-shirt or beach towel. Say hello to Mickey and Minnie or the Little Mermaid, fly off with Peter Pan, join the cast of *The Jungle Book*, or whistle while you work with one of the Seven Dwarfs. Turn the pages of history that have brought millions of smiles to kids of all ages.

WOODEN SOLDIER
Kearsarge St.
North Conway, NH 03860
603-346-7041; 603-356-6243 (customer service)
603-356-3530 (fax)
Catalog (full-color)

March right into a wonderland of perfection in children's clothing. An exceptional selection of classic traditional and graceful Victorian-style clothing and playful sportswear designed to tickle any child's fancy. A unique offering is their mother-child's coordinated collection—matching ensembles for formal or casual dressing. Clothing with a freshness of spirit and attention to detail, design, and quality. Toys, too! Ships via UPS. Offers overnight delivery and gift wrapping. Free catalog.

Family

AMERICAN T-SHIRTS
1228 Scyene Rd.
Mesquite, TX 75149
800-782-0214

There's nothing more un-American than paying full price for . . . anything! If you hand-paint or silk-screen T-shirts, isn't it about time you paid peanuts for your Picasso projects? Here, Hanes white T-shirts only, in sizes small, medium, large, and extra-large were $2.55; light colors $3.09; dark colors $3.32. Matching leggings in white were $6.49. Now price them in department stores and you'll see why we're so proud to be American fans.

BENETTON
Corporate Office: 343 W. Erie #330
Chicago, IL 60610
312-337-0283

Color their retail clearance stores green with your savings on Benetton's kids' sportswear, jeans, overalls, sweaters, and more, all considered "factory seconds." They will ship you an item from their outlet stores; just don't expect the color of choice to always be available and be aware that there might be a flaw (though generally it won't be discernible). Clearance stores are located in Appleton and Kenosha, WI (414-734-0773).

BOSTON TRADERS
Corporate Office: 315 Washington St.
Lynn, MA 01902
617-592-4603

Sip on the Boston Traders' special-tea by having a party at one of their outlet stores. Save big on the Boston Traders and Trader Kids sportswear and outwear labels at 30–70 percent off (including big and tall sizes). Locations include: Baltimore, MD; Freeport and Kittery, ME; Burlington, MA; Reading, PA; Central Valley and Woodbury Commons, NY; Manchester, VT; McLean, VA.

BUGLE BOY
Corporate Office: 15 Union St.
Lawrence, MA 01840
508-683-9083

Toot your horn at 20–60 percent off retail in the brands that strike up the band. Kids' clothes (boys and girls), juniors' and misses', young men's, and men's with such great sounding names as Bugle Boy and Vincente Nesti. Outlet locations in Boaz and Dothan, AL; Barstow and Vacaville, CA; Commerce, GA; Lawrence, MA; Secaucus, NJ; Lake George, NY; Lancaster and Philadelphia, PA; Pigeon Forge, TN; New Braunfels, TX; and Woodbridge, VA.

CHOCK CATALOG CORP.
74 Orchard St.
New York, NY 10002-4594
212-473-1929
Catalog $1; PQ

Chock is the source of much ridicule on my national book tours for they hold the world's most waist-full pair of men's boxer shorts . . . size 60. We have always given them high marks for keeping all the family in stitches (and pantyhose, and lingerie, and sleepwear, and underwear . . . names like Christian Dior, Martex, Oscar de la Renta, Calvin Klein, Jockey, BVD, Munsingwear, and more). For smaller soles, they carry Trimfit socks, and Chock even has a separate department for infants and kids with Carter's layette items, nursery needs, cloth diapers, and crib sheets. Boys love Hanes. Girls and boys sleep tight, too, for less. Save up to 35 percent through their 64-page catalog or call for a price quote for fast, courteous service by phone.

D & A MERCHANDISE CO., INC.
22 Orchard St.
New York, NY 10002
212-925-4766
Catalog $1.50

If your kids are used to royal-tee, introduce them to the King of Underwear. Since the 1940s, this New York mainstay has been the undercover source for cheap shorts everywhere. Men's, women's, and boys' (where's the girls'?) first-quality underwear in all the best brands at up to 35 percent off: Jockey, Bali, Christian Dior, Formfit Rogers, Lily of France, Lollipop, Maidenform, Olga . . . get the picture? For boys, the underwear supply is limited to BVD and Hanes.

DECKERS
Corporate Office: 666 West Ave.
Norwalk, CT 06850
203-866-5593

Only in Connecticut, but they will ship anywhere. A family affair when it comes to wear-and-tear in department store labels, Deckers has a stellar line-up of stars in infants' wear, toddlers', and children's sizes with such names as Gant, Izod,

Eagle, and others soaring at savings of 30–50 percent less than retail. Outlets located in Norwalk and West Hartford, or by phone.

FALL RIVER KNITTING MILLS SWEATER FACTORY OUTLETS, INC.
Corporate Office: 69 Alden St.
Fall River, MA 02723
617-678-7553

Cry me a river, but don't fall for full retail prices. That's the motto at Fall River where they've been knitting up a storm for many moons. Sweaters for men, women, and children with the Fall River label can be worn out the door at 20–60 percent less at the following outlets: Fall River, Falmouth, Hyannis, and Plymouth, MA; Wells, ME; North Conway and North Hampton, NH; Newport and Warwick, RI; and Quechee, VT.

FARAH OUTLET STORES
Corporate Office: 8889 Gateway West
El Paso, TX 79925
915-593-4444

The Gateway to the West is the home of the slacks that won the West. Separate the men from the boys at this outlet store in boys' sizes 4–7, 8–12, prep, husky, young men, and men. All Farah first-quality by name though the brands vary by location. Farah, W.F.F., Savanne, E'Joven, and N.P.W. at 35–40 percent off. Outlet merchandise available by phone or on location at Boaz, AL; Lancaster and Reading, PA; New Braunfels, TX; Kenosha, WI; and Puerto Rico.

GUESS?
1444 S. Alameda St.
Los Angeles, CA 90021
213-765-3100

Take the Guess? work out of shopping for guess what line of clothing? You guessed it. Guess? sportswear winds its way down the line to their outlet stores, even in children's sizes from size 8 and up. Sorry, no phone orders accepted. Visit their 18 outlets in person at Foley, AL; Cabizon, Eureka, and Los Angeles (The Cooper Building), CA; Ellentown, Orlando, and Sunrise, FL; Gurney, IL; Michigan City, IN; Kittery, ME; North Conway, NH; Central Valley and Niagara Falls, NY; Morrisville, NC; Philadelphia, PA; Chattanooga, TN; San Marcos, TX; Prince William, VA.

IZOD/FASHION FLAIR
Corporate Office: 13th and Rosemont
Reading, PA 19604
215-374-4242

For a fashion flair that's not on the endangered species list, join all in the family for an Izod or two. Also available through their national chain of factory stores are the labels Ship 'n' Shore, Monet, Gant, Lacoste, Evan Picone, and Palm Beach at 30–60 percent off. Outlet stores are all concentrated on the East Coast with the exception of Fremont and Michigan City, IN; Birch Run, MI; Branson, MO; and Kenosha, WI.

LANDS' END KIDS
Lands' End Lane
Dodgeville, WI 53595-0001
800-356-4444
Catalogs

From their humble beginnings in a basement on Chicago's waterfront in 1963, this powerhouse has land-end with an outlet division for what doesn't sell through their catalogs at up to 50 percent off. In their catalogs, watch for markdown pages where prices are up to 55 percent off and a kids' book for little ones dedicated to the traditional values inherent in saving money on quality items. Pennies from heaven don't have to rain on your children's parades. They even have a collection of rainwear and other outer gear to keep them dry. Recently a hooded slicker was $19.50, a pair of rain boots $22.50 and an umbrella $9. Kids' sizes and infants' (3 months to girls 14, boys 16) are covered in this kids' version of Lands' End favorites. Outlet stores are concentrated in the Chicago and Wisconsin areas and can be shopped by phone.

MIGHTY MAC FACTORY OUTLETS
Corporate Office: 90 E. 6th St.
Bayonne, NJ 07002
201-339-2424

Mighty Mouse would have been mighty proud had he discovered Mighty Mac's at 20–50 percent off. Children's outerwear (men's and women's, too) is included in the inventory at this mighty fine outlet as well as tops, pants, jams, and sweaters. Outlet locations at Branford, CT; Kittery, ME; Fall River, Gloucester, and Lawrence, MA; Keene and North Hampton, NH; Bayonne and Secaucus, NJ; and Lake George, NY.

NEW HORIZON SPORTSWEAR
Factory/Corporate Office: 113 Summit Ave.
Hagerstown, MD 21740
301-739-1288

Rounding the bases in a uniform that will suit the team to a tee is a winner in anybody's book. This manufacturer makes uniforms—soccer, baseball, hockey, basketball, even cheerleaders' costumes—and will sell direct to the team or to anyone who hasn't made the team if they order by the dozen. By eliminating the middle man, this source can make a Cadillac of a T-shirt, or a pair of shorts, at the price of a Ford. Stitch for stitch, patterns are custom-crafted and then it's on to the assembly line. Team emblems are applied. Sizes from diaper waists to 2X-3X-4X if dad's has expanded. Sweats, hats, jackets, jogging outfits, too, as well as Hanes, New Era, and Russell are sold through their outlet stores in Hagerstown, MD, and Waynesboro, PA (for savings up to 35 percent). For other orders, call or write the factory above.

PATAGONIA OUTLET/REAL CHEAP SPORTS
Corporate Office: 4880 Colt St.
Ventura, CA 93003
800-336-9090 (catalog request)

Strictly for the rugged enthusiast, this catalog's outlet stores are wonderful repositories of past seasons' catalog merchandise. But so what? When school starts in the fall, and it's 90 degrees outside, your children can stay cool in a pair of Patagonia shorts for as low as $9.50, or a baggy pair for $12.50 (retailing at least twice the price in the Patagonia catalog). Kids can dress like grown-ups in twill jeans and bombacha pants, with tees and polos (as low as $3 and $10 respectively). Keep your past seasons' catalogs handy, then call one of their outlet stores if you're not in the area of Ventura, CA; Freeport, ME; North Conway, NH; or Salt Lake City, UT. Patagonia donates 10 percent of their pretax profits or 1 percent of their sales (whichever is greater) to preserving and restoring the natural environment.

POLO/RALPH LAUREN FACTORY STORE
Corporate Office: 590 Commerce Blvd.
Carlstadt, NJ 07072
201-438-5900

Playing the field in a Polo can score big dividends at their outlet stores. Play carefully, though. Often the outlet merchandise is glaringly close to retail price. But still, the thrill of the hunt is to actually set foot inside a Ralph Lauren Outlet Store. Family apparel, footwear, and accessories at 20–50 percent off is their claim. Boys' clothing is included. Girls' is not. Outlets in Boaz and Foley, AL; Barstow and Eureka, CA; Durango, CO; Michigan City, IN; Eddyville, KY; Freeport and Kittery, ME; Lawrence, MA; Osage Village, MI; Billings, MT; North Conway, NH; Carlstadt, NJ; Cohoes, Lake George, Niagara Falls, Plattsburg and Watertown, NY; Reading and York, PA; Blowing Rock, NC; Rapid City, SD; Chattanooga, TN; El Paso, TX; Manchester, VT; Martinsburg, WV; Appleton, WI; Jackson, WY; and San Juan, Puerto Rico.

RED FLANNEL FACTORY
73 South Main
P.O. Box 370
Cedar Springs, MI 49319
616-696-9240
Catalog

Kids can turn their clocks back to Grandpa's days when this company was born. In 1949 the Red Flannel Factory first produced their now-famous pajamas, undergarments, robes, and shirts in white and red for the entire family (even the dog). Now past forty, but still going strong, their outlet offers their entire line at 20 to 30 percent less than retail. Write for free catalog and curl up and save right.

SOCKS GALORE & MORE
220 Second Ave. South
Franklin, TN 37064
800-626-SOCK; 615-790-SOCK (TN)
Catalog

This blockbuster sells socks, socks, and more socks in their more than 50 outlets across the country. If you are not near the socks you love, you can love the socks you're near via their catalog. Their unbranded (but coming from the same sources as those with designer names) best-selling models are sold at up to 80 percent off. Footloose and fancy-less footwear for the entire family from sport styles to tube socks, all-cotton socks to thick wool socks, argyles to support knee-highs, they make for great gifts at great prices. Order a "sock certificate" if you are at a loss for what to buy the kid who has everything.

THE SOCK SHOP
Sweetwater Hosiery Mills
P.O. Box 390
Sweetwater, TN 37874
615-337-9203
Price list

Sweetwater will be celebrating its 100th birthday soon, and you can help in the celebration but you don't have to wait for birthdays. Their everyday savings rate is up to 50 percent off the entire line of the Sweetwater brand of hosiery. From booties to knee-highs, girls, boys, and infants (parents, too) can sock-it-to-you for less. The lowdown on underwear includes cotton and nylon panties for girls (sizes 2–14) and Fruit of the Loom briefs and T-shirts for boys (sizes 2–20).

Their outlet store is in Sweetwater, Tennessee, at 818 N. Main Street. Write for their price list for orders by mail.

SPECIALS EXCLUSIVELY (LEVI'S)
Corporate Office: 1244 Boylston St.
Chestnut Hill, MA 02167
617-277-4800

Though not owned by Levi Strauss, these outlet stores are supplied exclusively with both Levi's and Dockers at 50 percent off the ticketed prices. Fashions for the family with irregulars and closeouts as their middle name(s). Factory locations include Boaz, AL; Ft. Pierce, Orlando, and Sunrise, FL; Byron, Commerce, Lakepark, and Savannah, GA; Edinburg, IN; Slidell, LA; Freeport and Kittery, ME; Buzzards Bay and Fall River, MA; Birch Run, Monroe, and Traverse City, MI; North Conway, NH; Niagara Falls, NY; Smithfield, NC; Lancaster, Morgantown, and Philadelphia, PA; Bluffton, N. Charleston, Sandee, and Spartanburg, SC; Pigeon Forge, TN; Lightfoot and Potomac Mills, VA; Martinsburg, WV; and Oshkosh, WI.

SPIEGEL/CRAYOLA KIDS
1040 W. 35th St.
Chicago, IL 60609-1494
800-345-4500
Catalog $2

Crayola Kids catalog is the newest joint-venture entry to the Spiegel family lineup. Fall asleep counting sheets and savings and everything else you buy for bedtime, clothes time, playtime, or work time. Shop catalogs from Spiegel, the granddaddy of all mail-order catalog shopping, which now boasts an entire collection of specialty catalogs: For You, women's sizes 12W–26W, $2; Proportion Petite, Ready to Wear (ready to unwind), sizes 2–14 for those under 5'4",

$2; Men, $2; comfortable clothes for men and women, $2; Together, exclusive but affordable designs that you won't see yourself cloned all over town in, $2; the Ultimate Outlet, offering, as its name implies, an avalanche of top-of-the-line and private labels at rock-bottom prices from their "big books." All fees for catalogs are refunded with purchase.

SUNGLASSES U.S.A.
469 Sunrise Highway
Lynbrook, NY 11563
800-USA-RAYS
Catalog (full-color)

You've got it made in the shade with a pair of Ray-Ban sunglasses at wholesale prices. Sunglasses U.S.A. sells them all at one-third off retail. That's 33⅓ percent off. See the world cheaper. And not for adult eyes only. Serious sunglasses for peek-squeaks, too. Three of the all-time best-selling glasses (Metal, Wayfarer, and Cats) in sizes just for kids. Look cool in your new shades. Call or write for particular prices on specific specs.

VF FACTORY OUTLET
Corporate Office: P.O. Box 1022
Reading, PA 19603
215-378-1151

This giant can stretch your budget as well as put you in a pair of Lee stretch jeans. Their outlets factor in many a side trip off the major highways in the country when you learn the roster of popular brand names: Vanity Fair, Lee, Kay Windsor, Jantzen, Bassett Walker, Big Ben, Heron Cove, and Li'l Lollipop. Save 50 percent on their huge inventory of sportswear, sleepwear, loungewear, intimate apparel (like training bras), and jeans. Make a stop over in Boaz and Monroeville, AL; Mesa and Tucson, AZ; Graceville, FL;

Carrollton, KY; Iowa, LA; North Dartmouth, MA; Tupelo, MS; Lebanon, MO; Wyomissing, PA; Crossville and Union City, TN; Corsicana, Hempstead, Kingsville, Mineral Wells, and Sulphur Springs, TX; and Draper, UT.

THE WOOL SHOP
High St.
Killarney, Co. Kerry
Ireland
Catalog

If you are not tired of having the wool pulled over your eyes, you will love the Aran-knit sweaters and vests for the entire family here. All garments are knit by hand and therefore only price *ranges* are printed in the catalog. An individual price quote is returned before the garment is made allowing for hand-stitching, oversizing, special sleeves, virtually any customization required. Prices range from $65 to $125 for pullovers, and hover around $67 for cardigans. Shipping worldwide.

Infant

ABSORBA
Corporate Office: 1333 Broadway, Room 1200
New York, NY 10018
212-947-6024

Absorb the full retail value of Absorba by shopping at one of their select factory-direct outlet stores for infants' wear *par excellence*. Save 30–50 percent off Absorba and Gentilbebe labels (owned by Oshkosh B'Gosh). Locations in Commerce, GA; Hendersonville, NC; Pigeon Forge, TN; and Hilton Head, SC.

THE B2 PRODUCTS
P.O. Box 1108
Haymarket, VA 22069
800-695-7073
Flier (price list)

Cheaper by the dozen? You betcha! B2 Products sells infants' undershirts (soon to expand to crawlers and older children) by the dozen to save TIME and MONEY! Imagine never having to wait for a sale or driving to the store only to find out they're sold out of the size you need. As a B2 customer, you'll receive: superior quality products, delivery within 15 days, special savings on personal care items, bonus coupons, packing list specials, updates on new product lines, gift wrapping on request, and a special monthly health newsletter. Sizes 3–36 months. Don't "B2" slow, or you'll miss out on a *Great Buy*! Call for free price list.

BABY WAREHOUSE
4617 S. Buckner, Suite H
Dallas, TX 75227
214-388-1201

Buckle up to this bargain warehouse where you can shop direct from the creator's workroom and never leave home. Choose works of crafty accessories for baby's room at 50–60 percent less than retail. Call for appliquéd fabric crib sets and accessories, monogrammed and custom-made headboards, comforters, diaper bags, totes, and bibs. Perfect for grandmas and shower gifts. Also children's clothing from newborn to 12 months, wall hangings, appliquéd letters, cribs, and furniture.

MAGIC WINDOWS
1046 Lexington Ave. (75th St.)
New York, NY 10021
212-517-7271
   and
186 Madison Ave. (87th St.)
New York, NY 10028
212-289-0028

Open these magic windows and say, "Ah-h-h-!" The Lexington store carries breathtaking infants' clothes through size 6X-7, though their forte is in layette and infant gift items. Their Baby Registry helps make it easier for friends and family to choose the right gift for baby or custom-make THE perfect gift baskets to delight both baby and mom. The Madison store carries infant through preteen sizes with an emphasis on wardrobe needs of the older child to size 14. Beautifully smocked dresses are a specialty as well as wedding and special-occasion outfits. Like proud parents, they brag about their great sales. And they are gr-r-r-eat! Delivery does *not* take nine months. Call for sale dates. And leave the shopping *and* shipping to them.

NEWPORT/KIDSPORT
Unique Infant Sportswear
10775 NW McDaniel
Portland, OR 97229
800-552-8447
Catalog

Dress 'em up in practicality for practically peanuts. Easy-to-slip-on and off capes for children make for heads-up innovation that'll top off any baby's wardrobe. And remember, with the cape, there are *no buttons or zippers* for on-off frustration. Add sheepskin pull-up leggings called Baby Ughs for fashion-forward warmth, comfort, and style, and you end up with a baby who's dressed for an Arctic blast at bargain prices.

RUBENS & MARBLE, INC.
P.O. Box 14900
Chicago, IL 60614-0900
312-348-6200
Brochure (free with SASE)

These are the folks that bring care to bare babies' bottoms. Supplying hospitals with infants' clothing for over 100 years, you can buy what "General Hospital" buys at up to 60 percent off. Send for their free flier (but be sure to enclose a SASE) and see for yourself sizes premie and newborn to 36 months for undershirts in every conceivable configuration (with sleeves, with mitts, with snaps, with ties, double-breasted, you name it). And from there, you can add training and waterproof pants, drawstring-bottom baby gowns, terry bibs, bassinet and crib sheets. And tell me, what baby can live with only a dozen kimonos? *Sayonara*, bargain babies.

ARTS AND CRAFTS

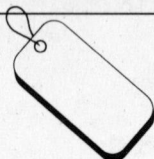

ALLEN'S SHELL-A-RAMA
P.O. Box 291327
Ft. Lauderdale, FL 33329
305-434-2818
Catalog $1 (receive $2 gift certificate)

Long for long walks along the ocean's shore? Want to build a subdivision of sand castles? Are shark's teeth, seahorses, and sand dollars among your passions? Do you find shells and exotic tropical air plants irresistible? You can add to a collection, at wholesale prices, with decorator, collector, and specimen shells, all novelties, and original kits (unavailable anywhere else) to choose from and spend many a day crafting away the hours.

ART SUPPLY WAREHOUSE INC.
360 Main Ave.
Norwalk, CT 06851
800-243-5038; 203-846-2279 (CT)
Catalog

Pint-size Picassos paint the town with savings of up to 60 percent by shopping by the book at Art Supply Warehouse. This 76-page catalog of name-brand and popular art supplies includes a palette of oils and acrylic paints and all the pigments, solvents, and fixatives as an accompaniment. For other mediums, psych yourself up with their huge selection of colored pencils, markers, chalks, oil pastels, brushes, inks, palette knives, easels, art boxes, and silk-screening supplies.

CHILDCRAFT, INC.
20 Kilmer Rd., P.O. Box 3143
Edison, NJ 08818-3143
800-631-5657; 800-367-3255 (customer service)
908-985-6761 (fax)
Catalog

Outfoxing them all, Childcraft has it all. A colorful collection of child-pleasin' creations from items to decorate a child's room (sheets, lamps, beanbag chairs) and sponge decorative kits for painting, to backpacks and pogo sticks. A multitude of merry-making's in store with costumes, crafts, clothing, learning toys, and even a Mini Mouse Makeup Line. Unconditional guarantee on all merchandise.

CRAFT KING, INC.
P.O. Box 90637
Lakeland, FL 33804
813-686-9600
Catalog $2

If I can't live in Lakeland, the most I can do is buy some after-school projects from their 100-page arts, supplies, kits-for-crafts catalog. Being a teacher and a former camp counselor and director, I never stop looking for a deal on macramé, cross-stitchery, pom-poms, doll making, fashion art, embroidery, ornaments, anything to keep nimble fingers out of trouble. And then, when the prices are slashed 30– 60 percent, that's where I draw the line.

DHARMA TRADING CO.
P.O. Box 150916
San Rafael, CA 94915-0916
800-542-5227; 415-456-7657
Catalog

Dharma gives off great karma when the subject of "to-dye-for" fashions comes up. Entire households get into the art of tie-dyeing practically everything once they get the rudiments of how-to-do-it-without-coloring-everything-purple. Dharma's 30-page catalog is one of the few catering to the textile arts—paints, dyes, resists, and fabrics. They not only sell you the tools of the trade, they also offer an extensive collection of 100-percent cotton T-shirts, skirts, pants, and vests in sizes for children and up, oversize shirts, and Habotai silk scarves. Savings of 50 percent are cut to order.

DICK BLICK CO.
P.O. Box 1267
Galesburg, IL 61401
309-343-6181
Catalog $3

Flick to Blick when the subject of art supplies and equipment comes up. Their gargantuan catalog is a giant in the industry. Over 20,000 items are listed in their 464-page one-stop art shop and the savings are up to 30 percent whether you're a Teacher (in school) or a teacher (as in "parent"). Looking for Crayolas? Liquitex paints? Kraft paper? Teachers and mothers go crazy with the possibilities here. Pick your project: silk-screening, découpaging, printmaking, leather-making, lapidary polishing, macramé weaving, or wood carving plus hundreds of books and videos on the subject of "how-to"! Stores located in Plainville, CT; Roswell, GA; Decatur, Galesburg, Moline, Peoria, Springfield, and Wheaton, IL; Iowa City, IA; Dearborn, MI; Emmaus and Wilkes-Barre, PA; and Henderson, NV.

ENTERPRISE ART
P.O. Box 2918
Largo, FL 34649-2918
813-536-1492 (mail-order customers)
813-531-7533 (local)
Catalog

Enterprise has been providing crafty customers a vast selection of materials and supplies to keep the nimblest of fingers busy for over ten years. Save by buying in bulk for jewelry-making projects (findings, rhinestones, mirrors, pearls), crafts (doll parts, miniatures, floral supplies), wearable art (tie-dye, metallic foil, fabric paint, bandannas), beads, and much more. Raffia straw for door wreaths, sequins to dress-up sweatshirts, or yarn to make a cuddly Raggedy Andy doll. When in Florida, you can visit their mail-order warehouse seven days a week at 2860 Roosevelt Blvd., Clearwater, FL 34620.

FROSTLINE KITS
2512 West Independent Ave.
Grand Junction, CO 81505
800-KITS-USA (800-548-7872); 303-241-0155 (CO)
Catalog $1

You don't have to know a thing about sewing to complete a Frostline kit! All you need is a sewing machine and one of Frostline's money-saving, superior-quality kits that come complete with everything you need—precut. Just sit down and sew according to their easy step-by-step instructions. If you do have a problem or question along the way, call their answer line (303-251-0155) for help. Mountain parkas and biking gear are their biggest sellers, but they also have kits for making baby bunting and clothes for hunting, bed quilts, booties, robes, even tents. Allow three to four weeks for delivery. In the event of faulty material, there is a six-month refund period.

GINGERSNAPS
3181 Mission #122
San Francisco, CA 94110
415-826-7518
Brochure

It's a "snap"! Personalized 4″ X 6″ postcards made from a child's work of art. Carefully reproduced in full color with personalized captions, these are great for custom correspondence, invitations, or gifts for parents, relatives, or friends. Each card has a caption on the back with the title and date of the artwork, and the name and age of the artist. Original artwork returned and satisfaction guaranteed or money refunded.

HEARTLAND CRAFT DISCOUNTERS
941 S. Congress St.
Geneseo, IL 61254
309-944-6411
Catalog $2

There's no need for boredom when the bargains are just around the corner. Over 6,000 items at 30 to 50 percent off will carve out some pretty handy and crafty items. Just about anything for the craft hobbyist: florals, glues, ribbon, wood cutouts, paints, needlecraft, doll parts. Your imagination is stretched to the outer limits for an endless creative project.

HERRSCHNERS, INC.
Hoover Rd.
Stevens Point, WI 54492
800-441-0838; 715-341-0560
Catalog

Twenty-four hours a day, 7 days a week, you can outfox even the craftiest. Since 1899, this has been one of the oldest and largest quality catalogs of craft kits in the country. Plenty of cross-stitching with a cat theme, afghans, baby items, calendars, crochet items, fabric, frames, needlepoint, paint, pillows, stitchery, threads, years of activities to work your fingers to the bone. When in Stevens Point, stop and shop firsthand at their catalog store.

KIDSART
817-566-6444

Call on this artist-in-residence who is one of the most sought-after teachers of art for kids in the north Texas area. Innovative classes for young artists—drawing, painting, "art after school," and other studio crafts foster creativity and self-esteem. Special workshops both for teachers and kids and a special art party can be arranged for a birthday party, school vacation, or on location at area recreation centers, churches, or your home (if you're in north Texas). If not, mail-order KidsArt kits, sketchbooks, and manuals provide additional stuff for an A-Z start to making your kid an arty-smarty. Call for details.

MAKIT PRODUCTS INC.
12221 Merit Dr., Suite 1030
Dallas, TX 75251
214-458-0954
214-458-0979 (fax)
Flier

Make a memory with Make-A-Mug and Make-A-Plate from Makit Products, Inc. Make sense? Well, it's simple. These keepsake art projects can be applied to a mug or a plate, are fun and easy, and make a welcome gift any time of the year.

Items can be used for everyday occasions or displayed with other childhood mementos. They're the ideal way to permanently frame your child's artwork. Kit includes cost of processing one original drawing. Write or call for store nearest you offering the Makit Products.

MICHAELS
P.O. Box 612566
DFW, TX 75261-2566
214-580-8242

Michaels is *the* arts and crafts store and a whole lot more. Outwit the craftiest of foxes with a do-it-yourself work of art, from scrumptious homemade candy to porcelain flower arrangements, stitchery to specialty T-shirts. Create a one-of-a-kind masterpiece and save big bucks over ready-made counterparts. Free custom framing (you only pay for materials), a kids' club, and the creative camaraderie of others "sew" inclined. Call or write for the store nearest you.

MORTON SALT
100 N. Riverside Plaza
Chicago, IL 60606
312-807-2000
Brochure

With just a pinch of salt and a little imagination, your kids can have hours of creative fun. Morton Salt offers a free brochure called "Saltcrafts" on how to create masterpieces with salt. So when it rains, pour on the salt!

PEARL PAINT CO.
308 Canal St.
New York, NY 10013
800-221-6845; 212-431-7932
Catalogs

This gem of a discounter offers more than just pearls of wisdom for the artistically inclined through their 8 catalogs a year. Offering discounts of 20–70 percent (off list) with a gem of a selection for kids' art sake and creativity. Since 1933, this company has been mixing the mediums in the art world with materials for every conceivable craft. Beginning artists' kits especially crafted for kids 12 and under. Their expanded children's department includes children's easels, lanyard lacing kits, modeling clay, crayons and markers, color wheels, coloring books, Walter Foster instruction books, fashion paints (for sneakers and tees), kits for marbleizing, fabric painting, and papier-mâché.

PUEBLO TO PEOPLE
2105 Silber Rd., Suite 101
Houston, TX 77055
800-843-4257; 713-523-1197 (Houston)
Catalog

This nonprofit organization provides products exclusively from South American cooperatives with its central goal to aid native artisans in selling and distributing their handicrafts. Catalog is filled with a bounty of ecologically sound and economically appealing items for kids. Sneak a peek inside the pages of a recent holiday catalog and taste a little girl's pocketed dress for $20; a Salvadoran mobile $17, and a cardinal hand puppet $15; a bag of 6 "Animalitos" for $9; handmade Mayan dolls, two for $19; plus baby baskets, sisal animals, alligator mittens, appliquéd and embroidered bibs . . . all perfect for gift-giving. When in Houston, visit their outlet store where discontinued items, irregulars, and closeouts are available at a fraction of the catalog price.

THE RIBBON OUTLET/ THE RIBBON MILL/ RIBBONS FOR EVERYTHING
**Corporate Office: 3434 Route 22, W. Fox Hollow #110
Somerville, NJ 08876
201-707-9800**

Tie one on in any one of their 80 stores across the country if you want bulk and precut ribbon, craft supplies, and hand-crafted gift items at 20–70 percent off. Over 3,000 varieties in ribbon and trim alone. Wrap up in gift wrap and top off in hair accessories. Call or write for locations in your area.

SAX ARTS AND CRAFTS
**P.O. Box 51710
New Berlin, WI 53151
800-558-6696; 800-242-4911 (WI)
414-784-1176 (fax)
Catalog $4 (refundable)**

For everything your art desires, consult this full-color catalog and you'll be creating custom jewelry and wonderful wear-ables, painting canvas dolls and toleware, and stitching up fresh new ideas for gifts for Mom and Dad and even for yourself. Learn to make baskets and porcelain flowers. Everything you need from start to finish is available. Order toll-free 24 hours, 7 days a week. Orders are shipped within 48 hours. Free freight with orders of $100 or more. Complete satisfaction is guaranteed.

SUNCOAST DISCOUNT ARTS & CRAFTS
9015 U.S. Route 19 North
Pinellas Park, FL 34666
813-577-6331
Catalog $2

From coast to coast, you can save up to 40 percent on arts and crafts supplies by shopping Suncoast. Over 300 pages of crafty and floral ideas can be mustered up with a little help from here. Think of all the productive hours that could stimulate creative minds. The list is endless: in the making—dolls, toys, rugs, jewelry, wreaths, hand-crafted calligraphed note cards, floral arrangements, cross-stitchery, quilted frames, macramé wall hangings, baskets, beadery, hand-painted T-shirts, and more. Page after page of possibilities with closeout specials soaring to 90 percent off retail.

SUPER YARN MART 1
Corporate Office: 1233 S. San Pedro St.
Los Angeles, CA 90015
213-749-7044

Weave a few tall tales for less (10–60 percent) and shop here for imported and domestic mill surplus and bulk yarns, as well as knitting, crocheting, needlepoint and embroidery supplies, and accessories. Most of the outlets are in California but you can mill about ones in Mesa, AZ; Denver, CO; Portland, OR; Salt Lake City, UT; and Seattle, WA, too.

VANGUARD CRAFTS, INC.
P.O. Box 340170
Brooklyn, NY 11234-9007
718-377-5188
Catalog $1 (refundable)

Vanguard has been the savior of the after-school pack when cries of "I'm bored!" start to sound like a broken record. Though primarily a source for teachers, a few ex-teachers have found them a wonderful aid to the rainy-day blues. Though the minimum order is $25 to qualify for the savings of up to 40 percent, it's not too difficult to meet the requirement after thumbing through their 68-page catalog. Kits and supplies for hundreds of hours of creative thinking. Foil pictures, shrink art, mosaic tiling, découpaging, copper enameling, stenciling, calligraphy, woodworking . . . and the tools to tool along. Basic art supplies also included such as the 3 P's: paint, paper, and pastels.

VETERAN LEATHER COMPANY, INC.
204 25th St.
Brooklyn, NY 11232
718-768-0300
Catalog $1.50 (refundable); PQ

Even a novice can find it easy to craft a project in suede or leather with some help from these veterans. A large assortment of leather-working accessories and tools are available including Osborne, Lexal, Original mink oil, Craftool, Midas, and Basic. Discounts of up to 30 percent. The minimum order is $25 and there is a 10 percent restocking charge on returns, unless the material is defective.

WIKKI STIX—OMNICOR, INC.
608 E. Missouri
Phoenix, AZ 85012
602-274-4550
602-248-8876 (fax)
Flier (full-color)

Sticks and stones shouldn't break your budget. And for relieving the boredom of long car trips, pick up some Wikki Stix. More fun than a toy! More creative than a craft! An excellent way to help develop hand-eye coordination, improve motor skills, and encourage self-expression. Perfect for quiet play and individual fun. Each package contains 48 eight-inch "Wikki Stix" either in 4 primary colors or 5 hot neon colors, complete with illustrations and ideas for use and play. Recommended for ages 4 and up.

ZIMMERMAN'S
2884 34th St. North
St. Petersburg, FL 33713
813-526-4880
Catalog $2 (refundable)

From A to Zimmerman, your child can create a crafty solution to the rainy day blues. "Have they got a deal for you!" This is the Ben Franklin of discount craft supply sources. Everything under the sun is found in sunny Florida. But for those away from the Sunshine State, shop at home and save. Beads, ribbons, yarns, macramé, dolls, books, crocheting and knitting supplies, and anything else to get the job done. Free UPS shipping anywhere in the U.S.

AUDIO AND VIDEO

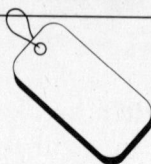

CRITICS' CHOICE VIDEO
800 Morse Ave., P.O. Box 549
Elk Grove Village, IL 60007
800-367-7765; 800-544-9852 (inquiries)
708-437-7298 (fax)
Catalog

Sit back. Relax. Even put your feet on the seat in front of you. Enjoy all the pleasures of home viewing without a line around the block. Save the cost of the ticket and overpriced candy, too. And if it's a favorite flick, you can watch it over and over again. The star attraction, of course, is saving money! Over 1,200 movies under $20; some overstock sale-priced as low as $7.88. A warehouse of choices, from comedies to classics, like *National Velvet* and *The Wizard of Oz*. UPS pickup at Critics' Choice expense if not completely satisfied. Free catalog. Pass the popcorn. Hold the (real) butter.

FOTO ELECTRIC SUPPLY CO., INC.
31 Essex St.
New York, NY 10001
212-673-5222
PQ

Sing the Foto Electric! Internationally acclaimed by satisfied customers, Foto Electric has been supplying photo enthusiasts with their audio and visual needs at a discount for over 30 years. The way to get a price quote, though, is to send your request in a letter (enclose SASE). Period. No other way to know exactly what blank videotapes are going for or what an Aiwa, Panasonic, Sony, or Phillips piece of audio or video equipment is going for, but expect at least a 30 percent price break.

FRONT ROW PHOTOS
Box 484
Nesconset, NY 11767
Catalog $1

Taking pictures at a rock concert is hazardous to your camera. If you want to keep the camera, and have a photo, too, this is your front row to success. Rock fans and photo collectors have it all from this source of thousands of photos at up to 50 percent off. Included with your catalog request will be a photo of Front Row's choosing. From the '60s to whoever's the current rage, a photo size 3½" × 5¼" will cost $1.60; 8" × 10" will cost $5.75. The more you buy, the more you'll save. Even the Grateful Dead would be grateful, Dad.

JCI VIDEO
21550 Oxnard St., Suite 920
Woodland Hills, CA 91367
818-593-3600
Catalog

Often wonder how to keep rambunctious children entertained? Tune in to JCI Video's children's line entitled "Video Wonders," two half-hour videos with two stories each. Geared for two- to six-year olds, these tapes have four elements: a read-along presentation with animated illustrations, an original song, a vocabulary lesson, and a booklet to read without the video. Stories include: *Home for a Dinosaur, The Monster Under My Bed, Maxwell Mouse,* and *The Great Bunny Race.* And for the prima ballerina, JCI offers *I Can Dance*—an introduction to ballet for ages 3 to 8. Toe shoes not included. Tapes are $9.95 each. Free catalog available.

KIDVIDZ
Special Interest Videos for Children
618 Centre St.
Newton, MA 02158
617-965-3345; 617-243-7611 (orders)
617-965-3640 (fax)
Flier

Live from Centre Street comes the kids' biz video king. This rising star in special interest children's videos has produced four award-winning video titles that inspire, teach, and entertain their young audiences. Each video features only kids as expert hosts, stars, and informants. This peer communication is a hallmark of the Kidvidz style. Two how-to tapes are offered—on cooking and arts and crafts—and the other two help children deal with new siblings or the experience of moving. Tapes priced at $14.95, plus $3.50 shipping and handling.

LVT PRICE QUOTE HOTLINE, INC.
Box 444
Commack, NY 11725-0444
516-234-8884
Mon.–Sat. 9–6 EST
Brochure, PQ

This price-quoting company provides a one-stop shopping call to over 75 major manufacturers at up to 30 percent off suggested retail prices. Since 1976, LVT has offered an excellent lineup of available brands: Amana, AT&T, Braun, Brother, Canon, Casio, Code-A-Phone, Eureka, Hewlett-Packard, Hoover, Mont-Blanc, Murata, Sanyo, Sharp, TI, and Zenith. For college life, bring a little order by sweeping your problems under the rug with a vacuum cleaner, or faxing home for help. And don't forget a microwave for the dorm room for late-night zapping of the night-before's pizza or an answering machine for a message to Mom as to where you are. Price quotes by phone or with SASE by letter. UPS shipping, handling, and insurance are included in quotes and all manufacturer's warranties are included. All sales final.

METACOM, INC.
Adventures in Cassettes
5353 Nathan Lane
Plymouth, MN 55442
800-328-0128; 612-588-2913 (MN)
Catalog

Turn the tides and return to the golden years of radio. Growing up with Baby Snooks (Fanny Brice) and Fibber McGee and Molly can be recalled by audiocassette. Curl up around the fire while the Lone Ranger rides again (for less silver) or hop aboard with Hopalong Cassidy and catch a few winks of Casper the Friendly Ghost. Introduce your children to your childhood memories and watch how both generations smile.

RICK'S MOVIE GRAPHICS, INC.
P.O. Box 23709
Gainesville, FL 32602-3709
904-373-7202
Catalog $3 (refundable)

If your hang-ups run the gamut from vintage to current movie posters, you'll love flipping the pages of this 80-page catalog of flicks. Posters average around $15, but that reflects a savings of 10–30 percent from other poster stores in town. Besides, you can cover a lot of wall for only $15 (plus framing). The savings are much greater in the vintage poster department (from 30 to 65 percent). Our choices ran from *Rambo* to *Rocky*, *Star Trek* to *Batman*, Disney titles to *Friday the 13th*.

STRAND VCI ENTERTAINMENT
3544 Troost Ave.
Kansas City, MO 64109
816-931-5341

The shining star in this company's offering of videos for children is host/narrator Ringo Starr and some cheerful toy train engines. *Thomas Gets Tricked & Other Stories* and *James Learns a Lesson* have a running time of 40 minutes each ($14.95 each). Both come with a *Thomas the Tank Engine* wristwatch and contain seven stories each, with titles like "Foolish Freight Cars," "Terence the Tractor," and "Thomas & Bertie's Great Race."

VIDEO TECHNOLOGY INDUSTRIES, INC.
380 W. Palatine Rd.
Wheeling, IL 60090
800-521-2010
Catalog (full-color)

Video Tech takes today's video technology and creates electronic toys and learning aids with a unique approach: an interactive capability with a basic preschool approach. Toys like "Sound Zoomer"—free-wheeling vehicles loaded with eight real action sounds and lights (ages 2 and up)— and "Video Smarts"—live action puppetry, colorful animation, and original music presented in an entertaining style. For the junior "techie" (ages 6 and up), Video Tech offers hand-held games, Electronic Battleship Command, Precomputer 1000 Junior, and more. Available at most major retail stores. Call for details.

WARNER BROS.
4000 Warner Blvd.
Burbank, CA 91522
818-954-6000

Jane Fonda's exercising her options again with her first two workout tapes for kids! For the three-to-seven-year-old set, there's "The Swamp Stomp," and for the seven-year-olds and older, it's "The Fun House Funk" (say that three times fast!). Each tape is introduced by Fonda and exercises are led by J. D. Roth of TV's "Fun House." Tapes ($19.95 each) are designed to hold the attention of youngsters while making exercising fun, with special attention paid to the safety of young muscles. Check at your local video store or wherever tapes are sold.

WHOLESALE TAPE AND SUPPLY COMPANY
P.O. Box 8277
Chattanooga, TN 37411
800-251-7228; 615-894-9427 (TN)
615-894-7281 (fax)
Catalog, PQ

As the name indicates, this is *the* source for wholesale prices on blank audio- and videocassettes and reel-to-reel tapes in all shapes and configurations. They are specialists in the audiovisual supplies and services business and have been duplicating their efforts worldwide since 1977. Six kinds of tapes available (from 12 to 122 minutes). Professional and studio-quality audio and video recording tape from Agfa, Ampex, Maxell, Memorex, and TDK is also available at applaudable savings. Their duplicating services, too, are excellent but the best prices are on orders of 50 or more. Minimum order $20. Price quotes also available by phone or SASE.

THE WHOLE TOON CATALOG
P.O. Box 369
Issaquah, WA 98027
206-391-8747
206-391-9064 (fax)
Catalog

The most comprehensive source of animated films and cartoons, animation art, posters, books, toys, buttons, mugs, and stickers available anywhere. The Whole Toon Catalog contains hundreds of rare, hard-to-find cartoons featuring such characters as Betty Boop, Amos 'n' Andy, old black-and-white cartoons from all the studios, and recent Disney, Bluth, and Warner Bros. releases. Adults as well as children will find this a fun catalog to peruse and use. After your first order of $100 or more, you become a "Toon Club" member and receive 10 percent off all future purchases. Call Monday–Saturday 9–6 (PST) for a free catalog.

WISCONSIN DISCOUNT STEREO
2417 W. Badger Rd.
Madison, WI 53713
800-356-9514; 608-271-6889 (WI)
PQ

"Hear this! Hear this!" This is how one call-in listener raked me over the coals for not knowing about Wisconsin Stereo. Thank you, wherever you are, dear ole Mrs. Calabash. But now, *Great Buys for Kids* readers will know this fabulous find where it's not unheard of to capture up to 70 percent off most major brands of electronics in the world! Call for prices on practically every audio component or portable stereo, and practically every piece of video or car audio equipment known to man, woman, or child. ADC, Aiwa, Bose, Clarion, Design Acoustics, Dual, Hitachi, JBL, Jensen, JVC, Kenwood, Marantz, NEC, Panasonic, Sansui, Sharp, Sony . . . are you listening? From 30 to 40 percent off and as high as 70 percent across the board.

BABY GEAR

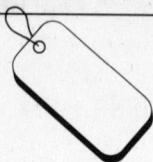

ALDEN COMFORT MILLS
1708 E. 14th St.
P.O. Box 860055
Plano, TX 75086-0055
800-822-5336; 214-423-4000
Catalog

For comfort, class, and creative cuddling, these crib down comforters are scaled-down versions of this manufacturer's larger comforters and are made with baby in mind. Approximate finished size is 40″ × 50″, fill weight of 5 or 9 ounces. Comes with matching down crib pillow. Your choice of colors. $44.95 plus $3 shipping and handling.

ARTSANA OF AMERICA, INC.
200 Fifth Ave., Room 910
New York, NY 10010
800-336-8697; 212-255-6977 (NY)
212-645-7143 (fax)
Catalog (full-color)

Chicco-Artsana offers learning and developmental toys, carriages and accessories for children, newborn to 6 years. In addition to their high-quality, classic strollers that come in a variety of styles and safety features, baby can sit up straight and walk tall in their innovative high chairs and baby walkers. These educational and stimulating toys help babies develop learning skills and challenge their capacities while still being entertaining. Can you imagine their fascination with their "First Discovery" mobiles or their "First Imitations"—toys that encourage simple imitations of the adult world? Call for a dealer near you.

BABY BUNZ & COMPANY
P.O. Box 1717
Sebastopol, CA 95473
702-829-5347
Catalog

If you've decided to use cloth diapers in lieu of disposables because of cost or environmental concerns, then you'll appreciate the prefolded diapers from Baby Bunz Co. Besides standard and fitted diapers, they carry the best-known covers by Nikkys, in soft lamb's wool, waterproof, and poly-lined cotton. Sizes range from newborn to chubby (super-large up to 32 pounds) at prices up to 30 percent below retail. Baby Bunz also carries its own line in three styles (contour, prefolded, and flat) at an average of 22 percent below retail. Layette wear from Wee Wear and Fix of Sweden, and everything from booties to bedding don the pages of their colorful catalog. Weleda baby-care products are also available. Catalog free with phone call, otherwise $1. Satisfaction guaranteed; refund or credit.

BANDAKS EMMALJUNGA, INC.
737 South Vinewood St.
Escondido, CA 92029
800-232-4411
Brochure (color)

"Let's Buggie" in a Bandaks Emmaljunga stroller offering the transportation command station for baby, twins, or small kids for the '90s. Beam 'em up, Scotty! Many styles to choose from and recognized worldwide for safety, durability, elegance, and practicality. Oversized understorage baskets, easy fold-down mechanism. Detachable bassinet can be used as a traveling bed. Newborns dream-ride into toddlerhood and beyond. Call for a list of stores in your area.

BEN'S BABYLAND
81 Avenue A
New York, NY 10009
212-674-1353
PQ

Bye-bye, baby, time to hit the road to dreamland. Don't cry, baby, mama can buy you a brand new crib, stroller, playpen, walker, layette ensemble. If it's for a baby's room, Ben's got it. Call or write (SASE) for price quote on specific items and expect a shipment to arrive at 20–30 percent less than retail on everything Ben sells: car seats, car beds, high chairs . . . we said everything *but* the baby's for sale.

THE COMPANY STORE INC.
500 Company Store Road
La Crosse, WI 54601
800-356-9367; 608-785-1400 (WI)
608-785-7037 (fax)
Catalog

You can expect a company in La Crosse, Wisconsin, to know how to keep warm in the winter, cool in the summer. It's easy to get covered either way from their 56-page color catalog of down bedding and other cover-ups. Bed down in down comforters of all weights and sizes, including the sought-after all-cotton varieties of bedding for those who prefer au naturel. Sheets, duvet covers, pillowcases, shams, bed ruffles—all accompaniments for the down comforters at down-home prices. There's a wonderful selection for babies (kids and doggies, too). The store's nursery department stocks bedding in pastel solids, and crib comforters, bumpers, pillows, and shams for down-filled heaven.

GRACO CHILDREN'S PRODUCTS, INC.
P.O. Box 100
Elverson, PA 19520
800-345-4109; 215-286-5951 (PA)
Brochure (full color)

Graco gives you the freedom of choice! A wide variety of baby-tested, parent-approved products with quality crafts-manship, proven reliability, and assured safety. Their product line includes swings, high chairs, playpens, strollers, walkers, booster seats, and baby carriers. Everything you need to meet baby's needs for travel, playtime, and naptime. Call for the Graco retailer nearest you.

KEL-GAR INC.
P.O. Box 796934
Dallas, TX 75379-6934
214-250-3838

Founder Gail Frankel had a better idea. Built around her own personal experience trying to straddle baby and brother, stroller and bottle, lemonade and her patience while shopping the mall, she designed the Stroll'r Hold'r to make shopping as easy as A-B-C. This plastic three-hook attachment fits onto any stroller bar and holds a multitude of stuff (bottles, bags, toys, and more). The Tubbly-Bubbly transforms a plain faucet into an elephant complete with a "trunk" dispenser full of bubble bath. The Squeez'r-Feed'r is a portable baby feeder that is a spoon and jar all in one. Eat, baby, eat, on-the-run for moms-on-the-go. Most items available at Toys 'Я' Us, or other fine discount toy retailers; also available through the Rite-Start Catalog, 800-Little-1.

LEACHCO
P.O. Box 717
Ada, OK 74820
800-525-1050; 405-436-1142 (Canada)
Flier (color)

The next best thing to mother's arms is this batch of innovative infant and child care products. Win the arms race hands down with a Wiggle Wrap for little "wiggle worms." Prevents slipping, standing, and sliding, and is self-adjusting for optimal support . . . great for baby at restaurants or down the aisle (at supermarkets). Also, "Kid Kaper," a giant-sized terry towel for sun, fun, bath, or snack time. This company also offers Genesis, a new baby-bottle line with up-to-date child care information like CPR instructions and a hotline number printed directly on the bottle (4 bottles for

$12). Member of the Juvenile Products Manufacturers Association. Call for retailer nearest you or order direct.

THE NATURAL BABY COMPANY
114 W. Franklin, Suite S
Pennington, NJ 08534
609-737-2895
Catalog

What is a Nikky? Well, it's a wonderful, natural alternative to plastic pants. You lay any kind of diaper in the Nikky and wrap the Velcro for a perfect fit. No pins. Waterproof. Feels like felt. And 100 percent cotton. $13.95 each for cotton; $16.75 each for wool. Recommended: 4 per day. Washable and can be handed down to new siblings. Other natural contributions in this catalog besides cute copy and handy how-to hints include terry velour diaper covers, the Rainbow diapers (the kind they use in diaper services), Velcro diapers, natural baby cosmetics like Weleda Oil and Tom's Honeysuckle shampoo, changing bags, baby carriers, booties, strollers, socks, nursing gowns, toddler terry robes, and information on their bargain lines of woolly long johns, dressy diaper sets, peasant blouses, and other items.

ON THE GO
P.O. Box 2352
Santa Barbara, CA 93120
805-965-1408

When the doctor orders you to take a hike, take your baby and the Hip Hiker Baby Carrier along for the ride. This carrier adapts the Indonesian sling technique for toting kids up to 40 pounds. By distributing the child's weight across your back diagonally to relieve stress on the back, this carrier allows you to walk safely and cuddle at the same time. Machine-washable and available in red, navy, or gray for $25 (regular), $28 (long).

QUILTS UNLIMITED
P.O. Box 1479
Williamsburg, VA 23187
804-253-8700
Catalog and photographs $6; year subscription $35

Don't feel guilty about saving up to 30 percent off what dealers charge for similar quilts. These are new, old, and antique quilts guaranteed to keep you covered in a style you and/or your baby should cover up with for years. Particularly pleasing for baby is their selection of crib coverlet quilts and wall hangings hand-stitched lovingly by Amish, Appalachian, and Mennonite women. If you're in the area, visit in Williamsburg at Merchants Square; 203 E. Washington St., Lewisburg, WV; Cottage Row at The Homestead Resort, Hot Springs, VA; and The Greenbrier, White Sulphur Springs, WV. Save $10 off the $35 regular subscription cost if you mention *Great Buys*.

RACING STROLLERS, INC.
P.O. Box 2189
Yakima, WA 98907-2189
800-548-7230; 509-457-0925 (WA)
Brochure

Don't race past this one! Combine fitness, family, and fun with the "Baby Jogger." Mom and Dad can stay in shape while the kids ride in style. This smooth-rolling, all-terrain stroller eases out the bumps and grinds and maneuvers easily. Carries infants to 4 years old. Choices also include the Walkabout style for quicker dismantling and the Twinner for twice the fun. Also modifies and custom-designs strollers for handicapped children. Ships via UPS unless otherwise specified. Offers great deals on demo and factory-second strollers. Call for details.

STAGES
345 7th Ave.
New York, NY 10001
$26.50 + $3.50 postage and handling

This is an incredible little gizmo that took a doctor's imagination to conceive. This is a warmer for wipes for baby's sensitive skin. Safely heats disposable wipes, and also acts as a nightlight. Consider one for every diaper area. Isn't that special!

TAMI'S DESIGNS OF CALIFORNIA
705-5 E. Bidwell St., Suite 104
Folsom, CA 95630
916-983-2547
Brochure (color)

At last, parents of the '90s can be protected from baby's messy mishaps. For generations, parents grabbed for the cloth diaper or blanket when baby drooled or burped or worse. Bye-bye, blankets and diapers. Hello, Baby Burp Cloth. A perfect size (13″ × 22″) for so many uses: under baby's head, on parent's shoulder, on the floor for diaper changes, or to gently shield baby when nursing. Baby Burp Cloth is 100 percent absorbent cotton-quilted flannel/poly-fill, machine wash/dry. Of course, available in seven designer patterns to fit every fashion-conscious baby. Refund or exchange within 30 days.

WEE BEE KIDS
800-676-5075; 718-645-5075 (NY)
Catalog

Custom-painted diaper pails with durable plastic childproof lids make for a clean sweep in the gift department. Available in many different designs and colors. Order the pail separately for $18, or a diaper pail gift basket with extra goodies for $25 and up.

BOOKS

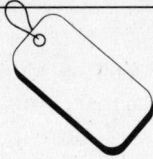

ABOUT ME
24 Lantern Lane
Norwell, MA 02061
800-827-READ; 617-659-1840 (MA)
Brochure

Build a love for reading . . . gift for a lifetime. About Me personalized children's books stimulate the imagination and encourage reading. With eight styles to choose from, these hard-cover, fully illustrated storybooks star your child along with friends and family members. From *The Circus Star* to *The Hanukkah Rescue*, your child commands the center of attention. Some are even available in Spanish and French. An introductory price of $11.95 (plus postage and handling) for your first order gets you any additional books at $8.95 (plus postage and handling). Massachusetts residents add 5 percent. All orders shipped within 48 hours.

BLACK IMAGES BOOK BAZAAR
P.O. Box 41059
Dallas, TX 75241
214-943-0142; 214-375-1733
Flier (order form)

Black Images Book Bazaar specializes in books, games, greeting cards, cultural prints, and artifacts from the black point of view. You are welcome to visit the store (call for address and directions) or order by mail. Some highlighted offerings include *Shake It to the One You Love the Best* (play songs and lullabies from the black musical traditions); *Tar Beach* (an enchanting, highly original picture book); and *Black Science Activity Book* (McDonald's salute to black inventors). A gift haven to support the black heritage. One-third down, full payment required in 90 days. A layaway plan is available and exchanges or refunds are accepted with receipt.

BOOKS OF WONDER
132 Seventh Ave.
New York, NY 10011
212-989-3270
Flier

Question: Where's one of the largest children's bookstores? Answer: New York City. The Big Apple has gotten to the core of the matter by offering an entire bookstore specializing in imaginative books for the young and young at heart, and all available by phone without a trip to Seventh Avenue. Browse through a distinguished selection of childhood classics (especially Oz books and memorabilia) and modern masterpieces to read and share. Most of the books are hardcover, but some are in paperback ($1.95 to $24.95). The store issues a monthly flier with notices of sales and in-store author autograph sessions. Also available for $3: a catalog of antique, first-edition collectibles and out-of-print materials.

db BOOKS AND THINGS
P.O. Box 1074
Fairhope, AL 36533
205-928-3846
Color brochure
Record free with purchase

Seeing is believing. Much more than just their names, their faces tell the story, too! Just imagine—your child the star. The subject of his/her very own book (or poster). Child's photo will appear on 23 pages of this 32-page, hardcover, full-color, soil-resistant book. Best of all, the cost is less than you would pay for many inexpensive gifts or toys. Satisfaction is guaranteed or money cheerfully refunded. Free brochure on request and, to our readers, a free follow-along record with purchase.

DOVER PUBLICATIONS, INC.
31 E. 2nd St.
Mineola, NY 11501
516-294-7000
Catalog

You'll find a circus of savings in this colorful catalog of over 550 books for children from Dover Publications, Inc. Children's classics like *The Tale of Peter Rabbit*, *Alice's Adventures in Wonderland*, and *The Wizard of Oz*, and even Shirley Temple paper dolls reproduced from rare original sets. You'll find cut-and-assemble books, paper dolls, stickers, educational activity books, posters and more, and most ranging from $1 to $5.95. A wonderful collection of children's books at terrific prices! Gift certificates available. Unconditional guarantee; return within 10 days for full cash refund. Telephone or credit card orders not accepted.

PUBLISHERS CENTRAL BUREAU
One Champion Ave.
Avenel, NJ 07001-2301
201-382-7960
Catalog

The savings are astronomical, reaching sky-high at up to 90 percent off retail. Book a bargain with one book or a hundred. Monthly catalogs arrive in your mailbox and offer books on every topic imaginable, as well as videotapes and records. For kids, there are pop-up books, magic books, craft books, animal books, beauty books, trivia games, and posters.

Resource Guides

AMERICAN CAMPING ASSOCIATION
5000 State Rd. 67 N.
Martinsville, IN 46151-7902
800-428-CAMP; 317-342-8456
317-342-2065 (fax)

Guide to Accredited Camps (1991–92), by the American Camping Association, for parents ($10.95, ISBN 0-87603-121-2): Roll out those sleeping bags! When it comes to camping, the American Camping Association has you covered with this comprehensive and current information guide to over 2,000 camps, for all ages and every income level, including how much it'll cost, operating seasons, capacity of the camp, and facilities available. Just remember to pack the bug spray.

AMERICAN LIBRARY ASSOCIATION
50 E. Huron St.
Chicago, IL 60611
312-944-6780

Children's book sales across the United States have almost quadrupled since 1982. For devoted bibliophiles, this is good news, heralded in part by the efforts of the American Library Association. In cooperation with sponsors like the California Raisin Advisory Board, the Clorox Company, and other diverse companies, the American Library Association sponsors summer reading and writing contests to encourage reading among children. Call or write for participating libraries in your area.

AMERICAN LIBRARY ASSOCIATION (ALA)
Service to Children
50 E. Huron St.
Chicago, IL 60611
312-944-6780
Pamphlets

"Notable Children's Books 1990 Edition" keeps parents current on new books. Send 50 cents and SASE to the ALA requesting your copy. "Books for the Youngest Child: Update." Another offering from the ALA on books available for children under 5. Free with SASE and 45 cents' postage. "The *New York Times* Parents' Guide to the Best Books for Children," Times Books, $9.95. This publication includes an annotated guide to more than 300 of the best children's books on the market.

WALDEN BOOK COMPANY, INC.
P.O. Box 10218 (201 High Ridge Rd.)
Stamford, CT 06904
203-352-2000

Tough Topics, by Sara Wilford, M.S., M.Ed., sponsored by Waldenbooks, for parents ($4.50): Used by libraries and community-minded organizations as well as parents, this booklet provides a recommended list of books in print that deal with "tough topics" like abuse, adoption, birth, death, divorce, drugs, handicaps, health care, separation, sex, and sibling rivalry. Each listing is accompanied by a brief introduction. Available at Waldenbook Stores or send $4.50 to above address.

BUYING SERVICES
WAREHOUSE CLUBS

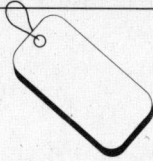

The warehouse club concept originated in 1976 in San Diego with the Price family and was aptly called the Price Club. Its appeal and growth have spawned numerous competitors, like Wal-Mart's Sam's.

The basic idea is simple. To join, you pay a small membership fee and purchase goods at a discounted price. The discount varies depending on whether you're a small- or medium-sized business, or whether you are an employee of a certain organization, government unit, or credit union.

Be prepared for a warehouse environment with forklifts and cartons stacked high. Merchandise is often limited in certain categories, and many food products are sold in institutional-sized quantities. (Having a carton of Doritos on hand is too tempting for me.)

Warehouse clubs generally stock family apparel, office supplies and furniture, small and major appliances, TVs, radios, home entertainment items, cameras, and books within 50,000 to 100,000 square feet.

Sam's is experimenting with an even larger store concept called the Hypermart, where employees skate around to replenish stock.

Warehouse clubs are among the "hot" retailing phenomena and will reach many more metropolitan areas in the 1990s.

Here are a few to watch for. Call or write to their corporate offices for the location nearest you.

bigg's
Corporate Office: 4450 Eastgate Blvd.
Cincinnati, OH 45245
513-753-7500

This French hybrid launched their first bigg's in Cincinnati, then spread to nearby Clarksville, IN; Florence and Middletown, KY; then skipped to Denver, CO. Watch them get bigg-er in Indiana and Kentucky. This hypermarket is a frenzy of activity with more checkout cashiers than any store in the country. General merchandise and food from all the major manufacturers like Procter & Gamble, Campbell's, Wrangler, and Nike. Save 15–20 percent.

BJ'S WHOLESALE CLUB
Corporate Office: One Mercer Rd.
P.O. Box 3000
Natick, MA 01760
508-651-7415

This chain is making its moves and checking them twice. Over 30 stores to date and plenty more on the drawing boards. Like its colleague Sam's, this warehouse club concept is similar in every way including size. Its general categories of name-brand items are limited in scope, but the price is right. Wholesale prices on both food and general merchandise.

C.O.M.B.
720 Anderson Ave.
St. Cloud, MN 56372-0030
800-328-0609 (orders)
612-654-4800 (customer service)
Catalog

First, order their catalog. Then order anything from their catalog (owned by the QVC TV Shopping Network). With that purchase you will automatically receive a monthly insiders' hotline list. This catalog is not called *The Liquidator* for nothing! Terminate high prices on a Sharp zoom lens camcorder, retail $1,999/their price $799; a 13-volume encyclopedia set for $49; a super woofer boombox, retail $139/their price $59; an Adidas Delta tennis racket, retail $234.14/their price $49; a free-standing bunk-bed set, retail $49.95/their price $199; a fluorescent table lamp, retail $49.95/their price $19. For school, for home, for work, for pleasure, get out your C.O.M.B. and untangle the snarls today. If in the Minneapolis area, visit one of their six closeout stores.

COSTCO WHOLESALE
Corporate Office: 10809-120th Ave. NE
Kirkland, WA 98033
206-828-8100

The Northwest and West Coast caught Costco customers in a web of substantial savings. From Anchorage, Alaska, to Van Nuys, California, and, of course, Washington and Oregon, to nearby Nevada and Utah, then on to Florida, then back to Honululu with a Costco Wholesale warehouse opening. Their game plan is anybody's guess, but rumor has it they're making their moves to Texas. Stores can be as large as 200,000 square feet or as small as under 10,000 square feet, but the message is the same. Name-brand groceries, baby food, diapers, chips and dips, electronics, office supplies, linens, appliances, plants, pet supplies . . . at 9–12 percent above cost. No, ma'am! Sam's not the only man in town.

DAMARK INTERNATIONAL, INC.
7101 Winnetka Ave. N.
Brooklyn Park, MN 55428
800-729-9000; 612-566-4940
612-531-0380 (fax)
Catalog

The UPS man thinks we own stock in Damark because of the number of packages with their mailing label delivered to our door. Their monthly "Great Deal" catalog, rivaling close-out heaven, regularly commands our attention. For example, we bought a 386 Cordata computer for $1,499/ retail $2,999; a Panasonic answering machine that was factory-reconditioned for $29; a 26″ remote control fire truck or police boat (retail $69.99/$39.99); a Synsonics Terminator electric guitar (retail $159/$69.99); a Greenleaf dollhouse and 30-piece furniture set (retail $196.93/$74.98); a 3-piece Oshkosh B'Gosh luggage set (retail $180/$49.99); and Bushnell binoculars (retail $159.95/$69.99)—and that's just for starters. The pages read like a parent's gift-giving shopping list with prices 50 percent—and sometimes up to 90 percent off.

FRED MEYER INC.
Corporate Office: 5100 SW Macadam Ave.
Portland, OR 97201

Over 125 stores in only 7 states concentrates the power buying in Alaska, California, Idaho, Montana, Oregon, Utah, and Washington. You can't live in the Northwest and not be a Fred Meyer fan. These superstores include groceries and drugstore items, as well as top brands of apparel and shoes, linens, books and magazines, electronics, appliances, sporting goods, and auto supplies. From Calvin to Corning, there isn't a stone left unturned. From specialty-store size (1,200 square feet) to over 200,000 square feet of value-oriented hyperstore proportions.

MEDCHOICE
Corporate Office: 480 Roland Way
Oakland, CA 94621
415-633-2020

A new niche is finally filled—medical, dental, and home- and health-care products, equipment, and supplies at savings of 20–40 percent. Showrooms in Arizona, California, Florida, and Texas. This should be the start of something big. When you have a choice between full price and discount, and your family's health is the question, the answer is perfectly clear: MedChoice.

PACE MEMBERSHIP WAREHOUSE
303-364-0700

Pace is outpacing many of the players in the warehouse club concept. With 50 stores in place, this Denver-based company is making its moves . . . stay tuned to this space for Pace's plans as they materialize. Apparel, appliances, auto accessories for starters. Food, toys, electronics, office supplies, and forklifts, of course. Stores so far include those in California, Colorado, Florida, Georgia, Iowa, Kentucky, Maryland, Michigan, Nebraska, North Carolina, and Pennsylvania.

PRICE CLUB
Corporate Office: 4649 Morena Blvd.
P.O. Box 85466
San Diego, CA 92117
619-581-4530

Warehouse clubs got their start in 1976 with the founding of the Price Club, and its founders were none other than the Price family. Today there are nearly 60 Price Clubs in operation with more on the drawing board. They, like Sam's, Costco, and Pace Membership, for example, continue to vie aggressively for prime real estate locations as they make their moves across the country. Locations thus far are in California, Arizona, New Mexico, Colorado, Washington, D.C., Virginia, New York, and Rhode Island. Expect to see name-brand health and beauty aids, groceries, wine, beer, liquor, appliances, housewares, linens, school and office supplies, electronics, clothing, books, and pet, auto, and lawn supplies.

SAM'S WHOLESALE CLUB
Corporate Office: 608 SW 8th St.
Bentonville, AR 72716
501-273-4668

Sam's the man who's turned the wholesale club shopping experience into the state-of-the-cart. If you can tolerate the long lines at the checkout counters, cases of Doritos waiting to be devoured, forklifts at every turn, bare-bones amenities, and an all-day shopping experience that will save you up to 50 percent and more, then Sam's the club to join. From eyewear to photo-finishing, reduced rates on long-distance and car telephone rates, name-brand electronics, appliances, clothing, dog food, cat food, people food, frozen food, even gourmet food. Over 150 stores nationwide but concentrated in the Southwest, Southeast, and Midwest thus far. But then Sam's the man who's behind Wal-Mart, so watch out. Uncle Sam wants you!

CAMERAS AND
SCIENTIFIC EQUIPMENT

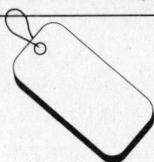

ABC PHOTO SERVICE
9016 Prince William St.
Manassas, VA 22110
703-369-2566
Catalog

Learning the sources for some of the best prices on film processing and photo printing is made as easy as ABC. Their catalog will enlarge on their photo-finishing services, but the prices are pretty simple. Save up to 30 percent on film developing for both color and black-and-white prints. Want a photo enlarged? Is 48″ × 144″ large enough? Duplication of slides, copy negatives, even prints from slides are offered. The standard finish is semi-matte unless you specify otherwise. Wedding album packages also available (but you supply the photos).

ASTRONOMICAL SOCIETY OF THE PACIFIC
390 Ashton Ave.
San Francisco, CA 94112
415-337-1100
Catalog (send two first-class stamps)

Following the stars is easy once you know where to look. The Astronomical Society of the Pacific is a nonprofit organization founded in 1889 strictly for the purpose of research and the appreciation of astronomical wonders. Stargazing through their 32-page catalog reveals a variety of wonderments from the heavens: slides, audiotapes, videotapes, books, maps, posters, charts.

B & H FOTO ELECTRONICS
119 W. 17th St.
New York, NY 10010
800-221-5662 (orders); 212-807-7474 (customer service)
PQ

When your Flash Gordon signs up for his camera badge for the Cub Scouts, be sure to lighten the load with a call here. Light up your life with flash systems by Nikon, Canon, Hasselblad, and a host of others. Choose from a host of light meters, tripods, and other camera gear. Everything's discounted (15–20 percent) and the prices are enough to make anybody's eyes shine. Fourteen-day exchange or refund policy; no restocking charge. Most orders delivered in about ten days.

EDMUND SCIENTIFIC COMPANY
101 E. Gloucester Pike
Barrington, NJ 08007-1380
609-547-8880 (orders)
609-573-6260 (customer service)
609-573-6295 (fax)
Catalogs

This company publishes two giant catalogs serving America's budding science community and they are both FREE. Their 112-page hobbyist edition and their 188-page industrial/educational catalog are jam-packed with an astronomical collection that would make any stargazer ecstatic. Tackle any science project with aplomb. Lasers, magnets, microscopes, optical tools and accessories, photography equipment, telescopes, measuring tools, weather and wind-speed instruments, even a helium fun party kit. Edmund distributes and manufactures over 200 different magnifiers alone, plus low-vision aids for the vision-impaired. Though not discount, it is *the* one-stop shopping source for science projects and the how-to-do books on the subject of making the grade, scientifically.

EXECUTIVE PHOTO AND SUPPLY CORPORATION
120 W. 31st St.
New York, NY 10001
800-223-7323 (orders only)
800-882-2801 (computer hotline)
212-947-5290 (NY, AK, HI, and all inquiries)
Catalog, PQ

You'll smile when you see the savings of 40 to 50 percent flashing across their 50-page catalog. Cameras, lenses, film, paper, and photographic accessories from names like Canon, Minolta, Nikon, and Hasselblad are part of their photographic inventory. Minimum order is $45, and it's usually delivered in 7–10 days. All manufacturers' warranties are included.

INTERSTATE/FLORIDA, INC.
P.O. Box 6536
Clearwater, FL 24618-6536
813-447-7766
Flier

Record memories of that first birthday party, that first tooth, that first step, that first date . . . the first of anything can last forever with a 3D photograph. The revolutionary new Nishika 35 mm 3D camera will give you breathtaking shots with standard 35mm color film that can be enjoyed without special glasses or viewers. One-year unconditional warranty. Also available: tripod, deluxe camera bag, camera strap, lens cleaner kit, and Nishika film. Call or write for more information.

MARDIRON OPTICS
The Binocular Place
4 Spartan Circle
Stoneham, MA 02180
617-938-8339
Brochure and price list (for 2 first-class stamps)
PQ

If your kid's taken a fancy to birdwatching, then fancy this. Mardiron Optics flies high in our book by discounting up to 45 percent on name-brand binoculars, telescopes, and opera glasses plus all the accoutrements to accompany their star-studded gazing. And the folks at Mardiron Optics are no bird-brains when it comes to knowing their scopes from their Steiner binoculars.

ORION TELESCOPE CENTER
P.O. Box 1158
Santa Cruz, CA 95061
800-447-1001; 800-443-1001 (CA)
408-464-0466
Catalog

Since 1975, Orion has been a bright constellation in the galaxy of telescopes and accessories. Their eye-catching 56-page catalog provides a road map to the stars at up to 40 percent off. Not only are products highlighted but articles on the subject of scoping are part of their catalog's universe. All the best brands are stocked: Celestron, Edmund, Meade, Orion, and Televue. Also binoculars. Visit their two stores in California, in Santa Cruz and Cupertino.

PORTER'S CAMERA STORE, INC.
P.O. Box 628
Cedar Falls, IA 50613
319-268-0104
Catalog

When you call on this Porter, you can expect first-class service on the best-selling names on the camera train. Their 112-page catalog wins hands down with price savings up to 65 percent off retail. Since 1914 the war has been won in cameras and darkroom equipment. Whether it be cameras or lenses, filters or film, cases or chemicals, batteries or bags, the names are industry leaders, from Agfa to Vivitar, Canon to Nikon. Knowledgeable personnel to answer you every step of the way. Visit their warehouse outlet in Cedar Falls, Iowa, if you're in the area.

RELIANCE COLOR LABS, INC.
Studio 386-5 Box 1000
Swansea, MA 02777

Talk about getting a rush job. For only $3, you can get 40 express photos in any combination (like 40 wallet-size; or 32 wallet-size and one 5″ × 7″; or 8 wallet-size and four 5″ × 7″ 's; or 2 custom 8″ × 10″ 's; or one custom 11″ × 14″; or 20 jumbo wallet-size. Ah. So many choices, so little time. Enclose check or money order with return address when you mail in photos or instant prints up to 8″ × 10″ (or negatives or slides—all will be returned). Add 95 cents for each set for postage and handling or $2 for rush express.

TASCO
P.O. Box 520080
Miami, FL 33152-0080
305-591-3670, ext. 322
305-592-5895 (fax)
Catalog (full-color)

Focus your attention on the telescopes and microscopes by Tasco. Superior quality and performance telescopes from $72 and up. For budding Galileos, peer in a microscope for as little as $9.60 (the basic Microscope Discovery Kits). All styles and sizes for your prospective scientists to discover the miniature specimens of nature, the universe, and beyond! Tasco also offers sports optics for the kid-of-the-wild. "Opti"-mum satisfaction guaranteed.

WALL STREET CAMERA EXCHANGE
82 Wall St.
New York, NY 10005-3699
800-221-4090; 212-344-0011
PQ

For the best insider information on Wall Street, shop Wall Street Camera Exchange and save from 35 to 75 percent on Nikon, Rollei, Hasselblad, Mamiya, Olympus, and Rolex. And if it's a Leica you're likin', their wall-to-wall collection includes cameras, lenses, accessories, camcorders (big selection), video cameras, personal copiers, typewriters, radar detectors, and more. A new division specializes in 35mm equipment. Trade-ins are welcome; they purchase outright or apply to a new purchase. Manufacturers' warranties where applicable and extended warranties available.

WESTSIDE CAMERA INC.
2400 Broadway
New York, NY 10024
212-877-8760
PQ

East Side, West Side, all around the town, the folks keep talking about this camera store. Since 1972, they've been shooting circles around the competition, selling cameras and darkroom equipment and supplies at up to 50 percent off. Some brands are well-known to amateurs; others only a pro would know: Agfa, Beseler, Bogen, Canon, Dax, Fuji, Gitzo, Hasselblad, Ilford, Kodak, Leica, Minolta, Nikon, Olympus, Pentax, Polaroid, Ricoh, and Yashica for starters. Minimum order ($25) is not hard to satisfy.

CAMPS

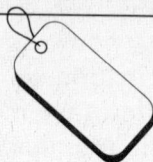

Educational

**THE BREAKERS: ETIQUETTE CAMP and MONEY
MANAGEMENT CAMP**
#1 South County Rd.
Palm Beach, FL 33480
407-655-6611
407-659-8403 (fax)
Brochure (full-color)

Manners and money management are the topics at these
two unique summer experiences for kids offered by the
Breakers Hotel in Palm Beach, Florida. Etiquette Camp is a
weeklong program where children 9–16 learn table manners,
their "Yes, sirs" and "No, ma'ams," correspondence, telephone etiquette, ballroom dancing, and more! Money Management Camp is for kids 12–15 and designed to be a fun
and informative method of introducing children to the stock
market and investments. There's a hitch, of course: a parent
or guardian must accompany the child. Call for details.

CAMP AMERICA—AMERICAN INSTITUTE OF FOREIGN STUDY
102 Greenwich Ave.
Greenwich, CT 06830
800-72-STAFF; 203-869-9090
Brochure (full-color)

Giving new meaning to the term "training camp," this subsidiary of AIFS is a selective staffing service of international camp counselors from around the world. They pride themselves on their proven ability to bring the right type of individuals to specific camps. Camps send staff requirement estimates and an experienced placement staff member responds with profiles of counselors who meet the needs of the inquiring camp at no obligation. After selection is made, Camp America will prepare, orient, and transport the counselor to the camp. It's that simple! Write or call for details. Affordable fees.

NATIONAL LAW CAMP
P.O. Box 811086
Boca Raton, FL 33481-1086
407-276-7577
Brochure

While other kids are practicing their swing at a tennis camp, future Perry Masons can be in full swing practicing prelaw. Instead of sitting around a campfire, they can sit around computers, take a field trip to a courthouse and jail, awaken to an alarm clock rather than reveille, and instead of standard camp T-shirts, wear polo shirts complete with scales of justice (sorry, alligators are left for real lawyers). National Law Camp accepts day and overnight campers. Tuition includes all linens and pillows, meals, all field trips, course materials, camp shirt, insurance, etc. Two divisions: high school and college (and over). Mock jury trials are held before National

Law Camp judges. Summer sessions are held on the campus of Barry University in Florida (June-July), and the campus of Georgetown University in Washington, D.C. (July-Aug.). Promotional videotape is available (prefaced by a reminder to return within 30 days or a $5 fee will be assessed). No hung jury on this verdict: a great summertime experience.

U.S. SPACE CAMP
One Tranquility Base
Huntsville, AL 35807-7015
800-63-SPACE; 205-837-3400 (AL)
Booklet (full-color)

5–4–3–2–1 . . . Blast off! U.S. Space Camp/Academy is an educational program that couples classroom instruction with hands-on activities. Trainees learn about space flight and the space program via lectures and seminars and then internalize this academic data to practical use with simulators and tours. The educational programs teach teamwork, decision-making and leadership. Programs available for grades 4–12; grades 4–9, sessions are 5 days; grades 10–12, sessions are 8 days. Tuition fee includes meals, educational programs, materials, accommodations, and T-shirts. Fly me to the moon with gossamer wings by calling 1-800-63-SPACE. Camps in Alabama and Florida (904-267-3184). These camps are run by the nonprofit U.S. Space Camp Foundation with franchises in the works for Japan, Belgium, and Montreal. Children in grades 4 to 7 can participate for a fee in Florida ($425–$550 per camper plus optional flight suits for $75); in Alabama, it costs $425–$750, plus $75 for the flight suit. Attendance varies from 24 to 150 and about one-third are girls. Field trips to the Kennedy Space Center, Brevard Community College Planetarium, the Astronaut Hall of Fame, and the NASA Rocket Garden at Spaceport USA.

Free or low-cost summer activities can be found almost anywhere:

- public pools or waterfront programs
- parks and recreation departments (they offer many arts and crafts, sports, theater, and recreational programs throughout the year and especially in the summer)
- art and science museum programs
- public library
- relatives or close friends in other cities may welcome a little visitor
- scholarships to camps are often considered based on merit; also volunteering as a camp counselor, especially if you have a particular skill, often nets a free stay, sometimes even a salary.
- the zoo often offers behind-the-scenes learning experiences, volunteer jobs, and field trips
- churches and synagogues sometimes have study or cultural arts programs
- local factories, businesses, and farms may offer a field trip or two; then there's the local TV or radio station, a water treatment plant, a public auction, a courtroom, a pet show, a nature safari, a brewery or bottling plane, a bakery for free fun to get out of the sun
- pick fruit or vegetables at a farm or orchard

Specialty

CAMP HUNTINGTON
P.O. Box 3789
Poughkeepsie, NY 12603
914-462-0991
Brochure

This coeducational camp for the learning-disabled, neurologically impaired, and mildly to moderately retarded has been operating for thirty years and is a member of the American Camping Association. Located in beautiful High Falls in the Catskill Mountains of New York State, this very special camp offers 2-, 4-, or 8-week sessions for very special children. Sessions are carefully supervised by a highly qualified staff of professionals under the direction of Bruria K. Falik, Ph.D. Write or call for dates, fees, and further details.

CAMP PENUEL
P.O. Box 367, Lake Killarney
Ironton, MO 63650
314-546-3020
Flier

Located in Missouri's beautiful Ozark Mountains, Camp Penuel helps kids of all ages escape from the "asphalt jungle" for some fishing, swimming, hiking, boating, tennis, basketball, and more. This is a nondenominational Christian, not-for-profit camp offering camping with a spiritual emphasis. The camp also has special projects geared to autistic and handicapped children. In addition to summer camping programs, Camp Penuel is available to churches and Christian groups as a retreat location. Member of Christian Camping International. Write or call for more information on the camp and its facilities.

CENTERSTAGE
602-242-1123

Impresario Michael Lancy is the creative force behind the most successful theater program for children and teens in the country. Since 1970, beginning as a summer camp program at the Phoenix Jewish Community Center, this has grown to several theater traveling companies touring simultaneously. The waiting list is long, the wait worth it. From *Wizard of Oz* to *Grease*, from contemporary musicals to original works, the children take their talent and the summer's theatrical production, including weeks of hard work behind the scenes, and hit the road to neighboring community centers, organizations, municipal auditoriums, and parks. Centerstage commands an SRO audience with equal applause to the staff and crew. Call for details but don't expect an answer during the summer months while all the buses are rolling.

EASTER SEALS CAMP HARMON
P.O. Box 626
Santa Cruz, CA 95061
408-338-3383
Brochure

This camp certainly gets our seal of approval. Easter Seals Camp Harmon in beautiful Santa Cruz, California, offers supervised coed summertime fun for campers from ages 8 to 60. Sessions operate from June 1 to September 30. Facilities include cabins that are barrier-free and able to serve even the severely disabled camper. Residents enjoy swimming, arts and crafts, environmental education, farming, hiking, drama, dance, archery, and softball. Sessions include 6-day and 12-day stays with fees starting at $300. Call or write for free brochure, or contact your local Easter Seals Society for similar camps in your area.

HEARTS BEND
P.O. Box 217
Newfane, VT 05345
802-365-7797
Brochure

The Hearts Bend Summer Farm Camp invites 65 campers, ages 4–15, to enjoy a wide range of Vermont summer activities centered on playing and working, where else but . . . down on the farm. This is a six-week coeducational program carefully planned to make campers feel comfortable in just being themselves. Self-esteem is enhanced with each day's activities and camaraderie. Hearts Bend Abroad, offered to children ages 12–19, is a coed travel program whose mission is peace and global understanding. The Hearts Bend motto is "One Earth, with all her children smiling." Call or write for details on dates and tuition.

HOOFBEAT RIDGE CAMP
5304 Reeve Rd.
Mazomanie, WI 53560
608-767-2593
Brochure

Horse lovers of America, saddle up. This family-owned and -operated coed camp for horse lovers ages 7–16 is located 25 miles west of Madison, Wisconsin. They provide horsemanship classes in English, jumping, and Western. Other activities available: complete horse care, trail rides, overnights, crafts, canoeing, drama, and sports. Fee varies with length of stay; 1–9 week sessions. Free video upon request.

NATIONAL EASTER SEAL SOCIETY
70 East Lake St.
Chicago, IL 60601
(312) 726-6200
(312) 726-4258 (TDD)
Brochure

For parents of disabled children, the *Parents' Guide to Accredited Camps* is a useful, comprehensive directory of camps that will accommodate children with disabilities. The guide is available at cost from the American Camping Association (ACA), 5000 State Road, 67N, Martinsville, IN 46151-7902, 317-342-8456. Copies are also available in many public libraries and through some community agencies. Included in the Easter Seals brochure are tips on questions to ask concerning health and safety procedures, camp philosophy and goals, counselor-to-camper ratios, and accessibility for children with limited mobility, all designed to help select a resident camp or day camp. You may also contact the Easter Seals Society in your area.

RONALD McDONALD FOR GOOD TIMES
520 South Sepulveda Blvd., #208
Los Angeles, CA 90049
213-476-8488
Brochure

This special camp is operated by the California Children's Cancer Service with a year-round operating session. The program is coed for those 6–18 and provides both 4- and 8-day sessions. The camp program and facility are designed to serve children with cancer and offers academics, swimming, hiking, scuba diving, drama, music, and individual and team sports. Facilities include dorms and cabins. All of this is free to children who have, or have had, cancer.

STAGEDOOR MANOR PERFORMING ARTS TRAINING CENTER CAMP
Star Route Karmel Rd.
Loch Sheldrake, NY 12759
914-434-4290
Free video

To camp, or not to camp? That is the question on every parent's mind when summer rolls around. So, pay attention all you would-be stage mothers. All the excitement of theater and fun of a summer camp is here under one roof. Stagedoor Manor Performing Arts Camp is the only camp of its kind in the world. You'll be puttin' on the Ritz with superb accommodations with carpeted rooms and an air-conditioned theater and dining room. With their hands-on tech theater program, you'll learn acting, musical comedy, dance, modeling, TV productions, voice, stagecraft, and costuming. Regular summer camp activities include swimming, tennis, volleyball, baseball, and horseback riding. Programs are coed for 8–18-year-olds and sessions run from June through August. The only catch is that Mom and Dad will have to pay at least $1,685 for a 3-week stay (but a small price for stardom). Hurray for Hollywood! Ten- and 12-week sessions also available. Call or write for free video.

Summer Vacations

CHELEY COLORADO CAMP
P.O. Box 6525
Denver, CO 80206
303-377-3616
303-377-3605 (fax)
Brochure (color)

If you like hiking, horseback riding, archery, riflery, crafts, and fishing, then Cheley Colorado Camp is calling you! Campers even get to sleep in covered wagons—rustic but comfortable. Weekly reports to parents come from the camp newspaper, *The Pack Rat.* One staff member for every three campers. Prices vary according to length of stay. Adventurous campers ages 9–17 can choose 4- or 8-week experiences. Call or write for camp dates and fees.

FRESH AIR FUND FRIENDLY TOWN PROGRAM
1040 Avenue of the Americas
New York, NY 10018
212-221-0900
Brochure

Summertime is Fresh Air time for thousands of underprivileged New York City children. The Fresh Air Fund is an independent, nonprofit agency providing free summer vacations to needy inner-city youngsters. Volunteer families host the visiting children each summer in rural and suburban communities for two weeks or more in 326 Friendly Towns across 13 Eastern Seaboard states from Virginia to Maine and Canada. Check for similar programs in your "friendly town," or call the Fresh Air Fund in New York for assistance in organizing one for your area.

MARINE MILITARY ACADEMY
320 Iwo Jima Blvd.
Harlingen, TX 78550
800-677-7607; 512-423-6006 (TX)
Information packet

Sorry, girls! This one's just for the guys. Break the summertime blues and blow 'em away with the Marine Military Academy's Summer Military Training Camp. Athletics, physical education, and a healthy dose of pure fun for boys 13–17. (Also offers a regular year-round academy with standard academic curriculum; $50 registration fee.) Write or call for tuition and fees list. Free complete information packet upon request.

YMCA CAMP FLAMING ARROW
P.O. Box 286
Hunt, TX 78024
512-238-4631
Brochure

Your little camper is sure to hit the bull's-eye when it comes to having fun at Camp Flaming Arrow. Rolling woodlands and open spaces in the historic Hill Country of the Guadalupe River above Hunt, Texas, create a wonderful setting for a rich and varied program of activities for children and teens ages 7–15. The emphasis is on fun. Camp Flaming Arrow offers swimming, river rope plunges, horseback riding, hiking, crafts, sports, carnivals, special nighttime activities, and a wilderness program. A qualified camp nurse is in residence and a physician is on call. Sessions run from June through August and range from $275 to $450 depending on duration of stay. For an additional $5, campers go home with a 24-page memory book of one excellent summer spent at Camp Flaming Arrow. Write or call for dates and registration forms.

Weight Loss

CAMP VERMONT/CAMP LA JOLLA
13671 Chalk Hill
Healdsburg, CA 95448
800-825-TRIM
Brochure (color)

Want to send those extra pounds packing? Camp Vermont offers an easy three-step method that allows you to have a positive attitude toward changing poor eating habits. The camp provides a wide range of outdoor activities, aerobics, special events, movies, self-defense training, goal-setting, and exciting field trips. You'll also receive counseling and a unique at-home follow-up program. A camp that makes your child's health and happiness its number-one priority! Also represents Camp La Jolla in California (800-825-TRIM). Talk to Nancy Lenhart, camp director, one of the foremost authorities on childhood obesity.

SHANE TRIM DOWN CAMP
12734 RDI, Box JH
Ferndale, NY 12734
914-292-4045
Brochure

Tired of being overweight and overlooked? Shed those unwanted pounds and build self-esteem at Shane Trim Down Camp. Superb weight-loss program includes calorie-controlled diets, aerobics, diet education, cooking classes, sports, field trips, performing arts, crafts, and evening activities. This coeducational program is for ages 7–16 and includes a young-adult program for girls 17–25. Sessions run from June through August. Prices vary, depending on length of stay. Call or write for free brochure.

WEIGHT WATCHERS CAMPS
183 Madison Ave.
New York, NY 10016
800-223-5600; 212-889-9500 (NY)
212-481-8624 (fax)
Brochure (full-color)

No gain. All loss. And never say die(t). Have fun in the sun as the pounds come tumblin' down. Summer camp is the perfect setting to learn a lifelong skill of proper nutrition and a method of weight control. The acquisition of a new sense of worth as well as the mastery of controlling eating habits once and for all are both part of the master plan at a WW camp. Don't be surprised if you even bump into a Georgie Girl. Eight locations throughout East and West coasts. Campers ages 10–25. What a weigh-to-go!

CHILD CARE

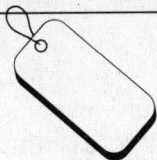

A CHOICE NANNY
8950 Route 108, Gorman Plaza, Suite 217
Columbia, MD 21045
800-73-NANNY; 301-730-2229 (MD)
Brochure

Given a choice, you can't afford *not* to be choosy when it comes to choosing a child caretaker. This firm offers child care needs assessment, a customized nanny search, and a valuable information packet to parents seeking quality, in-home child care. Nannies are interviewed by child care consultants, their references are checked, they are trained in Red Cross procedures and their backgrounds thoroughly investigated. A Choice Nanny offers full-time or summer-only nannies, and even provides for nannies on location for corporate care. Offices expanding nationwide. Call for complete location list and free brochure.

CHILD CARE TRAINING SYSTEMS, INC.
P.O. Box 871503
Dallas, TX 75287-1503
214-243-1285
214-350-1158 (fax)
Flier

Learn the ABC's of child care whether you're a parent, educator, or child-care professional. This innovative system of Child Development Training Workshops is state-certified and self-instructional. Accredited for 22½ clock hours of training, these professional workshops have been designed for use by both beginning and experienced group caregivers. Each video workshop and workbook supplied provides everything needed to meet early childhood training requirements. Clock hours received from Child Care Training Systems workshops can also be applied toward the 120 clock hours of formal training required to be eligible for CDA credentials. Training includes infant and toddler development and child guidance. C.T.S. has been a child-care consulting firm since 1981, a nationwide training system correspondence school since 1989.

CLASSIC PERSONNEL, LTD.
264 H St., P.O. Box 8110-447
Blaine, WA 98230
1-800-663-6128; 604-263-3621 (WA)
1-604-263-4139 (fax)
Brochure

Move over, Mary Poppins! Classic nannies have arrived. Established in 1974, Classic Personnel offers an experienced and perceptive selection in matching families with available applicants. It established a set of working conditions that form the basis of a cooperative team effort between employer and employee. Processing time is up to 6 weeks, and the duration of the contract is generally 12 months. A copy of

The Nanny Handbook, a comprehensive reference guide containing ideas for creative play with children, pointers on overall home management, a discussion on home safety and nutrition, plus a set of guidelines for employer and employee, is free of charge to Classic employers. Detailed information on fees, guarantees, and refund or replacement policies available at no charge. Full-time, live-in helpers earn $175 per week plus room and board. There's an $800 fee for placement with a 3-month guarantee (including a police report). Nannies work a 5-day week and no more than 10-hour days. Whew!

DR. BABY PROOFER, INC.
P.O. Box 595834
Dallas, TX 75359-5834
214-824-3964
Checklist for safety-proofing your home $5.

Thomas and Sue Golden learned firsthand the hazards of *not* baby-proofing your house while they were emergency room nurses in a major metropolitan hospital. After the birth of their daughter, they got their Ph.D.s in the baby business. Household dangers are the subject of their 300 item–plus checklist. Product recommendations are included.

You don't have to be Jewish to love a bagel. And teething babies get more relief from chewing on a frozen bagel than on a traditional teething biscuit.

KIDSAFE
P.O. Box 204
Cedarhurst, NY 11516
516-265-3311; 516-569-5334
Flier

Safe kids are no accident! Strange, our pets carry more identification than our children. The Kidsafe Safety Net program serves a definite need for a child's ID tag providing police, hospitals, and other authorized agencies access to vital medical and identification information 24 hours a day. This is one of the most extensive and comprehensive identification programs available today for your child's protection. The yearly registration fee is $20 per child. To enroll, you complete a confidential emergency information record form and return it to Emergency Response Centers. Your child is then registered with Safety Net and assigned a personal identification number. You will receive a set of 25 iron-on clothing labels imprinted with ID number and toll-free hotline numbers. Send SASE for information.

KIDTALK—LONESTAR COUNCIL ON CAMP FIRE
4209 McKinney Ave., Suite 100
Dallas, TX 75205
214-521-CAMP; 214-522-1144 (KIDTALK)
214-522-1188 (hearing-impaired)
Brochure

One ringy-dingy is all it takes to make a home-alone kid feel okay. Who talks to these kids after school when something frightens them? Or if they're lonely and just want someone to share the latest news? Kidtalk to the rescue! Kidtalk is a free, confidential telephone line for kids who are home alone, either regularly or occasionally. Trained volunteers make referrals as well as help children develop valuable decision-making skills and overcome momentary fears. It is a supplement to family support and not meant to replace established family emergency procedures. Also available for the hearing-impaired. For more information, to volunteer, or to contribute to a program in your area, call or write to the address above.

NANNIES OF CLEVELAND, INC.
15707 Detroit Ave.
Lakewood, OH 44107
216-521-4650
Complete information packet

Where's Mary Poppins when you need her? Well, try loving Nannies of Cleveland if she's flown the coop. The Nannies of Cleveland School offers an educational program with a wide range of subjects designed to prepare nannies with the skills, knowledge, and professional commitment required by families seeking the best in child care. Approved for college credit; free housing with host families may be arranged for out-of-town applicants. Offers a six-month comprehensive training period with placement nationwide. Nannies of Cleveland offers ongoing support and consultation to its graduates. For the thoroughly modern American parent in search of the thoroughly modern method of quality child care, call on a nanny, if you can!

RED CROSS NATIONAL HEADQUARTERS
17th & D St., NW
Washington, DC 20006
202-737-8300

Alas! Summer is upon you and you're minus a sitter! Here's a daycare solution for procrastinating parents. Local Red

Cross chapters across the United States hold classes for youngsters interested in baby-sitting. While they may not be able to give you names, they can pass your name along to some of their graduates. For specifics, contact the local Red Cross nearest you.

SAFE-SITTERS
1500 N. Ritter Ave.
Indianapolis, IN 46219

Patricia Keener, M.D., founded this nonprofit network to provide safety and child-care training to the millions of kids who are baby-sitters (or want to be). It's a course designed to instruct them on the art of everything from diapering to more serious matters like rescue breathing. Give your sitters all the ammunition they might need to handle any situation or any emergency. Write for more information.

Au Pairs

Today's child caretakers come from around the world offering a special international kind of TLC. Known as au pairs, they not only provide child care and some domestic duties, but you and your children have the opportunity to share in the life of another culture and language. There are several government-authorized programs that have established certain guidelines for au pair work visas: a one-year stay, an average cost of $165 per week, and up to 45 hours of live-in child care. These au pairs are between the ages of 18 and 25, and are carefully screened and selected from European countries. They are mature, responsible individuals with child care experience and English speaking skills. Following is a list of au pair programs you can contact.

The Safe Nursery, published by the U.S. Consumer Product Safety Commission, states that "more infants die every year in accidents involving cribs than with any other nursery product and thousands more are injured seriously." Cribs manufactured before 1974 did not follow certain protective guidelines. Following is the commission's safety crib checklist:

- slats are spaced no more than 2⅜″ apart
- no slats are missing or cracked
- mattress fits snugly (less than two fingers' width between edge of mattress and crib side)
- corner posts are no higher than ⅝″
- no cutouts in the head and footboards
- drop-side latches cannot be easily released (by baby)
- all screws and bolts are securely fastened

Furthermore, it is recommended that cribs not be placed near draperies or blinds. Be sure to leave pillows out of the crib; instead, add bumper pads, which are good for extra safety.

AU PAIR CARE—CULTURAL EXCHANGE
One Post St., Suite 700
San Francisco, CA 94104
800-288-7786; 415-434-8788 (CA)
415-986-4620 (fax)
Application and information packet

AU PAIR IN AMERICA—AMERICAN INSTITUTE OF FOREIGN STUDY
102 Greenwich Ave.
Greenwich, CT 06830
800-727-2437; 203-863-6123 (CT)
Application and information packet

AU PAIR HOMESTAY
202-408-5380

This is a nonprofit program run by the Experiment in International Living. Since 1986, qualified au pairs from Europe have been placed with thousands of American families. With one phone call, you can arrange an international live-in who is qualified as a child caretaker according to this organization's standards.

CLUBS

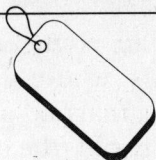

THE ACTIVITIES CLUB, INC.
P.O. Box 9104
Waltham, MA 02254-9104
800-873-5487
Flier (color)

When your kids say, "I'm bored," contact the Activities Club. Providing fascinating projects and activities designed to appeal to a kid's curiosity and sense of exploration, and at the same time building direction and self-esteem, this club offers kits filled with ideas for things to do. Choose a series of kits or try them individually. Each kit contains a project, a newsletter, collectible cutout activity cards, and an iron-on theme badge. Each kit introduces a new hobby and costs $12.95, plus $2.95 shipping and handling. Get a free copy of *All the Best Contests for Kids* when you pay for a series of kits. Geared for children ages 6–12. Join the club and help stamp out boredom!

INTERNATIONAL PEN FRIENDS
Box 290065
Brooklyn, NY 11229-0001
SASE

Fun and friendship from across the seas can be yours through International Pen Friends, whose doors are open to young and old, male and female, married and single. The youngest member is only eight years old (the oldest was born in 1893). Membership is for one year and during that period your name will be passed on to 14 persons in your own age group. Each subscriber may be assured that from among IPF's 250,000 members, they will be provided with many new, exciting, and interesting friends just as quickly as the enrollment form can be filled out and returned. Be sure to send SASE with request for information.

JUNIOR PHILATELISTS OF AMERICA
P.O. Box 1600
Trenton, NJ 08607
Newsletter

This is a great way to lick those humdrum hobby blues! Join the Junior Philatelists of America. Now, that's a mouthful! This club is specifically for kids who like to collect stamps. Send for a newsletter to learn all the latest information. You must enclose $1 and SASE.

KIDS MEETING KIDS
P.O. Box 8H, 380 Riverside Dr.
New York, NY 10025
212-662-2327
Newsletter (annual)

Pen pals for peace! Orignially the work of one family, this organization now includes thousands, with more than

350,000 children from all over the U.S. and the U.S.S.R. writing to one another. This fostering of international understanding allows kids to learn about what life is like in each other's countries. Enclose $3 with each letter you send to Kids Meeting Kids to receive the address of your penpal; this helps cover postage for the boxes of letters sent to the Soviet Union and to pay the cost of the annual newsletter. (However, KMK will accept letters from *all* kids—even those who cannot afford a contribution.) Everyone who sends a letter automatically becomes a part of the Kids Meeting Kids network and receives an annual newsletter. If you are interested in knowing more, call or write.

MICKEY MOUSE CLUB
Membership Headquarters
P.O. Box 2068
Marion, OH 43305
Flier (color)

M-I-C-K-E-Y M-O-U-S-E! You've got it! Access to that famous little mouse's club will cost $12.95. Official kit includes the newest, wildest club watch you've ever seen, membership card and certificate with your child's name on it, a collector's edition of *The Club Magazine* with the latest scoop and photos of the cast, club stickers, and club coupons with over 20 great offers including toys, games, travel discounts to Disney theme parks, plus a bunch of "ultra-rad" surprises! Sign up now!

NEW YORK TURTLE & TORTOISE SOCIETY
   (NYTTS)
153 Amsterdam Ave., Suite 365
New York, NY 10023
212-459-4803
Flier

With the rage of Teenage Mutant Ninja Turtles, half-pints on the half-shell have become favorite pets for kids. The New York Turtle and Tortoise Society is a nonprofit organization dedicated to the conservation, preservation, and natural reproduction of turtles in captivity. It publishes a bimonthly journal and sponsors an annual seminar, field trips, educational activities, and an annual turtle and photograph show. Membership is $15; children are encouraged to join under the supervision of adults.

THE JULIETTE GORDON LOW
   GIRL SCOUT NATIONAL CENTER
142 Bull St.
Savannah, GA 31401
912-233-4501
Brochure

This is the national center for the Girl Scouts of America, the largest voluntary organization for girls and women in the world. Membership is open to all girls ages 5 through 17. A continuous learning program offers girls a broad variety of activities addressing both current interests and future roles as women. The Juliette Low Center's purpose is to serve as a memorial to the organization's founder. There are 333 councils offering jurisdiction over 196,000 troops worldwide. Call for information on local chapters.

STUDENT LETTER EXCHANGE
215 5th Avenue S.E.
Waseca, MN 56093

Enclose SASE to get information on how to join the Student Letter Exchange where you can get a penpal from almost any foreign country or any state in the United States (ages 10–22). It'll cost you $1 for each penpal, with a minimum order of two, but the information about how to get started is free.

THE SURPRISE GIFT-OF-THE-MONTH CLUB
55 Railroad Ave.
Garnerville, NY 10923
914-429-2102
914-429-2792 (fax)
Brochure

Surprise! Surprise! This club boasts 50 percent or more savings on all inventory plus a free gift each month. Cost is $2 per month for postage and handling, a $24 drop in the bucket for a one-year subscription. As a member of The Surprise Gift-of-the-Month Club, you'll receive a unique and often unusual gift every month worth more than you paid. How do they do it? The club obtains many different items from manufacturers that have gone out of business; also overruns, closeouts, and new products seeking an introduction. Examples have included a distinctive, handmade latch hook rug wall hanging, suggested retail $20, your cost $3; or a genuine leather belt adjustable to all sizes in a rainbow of colors, retailing for $20, your cost $2. Full refund on returns with all items fully guaranteed.

U.S. CHESS FEDERATION
186 Route 9W
New Windsor, NY 12553-7698
800-388-KING
Annual dues $15

"Check" this one out, "mate"! If you are a chess enthusiast, or the parent of one, enroll yourself or him/her in the U.S. Chess Federation, America's only coast-to-coast chess club. Members under 19 pay $15 a year, which includes 12 issues of *Chess Life*, eligibility for tournaments and postal chess, and product discounts. It's your move!

COMPUTERS
AND SUPPLIES

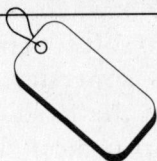

COMPUADD
800-477-4717
Catalog

It always computes to visit CompuAdd. Their prices rival
their customer service, and that's no easy task! They bring
the world of software (and hardware) within reach by
representing over 400 titles at the lowest prices in the
industry. What more could you want? How about four to
five name-brand software applications bundled into one big
bargain price? And for kids (or adults who still feel like
kids), there's a great collection of Game Paks, Learning Paks,
and Joystick Games. A sampling of software packages available: Chip 'n' Dale Rescue Rangers, Geo Jigsaw, Jetsons
Game, Jetsons and Flintstones Kit, Math Rabbit, and for the
sports enthusiasts, John Madden Football, Micro-League
Baseball, and Micro-League Football. CompuAdd also manufactures their own line of PCs as well as being one of the
largest discounters of name-brand computer hardware and
software in the country. Shop by catalog if there's no
CompuAdd in your area (Mon.–Fri. 9:00 A.M.–6:00 P.M.;
Sat. 9:00 A.M.–5:00 P.M. CST).

COMP USA (formerly Soft Warehouse)
15160 Marsh Lane
Dallas, TX 75234
800-451-7638
Catalog

Trying to hold down the hard costs of computers? Well, the folks at CompUSA are no soft touch, no doubt about it. This funland of "floppies" is superstar for both products and technical assistance when the hard drive goes soft. Toshiba laptops and Dell desktop computers drive a hard bargain here. Save 30–80 percent on over 5,000 computer-related products. Their collection of software geared specifically for children includes Disney Sticky Bear series for math and reading; Davidson's Student Organizer for 12 years to adult; Word Attack Plus—Vocabulary, Grammar Gremlins; Alge-Blaster Plus; Math Blaster Plus; and a whole lot more. Free catalog available. Check in and check 'em out! Twenty stores nationally and still growing.

COMPUSERVE
5000 Arlington Center Blvd.
Columbus, OH 43220
614-457-8600

An online data base service offering 1,500 different data bases. For kids, there's *Grolier's Encyclopedia*, Research Data, and ERIC—Education Information Center—a must for to-day's computer-literate society demanding instant information. Also, hundreds of online games and forums where kids can talk (computer-to-computer) with other kids and grown-ups from all over the world on almost any subject imaginable. All junior needs is a modem and phone line to "boot up" to a world of knowledge. Membership is $39.95 for a lifetime of data, and hourly "connect" charges apply. Call for further details, or visit your local computer software store for a membership kit.

COMPUTER MAIL ORDER
101 Reighard Ave.
Williamsport, PA 17701
800-233-8950; 717-327-9575
717-327-1217 (fax)
PQ

CMO commands SRO when it comes to computer systems, disk drives, printers, modems, software, and such. Save up to 40 percent when you want a WordPerfect bottom line. Their in-house computers also are noteworthy in the XT, 286, and 386 models. Insert, merge, macro, display, stop, print with computer goods, alphabetically speaking, from A to Z: Amdek, AST, Bernoulli, Curtis, Epson, Hewlett-Packard, IBM, Kensington, Lotus, NEC, Okidata, Panasonic, Star Micronics, Xerox, and Zenith.

EASTCOAST SOFTWARE
48 Derrytown Mall
Hershey, PA 17033
800-877-1327
Catalog

Take a byte out of this Hershey software catalog and watch the prices melt with every purchase. Specializing in software (educational, recreational, and business) for the Apple, Macintosh, Commodore 64, Amiga, and IBM-compatibles. Choices number in the thousands. Save also on peripherals like computer and printer stands, disks, and paper.

GREAT WAVE SOFTWARE
5353 Scotts Valley Dr.
Scotts Valley, CA 95066
408-438-1990
Brochure

Take the byte out of computer software for kids. Little hands can at least experience disk-counts. The quality comes from combining programming talent with the insight of experienced educators and master graphic artists. The result is educationally sound software that is also fun. Macintosh programs include American Discovery—uses interactive graphics, sound, and animation to teach and reinforce U.S. geography and history (remember how boring it was to be drilled on where the states were?); Kids Math—teaches math concepts and learning skills; Kids Time—enjoyed by children of all ages, it encourages creativity, learning and computer skills; Number Maze—supports learning critical reading skills; and Number Maze Decimals and Fractions—includes eight math curricula and covers 18 math skills. Kids Time also available in Apple IIGS, IBM, and Tandy versions. For music lovers, listen to Great Wave's Sound Waves Concertware (for the Macintosh only). For a demonstration or to purchase these products, visit your local dealer, or order direct.

LEARNING ADVENTURE COMPUTER CLUB
925 Oak St.
Scranton, PA 18515
717-342-7701
Flier (color)

Launch your children on a spectacular learning adventure. As a charter member of this club (similar to a book or cassette club), receive a newsletter about every four weeks, accompanied by a recommended software selection, plus alternate selections. Alternate selections should be requested

10 days prior to usual delivery date; main selections are sent automatically. Pay just $9.95 plus $2.95 postage and handling for your first choice of popular children's computer software programs valued at $59.95, and then be billed at regular Club prices, usually $29.95 and up, depending on the program. Minimum of three selections annually. Programs available for IBM compatibles and Apple II computers. Turn leisure time into learning time with the Learning Adventure Computer Club (a subsidiary of ICS—International Correspondence Schools). Remember, though: you must respond promptly with your intentions NOT to buy; otherwise you may be receiving a program that you hadn't counted on.

NATIONAL LEARNING SYSTEMS
925 Oak St.
Scranton, PA 18515
800-828-2917
717-343-8041 (fax)
Brochure

Attention future Wall Streeters and bargain barons. Learn Lotus 1-2-3 for much less than the cost of a single class or seminar. Micro-Tutor Software is a self-paced tutorial program for IBM and compatibles backed by the National Education Corporation. Other programs available include dBASE III PLUS, MS-DOS, WordPerfect, and more at just $49.95 each, plus $2.95 shipping and handling (PA and CA residents add 6 percent). Thirty-day money-back guarantee.

DEPARTMENT STORES/ OFF PRICE AND CLEARANCE CENTERS

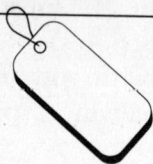

BURLINGTON COAT COMPANY
1830 Route 130 North
Burlington, NJ 08016
609-387-7800

Yes, they have coats. And more coats than you can shake a stick at. For kids wanting to cover up for 20–60 percent less, try on hundreds of coats, jackets, ski jackets, vests, sweaters . . . If it's meant to be worn outside, step inside one of the 170 Burlington stores nationwide. But that's just the tip of the iceberg. Their children's department includes the works, starting at the bottom with shoes and going on to tops, dresses, sportswear, activewear, everything that's meant to be worn in infant, toddler, boy, girl, preteen, and junior sizes. Furniture is included in about half their stores (they will special-order if there's no selection in your store) and includes cribs, strollers, high chairs, car seats, carriers, bedding, wood and metal furniture, and mattresses . . . everything for baby: Childcraft, Bassett, Luv, Perego, Combi, Aprica, and Evenflo. Don't overlook their selection of baby gifts, toys, children's books, and videos.

FAMILY DOLLAR
Corporate Office: P.O. Box 1017
Charlotte, NC 28201-1017
704-847-6961

With over 1,600 stores across half of the country, and more planned each day, surely there'll be a Family Dollar store near you one of these days. The budget store concept of the '90s, this family store outfits the whole family in clothes, shoes, and more, plus housewares, health and beauty aids, and toys in brand names as well as private labels. Check phone directory for store nearest you.

GOODY'S
Corporate Office: 400 Goody's Lane
Knoxville, TN 37933-2000
615-966-2000

Even a Goody Two-Shoes has a foot up on the competition. Family apparel and accessories like Levi's, Lee, Gitano, and Jordache at 20–25 percent off retail, Goody, Goody! Over 100 stores concentrated in Alabama, Georgia, Kentucky, Mississippi, North Carolina, Ohio, South Carolina, Tennessee, and Virginia.

HILLS
Corporate Office: 15 Dan Road
Canton, MA 02021
617-821-1000

Head for the Hills when you want to save 20–40 percent on name-brand family apparel, accessories, housewares, jewelry, linens, shoes, and toys for little girls and boys. Oshkosh B'gosh and everything nice, that's what little boys and girls are made of. Over 200 stores concentrated in Alabama, Georgia, Illinois, Indiana, Kentucky, Maryland, Massachusetts, Michigan, New York, Ohio, Tennessee, Virginia, and West Virginia. Check phone directory for one near you.

J.C. PENNEY OUTLET STORES
Department Store/Catalog Clearance
Corporate Office: P.O. Box 659000
Dallas, TX 75265-9000
214-591-1000

A penny saved at a J.C. Penney clearance center is a penny earned. You'll save more than pennies, though. Savings compute from 10–60 percent and are available by shopping the following locations: Tempe, AZ; Los Angeles, CA; Hartford, CT; Atlanta, GA; Chicago, IL; Boston, MA; Kansas City and St. Louis, MO; Reno, NV; Cincinnati and Columbus, OH; Philadelphia, PA; and Milwaukee, WI.

MAC FRUGAL'S (formerly Pic 'n' Save)
Corporate Office: 2430 E. Del Amo Blvd.
Dominquez, CA 90220-6306
213-537-9220

Closeouts from heaven have been picked for you to save. Almost 200 stores from California to Florida, with savings on general merchandise from 40–70 percent. Merchandise moves with the tide as the closeouts rise and fall. Toys, gift items, paper products, cosmetics, candy—what you see is what you get!

MARSHALLS
200 Brickstone Square
Andover, MA 01810
800-MARSHALLS

Since 1956, the Marshall plan has been taking the country by storm. Today they are the biggest and one of the best off-price chains linking Americans to the concept of name brands for less. Save 20–50 percent (and sometimes more) on a department-store selection of men's, women's, and children's apparel, jewelry, cosmetics, accessories, lingerie, shoes, bags, gifts, and bed and bath items. Anyone who is paying full price for children's clothes, underwear, even shoes for more than peanuts these days is nuts. This one-stop emporium offers a plan for an economical statement, where the bottom line is savings without sacrificing style, selection, or service. Call or write to find the store nearest you.

MERVYN'S
Corporate Office: 22301 Foothill Blvd.
Hayward, CA 94541
415-785-8800

This division of Dayton-Hudson is the home of family apparel that's at least 20 percent off. Promotional labels and name brands are their back-to-school stock in trade. Over 225 stores in Arizona, California, Colorado, Florida, Georgia, Idaho, Louisiana, Michigan, Nevada, New Mexico, Oklahoma, Oregon, Texas, Utah, and Washington. Call 1-800-MERVYNS for the one nearest you.

MONTGOMERY WARD CLEARANCE
OUTLET STORES
Corporate Office: One Montgomery Ward Plaza
Chicago, IL 60671-0001
312-467-2000

Stop monkeying around and paying full price for furniture
for the kid's room. From cribs to cradles, rocking chairs to
bunk beds, if it hasn't sold at full price in a Montgomery
Ward store, it might make its final performance at one of
their clearance store outlets at 10–60 percent off. Included
may also be a ceiling fan or two, a stereo, or a room air-
conditioner. Visit outlets in Phoenix, AZ; Los Angeles and
Sacramento, CA; Washington, DC; Tampa, FL; Chicago, IL;
Kansas City, KS; St. Paul, MN; Albany, NY; Portland, OR;
Pittsburgh, PA; Ft. Worth, Houston, and San Antonio, TX.

NORDSTROM RACK
Corporate Office: 501 Fifth Ave.
Seattle, WA 98101-1603
206-448-8522

Rack 'em in, nice and easy, from this giant in the department
store business. Nothing fancy about it, kids, except you can
expect the kid-glove treatment (Nordstrom is famous for
their service and their selection). Stacks and stacks are racked
in their clearance-store division chain numbering 14 in
Chino, Colma, Daly City, San Diego, Santa Ana, San Leandro,
and Topanga, CA; Clackamas and Portland, OR; Salt Lake
City, UT; Woodbridge, VA; Lynnwood, Seattle, and Spo-
kane, WA. The selection of kids' stuff is growing as fast as
your kids are. They've even added a children's shoe department, one of the few in the country to start 'em saving from
the ground floor. First quality and recognizable department
store labels abound, from infants to preteen. Save 30–70
percent every day. Get to know your sales person so your
name will be added to the Rack Preview Sale where mark-

downs are 50–70 percent off the already discounted price. Nautica, Esprit, Baby Boxer, Motto Red Dot, Iya, Ultra Pink, Safari, Bugle Boy, Norsport (private label), Polo, and Tic Tack Sox are just a few of the many popular brands. Charge it and they'll ship it!

PAMIDA
Corporate Office: 8800 F Street
Omaha, NE 68127
402-339-2400

Call out the F troops from F Street when it comes time to blow the horn on full prices. Save 10–30 percent on name brands for the family and home in brands from Wrangler to Lee. Stores located in Illinois, Iowa, Kansas, Michigan, Minnesota, Missouri, Nebraska, South Dakota, Wisconsin, and Wyoming. More's in store.

ROSS DRESS FOR LESS
Corporate Office: 8333 Central Ave.
Newark, CA 94560
415-790-4400; 800-345-ROSS

Why pay department store prices when there's a Ross around? Dress 'em up for less at this company. Over 200 stores in the Northwest, West, Southwest, and now expanding to the East Coast, Florida, Georgia, Virginia, Washington, D.C., Maryland, North Carolina, New Jersey, and Pennsylvania. Whoopee for their selection of name-brand wear for infants and toddlers, girls (4-6X; 7-14) and boys (4-7; 8-20). Save 20–60 percent on Jordache, Bugle Boy, Camp Beverly Hills, Lee, No Excuses, and Cherokee, to name-drop a few. Call their 800 number for store nearest you.

SEARS SURPLUS STORES
Corporate Office: Sears Tower
233 S. Wacker Dr.
Chicago, IL 60684
312-875-2500

Overstocks and discontinued items from Sears are collected at their more than 100 clearance stores nationwide at 10–70 percent off. Check your directory for store nearest you.

SOLO SERVE/SOLO STORES
Corporate Office: 1610 Corner Way
San Antonio, TX 78219
512-225-7163

This is like a Grimm's fairy tale with a happy ending. Everything for the entire family is waiting to be served on a plain vanilla platter. Their menu is strictly the South/Southwest: Texas, Louisiana, and Alabama. There is something for everyone when the subject is clothes, accessories, and shoes. Some of the class acts were Guess?, Jobo, Jordache, Bugle Boy, Polo, and Dockers.

STEIN MART
Corporate Office: 1200 Gulf Life Drive
Jacksonville, FL 32207
904-346-1500

Though no relation to Gold Stein, this Stein is still worth its weight in gold. Its boutique, upscale-department-store atmosphere belies the bargains in store. Lots of labels not usually found in other off-price stores but whose names remain silent to protect Stein Mart's vendor relationships. Clothing and accessories for infants, toddlers, girls and boys, from the basics like socks and underwear to designer outfits. Save 25–60 percent off department and specialty store prices.

Their 44 stores are concentrated currently in the Southeast and the Southwest, but more on the way.

TUESDAY MORNING, INC.
Corporate Office: 14621 Inwood Road
Dallas, TX 75244
214-387-3562

Tuesday Morning is not just another day of the week. Their seasonal sales are actually on an almost continual basis, and a shopper who's not interested in saving 50–80 percent should take a flying leap elsewhere. This is the king of closeouts for the entire family, but particularly appealing when your little prince or princess commands an audience with Santa year-round. Ask and ye shall receive. Gifts and gift wrap, clothes and accessories, toys and school supplies, and other good things for girls and boys. The only difference is the price. From an Orrefors crystal picture frame, to a Ralph Lauren beach towel, a Cabbage Patch doll, or a pint-size ski outfit, you can shop 'til you drop. Over 150 stores nationwide, though concentrated in the Southeast and Southwest, with a few in the Midwest, the Washington, D.C., area, and California. Soon to be in the Northeast. Call or write for locations nearest you.

VALUE CITY/SCHOTTENSTEIN'S
Corporate Office: 1800 Moler Road
Columbus, OH 43207
614-221-9200

There are millions of deals in Value City, so map out your shopping strategies with a stopover here. Any which way you turn, you will average savings of 25–75 percent on name brands for kids: tops, bottoms, dresses, outerwear, layette items, baby necessities like nipples and rattles, plus baby basics like furniture, bedding, and coordinating groupings.

Outfit them from infants, toddlers, boys to 18, and girls 4-14. Complete the family's outing with appliances, domestics, furniture (in some stores), electronics, housewares, lingerie, shoes, jewelry, health and beauty aids, toys, and gifts. Current and overstocked merchandise makes the fast track to one of the over 60 stores in Delaware, Illinois, Indiana, Kentucky, Maryland, Michigan, Ohio, Pennsylvania, Virginia, and West Virginia. Check the phone directory for store nearest you.

DIAPERS

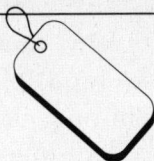

BIOBOTTOMS
P.O. Box 6009
Petaluma, CA 94953
800-766-1254; 707-778-1948
Catalog (full-color)

Comfortable, breathable, super-absorbent, and pin-free, who could ask for anything more? Biobottoms are full-felted woven wool and cotton diaper wraps in stylish patterns with an emphasis on eliminating diaper rash. Great styles to choose from: Classic Biobottoms, Rainbow Classic, and now Rainbow Bikini—cut higher on the legs for extra freedom and a more versatile shape for chubby or thinner legs. They also offer training pants and casual, colorful, and comfortable clothing for sizes infant to 14. The older kids' line features double-dyed fabrics from Africa and South America. Shoes, too! Fresh-air wear for kids. (Offers a free diapering booklet, "All About Diapering," and Bio Suds for conditioning cleanup of "dirty duds.") Call for your free catalog.

BUMKINS FAMILY PRODUCTS
1945 E. Watkins
Phoenix, AZ 85034
800-553-9302
Flier

Need a better idea for baby's bum? Meet Bumkins, a reusable, environmentally safe, "all-in-one" diaper. No pins, no plastic pants, or diaper covers needed. Machine wash and dry. Save $10-$15 a week otherwise spent on disposables or diaper services. For easier cleanups, 100 percent cotton liners make it quick and easy. (No more "toilet dunk"!) Bumkins come in all sizes and can be purchased in colors, patterns, and whites in three-packs and six-packs. Available at many juvenile retailers.

DIAPERAPS, LTD.
P.O. Box 3050
Granada Hills, CA 91344
(800) 251-4321; (800) 447-3424 (baby care counseling)
Brochure

Wrap it up in diapers for the '90s. If you're tired of being bottomed out, these cotton diapers are for you. Cloth tabs hold them securely in place with patented construction allowing air to circulate, while a foam inner lining helps reduce diaper rash. These innovative bottom huggers come in sizes NB (newborn) to T (toddler), solid colors of yellow, pink, white, and blue, and lamb, bear, tugboat, and circus prints. Diaperaps are convenient, comfortable, cost-effective, and environmentally safe. Washable, too! Next-day shipping with 100 percent money-back guarantee. Minimum order on credit card orders. Sorry, no CODs. Also available at stores near you.

HAPPY ENDINGS
12391 S.E. Indian River Dr.
Hobe Sound, FL 33455
407-546-1278; 407-283-1042
Brochure

Look, Mom! An adaptable diaper for growing babies complete with tips on diaper care and a guide to folding. By folding in both ends, you've got newborn diapers; fold in one end and there's a medium version; with a third fold, it becomes a toddler-sized diaper. These "diaper duds" come in all white or a choice of trimmed shades and sell for under $30 a dozen (up to 30 percent lower than prices on similar products). Minimum order one dozen. Call or write for brochure.

NATURAL BABY CO. INC.
114 W. Franklin Ave.
Pennington, NJ 08534
800-388-BABY
Catalog

This shop-at-home diaper service offers 100 percent cotton diapers plus diaper covers from $3.95 to $16.95 each. There's also a complete selection of shampoo and bath items.

TENDER CARE—R MED INTERNATIONAL, INC.
5555 E. 71st St., Suite 8300
Tulsa, OK 74136
800-34-IM DRY
Brochure

Do you realize your baby will spend approximately 20,000 hours in diapers? Most super-absorbent disposable diapers use acrylic acid polymer salts to keep baby dry. These chemicals turn into a gel that sits right next to baby's skin.

Chemicals are not listed on packages because the FDA does not regulate infant diapers. Fret not, mothers of America! Now there's chemical-free Tender Care, a new disposable super-absorbent diaper that's soft, comfortable, free of absorbing chemicals, perfumes, and deodorants. These diapers come in five sizes and styles including newborns (U-shaped, cut out around the navel for better healing of the umbilical cord). Better care for better bottoms, and environmentally pleasing, too. Automatic reorder when you join the Tender Care Diaper Club. Next-day service via UPS.

DOLLS AND COLLECTIBLES

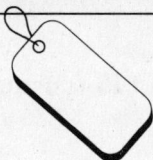

ASHTON-DRAKE GALLERIES
9200 N. Maryland Ave.
Niles, IL 60648-1397
312-664-4650 (client services)
Flier

Ashton-Drake is the world's only gallery exclusively featuring premier grade collector's dolls. Hand-painted porcelain dolls with hand-crafted period costumes are individually hand-numbered and bear the artist's signature, with certificate of authenticity. For those collectors interested in heirloom-quality dolls with investment potential, these are the doll babies to cradle. Market values have generally exceeded purchase prices. One-year unconditional guarantee (full refund or credit).

AUTOGRAPH ADDRESS LIST
Collectors Club
P.O. Box 467
Rockville Center, NY 11571-0467

Sign in, please. If you are an autograph hound, this is an inexpensive source to start your collection. Send 50 cents and a long SASE and start signing today. Movie stars, rock stars, TV stars . . . 35 names and addresses will be sent upon request.

BARRONS
P.O Box 994
Novi, MI 48376-0994
800-538-6340; 800-762-7145 (customer service)
313-344-4342 (fax)
Catalog (full-color)

For gifts that evoke a bygone, romantic era, Barrons offers hand-crafted crystal, heirloom-quality silver and china, and Royal Doulton hand-painted porcelain miniatures in mirrored display cases for doll collectors or a little girl's room. Choose also playful presents for little ones: music boxes, diaper bags, mobiles, and children's room accessories. Gifts in good taste from Barrons. Satisfaction guaranteed. Full refund, credit, or exchange.

CAROLLE—SPECIAL DOLL DIVISION
   OF MATTEL, INC.
333 Continental Blvd.
El Segundo, CA 90245
800-421-2887
Brochure (full-color)

Vive la France. These were all created and hand-crafted there and they are *the* tour de France when it comes to dolls. Carolle dolls are as special as their ultimate owners. Faces are sculptured after real children. The dolls' skin is specially molded vinyl and scented with vanilla. Bald babies are machine-washable; those with rooted hair are surface-washable. Special moments with these dolls will create fond memories for a lifetime. Great for collectors since their

lifelike features and attention to detail make exquisite treasures and precious playmates. Call for retailer nearest you.

CHILDREN'S GALLERY
599-A Washington St.
Dorchester, MA 02124
800-526-9253; 617-825-4141
Flier (order form)

This is your typical rags-to-riches story. The Children's
Gallery ethnic rag dolls are the epitome of success representing an entire world of children and their love of dolls.
A United Nations–like collection is designed to help children
realize that each race is different, yet alike. They are hand-
crafted and come in three sizes and three ethnic groups:
Asian, black, and Hispanic. "Raggs" is the female rag doll,
with calico dress and bloomers. "Patches" is her male coun-
terpart bedecked in a calico pantsuit. They've been featured
on NBC's "Cosby Show" and ABC's "Family Matters." Indeed, it's a small world after all. Write or call for further
information and order forms.

DOLLSVILLE DOLLS AND BEARSVILLE BEARS
461 N. Palm Canyon Drive
Palm Springs, CA 92262
800-CAL-BEAR (credit card orders only)
619-325-DOLL; 619-325-2241
Catalog

Cuddle up and collect 20 percent and more in savings on
collector teddy bears and dolls, doll houses and accessories,
doll and bear books, clothing, and jewelry. This company
will beat any advertised price, plus throw in free shipping.
Specials on Dakin "Elegante" dolls, World dolls, New Gorham
dolls, Carolle French dolls, and Lenci dolls pre-1986.

HUSTON DOLLS
7969 US Route 23
Chillicothe, OH 45601
Catalog $2

Though not from the heart of Texas, these Huston dolls are still lone stars in the category of lovable dolls. Sixty-plus years ago, Melvina Huston turned her hobby into one of the grandest doll collections in the world. Still run by her children, this catalog sells both kits and fully dressed dolls. For example, the Melvina doll is $60 but as a kit is $19. Over 250 dolls to dress up (or down), babies to Madame Butterfly, clowns to cherubs, and all crafted with precision and pride.

LENOX COLLECTIONS
One Lenox Center, P.O. Box 519
Langhorne, PA 19047-0519
800-233-0313
Flier (color)

What a dish! Now fine bone china connoisseurs can collect dolls and figurines from the same manufacturer who has been serving up fine china dinnerware forever. These fine porcelain collectibles are the perfect conversation pieces to display in your child's room. "Bedtime Prayers," an original sculpture of hand-painted porcelain, captures the serenity and beauty of a timeless moment between mother and child, and is just one of the delicate samples from their Mother and Child Collection. For personal collections or special gifts, call for details.

PLEASANT COMPANY
8400 Fairway Place, P.O. Box 998
Middleton, WI 53562-0998
800-845-0005; 608-836-4348 (WI)
Catalog (full-color)

This oversized catalog collects some of the most beautiful exquisite, delicate, and enchanting dolls for you to curl up with. You can collect the Three American Girls, as well as read about their adventures in a series of eighteen beautifully illustrated books. Called "The American Girls Collection," each doll brings to mind the traditions of girlhood with words and picture books, toys, dresses, and accessories. The "New Baby Collection" is crafted especially for toddlers who are anticipating the arrival of a new baby. Complete with a pop-up book, beautiful baby doll, and imaginative toys, toddlers learn special caretaking skills for the new sibling. The dolls are available only through the catalog. The books are available in bookstores.

SAXKJAERS
53 Købmagergade
1150 Copenhagen K
Denmark
011-45-331-10777
011-45-333-27210
Catalog $2 (by air); refundable

For devotees of collector's plates, this source is nearly a century old and provides platefuls of Hummel, Royal Copenhagen, and Bing & Grøndahl at 40 percent off and more. Start early and collect the porcelain animals or Mars Jonasson crystal "portraits," animals exquisitely etched in blocks of lead crystal. These pieces sell for considerably more in uptown galleries and are real chips off the old bargain block for anyone interested in a *great buy*. Also dished up were the popular Hummel figurines, Georg Jensen silverware and gifts, and Danish dolls. Though Danish is not served with each order, prompt and courteous service is. Shipped worldwide by surface mail; insurance is included.

WARNER BROS. COLLECTION
P.O. Box 60048
Tampa, FL 33660-0048
800-223-6524
Catalog

For fans of Warner Bros. animation, TV shows, and films, this is the one and only *complete* source for collectibles. All the Looney Tunes, Merrie Melodies, and Tiny Toons novelties imaginable, plus bomber jackets, bathrobes, T-shirts, ball caps, sweatshirts, key chains, coffee cups, watches, wall hangings, and more from movies like *Robin Hood*, *Batman*, and *Beetlejuice*, as well as memorabilia from "The Flash," "Growing Pains," "Full House," and other Warners TV shows. One of our favorite items is the Acme alarm clock/ time bomb that gives you just two chances to get up (in English, French, or Spanish) before "blowing up" ($48).

EDUCATIONAL
PROGRAMS

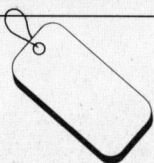

AMERICAN INTERCULTURAL STUDENT
   EXCHANGE
National Headquarters
7720 Herschel Ave.
La Jolla, CA 92037
(800) SIBLING; (619) 459-9761 (CA)
(619) 459-5301 (fax); telex 697927
Brochure

As a nonprofit, tax-exempt educational foundation for high school students, American Intercultural Student Exchange (AISE) offers education without national boundaries and is dedicated to the fostering of international understanding. As a host family for an AISE student from another country, you will have the opportunity to reach across cultural barriers and gain many new insights and an understanding of the world's people. Students pay for all fees and airfares necessary to participate. A $250 scholarship will be given to each American student who goes abroad in the overseas exchange program if the parents host an exchange student. Spend a year or summer abroad with a host family and experience Sweden, Norway, Denmark, Finland, Spain, Italy, Germany, Switzerland, England, or Australia. If you are between the ages of 15 and 18, reach out and touch someone halfway around the world. Brochure details information and a complete list of AISE offices nationwide.

CHILDREN'S EXPRESS
245 Seventh Ave., 5th Floor
New York, NY 10001
212-620-0098
Brochure

Extra! Extra! Read all about it! This is a nonprofit news organization for young reporters covering national and international children's issues. CE offers young people a unique opportunity to participate, during after-school hours, in hard-edged journalism through interviews with political leaders and experts in children's issues. Interactive round-table discussions cover topics ranging from drugs to the environment. Articles are written by kids 8–18, edited by teenagers and adults, then syndicated to major newspapers across the country. CE publishes a news quarterly and maintains a board of directors and medical advisory board. Children's Express is "expressly written" *by* children *for* everyone. Maintains bureaus worldwide. Write or call for more details.

DEEP SPRINGS COLLEGE
HC 72, P.O. Box 45001
Dyer, NV 89010-9803
619-872-2000
Brochure (full-color)

One of the best bargains available in higher education turns out to be at the smallest college in the United States. Deep Springs College in Deep Springs, California, no doubt qualifies as the smallest for the *Guinness Book of Records* with a staggering enrollment of 24 (and everyone male)! This college is situated on a working ranch adjacent to Death

College Degrees by Mail, by John Bear, Ph.D., for ages 18 and up ($11.95, ISBN 0-89815-379-4, Ten Speed Press/Celestial Arts): This is a great resource book for anyone in search of a college degree, but lacking the time and money to go back to school. A concise list of 100 reputable schools which offer bachelor's, master's, doctoral, and law degrees by home study. The time can be as short as three months, and the cost can be as little as $500. The author details information about each program, including tuition, majors and degrees offered, key contact persons, address, phone, and fax . . . plus a personal evaluation of the school. (Also includes a long list of schools to avoid.)

Valley, where the entire student body works at the ranch, functioning as admissions and hiring committees, cooks, dishwashers, and librarians. The curriculum is liberal arts with the usual school term of 12 weeks, with a week off at the end of every term. Don't expect to cut classes undetected and don't expect to pay tuition. Deep Springs is entirely FREE! So are room and board. The school pays for itself through bequests, gifts of parents and alumni, and the operation of the ranch. After two years, students are practically guaranteed admission to Cornell University and just about any other top school to which they apply. Tuition: zero $; room and board: zero $. For more information, write or call (but not collect).

FATHER FLANAGAN'S BOYS HOME
Public Service Division
Boys Town, NE 68010
800-448-3000 (national hotline)
402-498-1580; 402-498-1140 (Visitors Center)
Brochure (order form)

This privately supported, residential-care facility is touted as America's natural resource for abused and neglected boys *and* girls. At the heart of the program are specially trained and certified married couples, called Family Teachers. Six to ten youngsters, mixed by age and race, live in real homes along with these Family Teachers. Boys Town has four direct-care programs: Home Campus Program—educational and residential-care facility; Boys Town National Institute —research hospital for children with hearing, speech, and learning disorders; Father Flanagan High School—an inner-city high school for troubled youth; and Boys Town USA— wholly owned and operated campus sites around the country. As an incorporated village of the state of Nebraska, Boys Town has its own post office, fire and police departments, two churches, and three schools. Publications and films have been produced by the Public Service Division at Boys Town to help parents, teachers, counselors, and youth-care professionals. Send inquiries to the above address for additional information.

INVENT AMERICA
510 King St. Suite 420
Alexandria, VA 22314
703-684-1836
Sample packet

Rekindle the spirit of American ingenuity with Invent America, a program designed to stimulate creativity and develop kids' problem-solving skills. Winning inventors are eligible for national awards and a free trip to Washington, D.C.

Parents and teachers get a free ride, too. Information needed to implement the "Invent America Program" in your school is available through the above address. Write or call for a sample packet.

THE KIDS ON THE BLOCK—EACH AND EVERY ONE PROGRAM
9385-C Gerwig Lane
Columbia, MD 21046
800-368-KIDS; 301-290-9095 (in MD)
Flier (order form)

Not to be confused with the popular singing group New Kids on the Block, this is a child-sized troupe of puppets with disabilities that are used in schools across the country to teach healthy children how it feels to be different. As part of the Each and Every One Program, children in primary and intermediate grades experiment with being blind, wheelchair bound, or otherwise impaired. This disability-awareness program is available to parents, teachers, and schools throughout the United States. For information on implementing one in your community, call (800) 368-KIDS.

OAK PLANTATION PRESS
P.O. Box 640
Rockwall, TX 75087-0640
214-722-BOOK
Brochure (order form)

Give your child a head start in school with *Teach a Beginning Reader with Common Sense and a Cookie Sheet*. Wow, that's a mouthful! In kitchens and cars across America, parents are teaching young children how to read using this unique book as their guide. Applying a phonics-made-fun approach that includes using magnetic letters on cookie sheets, having the child write in sand or cornmeal on a cookie sheet, and making reading games out of sentence strips, story cards, and the like, reading is as easy as ABC. Available from Oak Plantation Press, 1–9 copies are $9.95 plus $2 postage and handling, plus sales tax. Quantity orders, 40–50 percent off. Shipping is free if order is prepaid.

TEEN AID OF TEXAS
401 S. Sherman St. Suite 215
Richardson, TX 75081
214-480-TEEN
Flier

This nonprofit organization is dedicated to teaching teens and their families how to achieve goals, strengthen self-image, and build healthy relationships through rap sessions, seminars and workshops, psychological and educational evaluations, relationship counseling, individual and family counseling, and family participation courses like the "Ropes Course." This two-day adventure for teens and parents combines wilderness adventure with new ways to build trust while improving self-confidence and personal performance. Program is bilingual, offers services to the hearing-impaired, and uses a sliding-scale fee structure.

SKIDAWAY MARINE SCIENCE COMPLEX—
   UNIVERSITY OF GEORGIA MARINE EXTENSION
   SERVICE
P.O. Box 13687
Savannah, GA 31416
912-356-2496
Flier

This marine extension program covers a wide range of educational activities, including elementary and secondary (K-12) programs; teachers' workshops; and adult short courses. A major function of the program is to provide assistance for teachers who wish to include field study as a part of science and social science classes. Samples of some of the field studies included a tour of a 10,000-gallon aquarium and exhibits, marsh studies, a barrier island study, dock-, plankton-, and boat-based studies, and an extensive collection of both coastal fossils and local Indian artifacts. A must if you are in, or touring through, Savannah, Georgia.

EDUCATIONAL SERVICES ORGANIZATIONS

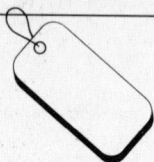

COLLEGIATE CHOICE WALKING TOURS
41 Surrey Lane
Tenafly, NJ 07670
201-871-0098
Flier

Attention, prospective college students! Here's a special you shouldn't pass up. Students can visit the college campuses of their choice, without leaving home, for just $20! One of the often overlooked start-up costs of choosing a college is the initial visit to check it out. Wouldn't it be nice if students and their parents could take a campus tour of any college in the country without the inconvenience, time, and expense of travel? Collegiate Choice Walking Tours offers the next best thing to being there. The cost to families is $20 for the first tour and $15 for each additional tour. Choose from almost 300 listed colleges in 20- to 120-minute-long, non-promotional, detailed videos of campus facilities. An excellent low-cost way to do your college shopping. Friendly staff to answer any questions.

THE COMPLETE COLLEGIATE, INC.
490 Route 46 East
Fairfield, NJ 08004
201-882-9339
Catalog

Got a kid going away to college? This mail-order company specializes in packing them off right from the start with such necessary items as oversized laundry bags that are divided by light and dark dirty clothes. If they'd rather not show their dirty laundry to their roommate, how about an underbed storage container? Visit their showroom and warehouse when in the area and see everything from backpacks to goodie bags packed with tea and cocoa. Many items personalized for free.

HOMEWORK HOTLINE
c/o Sam Massey, Principal
Beech Elementary School
3120 Longhollow Pike
Hendersonville, TN 37075
615-824-2700

How many excuses have you heard from Junior for why he didn't do his homework? Or what's his reason for not showing up in class? No chance to skip out on responsibilities at this school. To find out about homework assignments, all a parent has to do is call this school's toll-free, 24-hour computerized Homework Hotline and punch in the code for the child's teacher. Adapted voice mail and voice bulletin board technology provide not only homework information, but also lunch menus, schedules of athletic events, notices of PTA meetings and advice on how to help kids at home. According to Mr. Massey, initial cost for his school's system was somewhere in the neighborhood of $6,000 to $7,000. A great tool for noncustodial parents or grandparents who wish to keep up with children's activities. For more information on implementing the system in your child's school, contact Mr. Massey at the above address, or the Betty Phillips Center for Parenthood Education at Vanderbilt University in Nashville, 615-322-8080.

NATIONAL PTA
700 N. Rush St.
Chicago, IL 60611
312-787-0977
Booklet

Studies have shown that parents who actively participate in their children's school activities produce children who are much more motivated in academic pursuits. The national PTA offers a booklet, *The Busy Parent's Guide to Involvement in Education*, with tips on how to get involved when time is so restricted (especially when both parents work outside the home). Send SASE to *Busy Parent's Guide*, c/o National PTA at address above.

NATIONAL ASSOCIATION FOR EDUCATION OF
YOUNG CHILDREN (NAEYC)
1834 Connecticut Ave. NW
Washington, DC 20009-5786
800-424-2460; 202-232-8777
202-328-1846 (fax)
Catalog

NAEYC is an information-packed service providing a wealth of sources on child care. Acting as a referral network, it directs parents and educators to organizations, publications, and projects that deal with specific child-care topics. This service also offers information on demographics, licensing provisions, and contacts for a variety of provisions for the maintenance of high-quality early-childhood programs. Some examples: "Off to a Sound Start: Your Baby's First

Year" and "Teaching Your Child to Resist Bias: What Parents Can Do." Call or write for free catalog of resource material.

NATIONAL COMMITTEE FOR CITIZENS IN EDUCATION (NCCE)
10840 Little Patuxent Pkwy., Suite 301
Columbia, MD 21044
800-NET-WORK; 301-977-9300 (in MD)
Booklet

One of the most effective ways to bring about change in the public schools is to work as a group with other parents. Collectively, parents can voice their concerns with much more impact than one-on-one. NCCE offers advice on how to organize effective parents' groups and suggests additional resources which may assist in this effort. Through the group, parents can make a positive contribution toward improving the quality of education. If there are no PTA or PTO organizations in your child's school, contact NCCE for assistance.

NATIONAL COMMITTEE FOR PREVENTION OF CHILD ABUSE
332 S. Michigan Ave., Suite 1600
Chicago, IL 60604-4357
312-663-3520
Booklet; catalog

This organization assists in the prevention of child abuse through a variety of public awareness campaigns, education, advocacy, and research. Write or call for their booklet with basic information on child abuse and an introduction to NCPCA's approach to preventing abuse. Catalog of literature and special subject materials available for children, parents, and educators. Call or write for further details.

THE STEWART HOME SCHOOL
P.O. Box 26
Frankfort, KY 40601
502-875-4664
Brochure

A year-round program of progressive education in a home environment for the mentally handicapped child or adult is available at the Stewart Home School, set on a 600-acre estate. Established in 1893, and under the supervision of a resident physician, "special care for special people" has been the cornerstone of this uniquely designed, multilevel recreational and social approach to treating the mentally impaired.

ENVIRONMENTAL
AND ECO-SOURCES

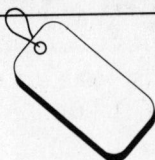

AMERICAN FORESTRY ASSOCIATION (AFA)
P.O. Box 2000
Washington, DC 20013
202-667-3300
Free pamphlets

The AFA is concerned with the management and enjoyment of forests, soil, water, wildlife, and other natural resources. To that end, they offer educational materials for both students and teachers, such as "The Global Releaf Report" and a newsletter informing children how they can initiate tree-planting projects and other ecologically motivated pursuits in their school, neighborhood, or city.

AMERICAN OCEANS CAMPAIGN (AOC)
235 Pennsylvania Ave. SE
Washington, DC 20003
202-544-3526
202-544-5625 (fax)
Flier

AOC is a nonpartisan, nonprofit organization dedicated to the restoration and preservation of America's oceans. It is committed to making the public aware of the plight of the oceans and the need for a national ocean policy with the creation of a multimedia educational campaign utilizing print, video, and film. It supports the activities of local and regional coastal organizations and concentrates on three major action areas: coastal pollution, offshore oil drilling, and driftnet fishing. Offers a $3 "Household Hazardous Waste" wheel that identifies toxins in the home and suggests effective substitutions. Also has an office at 2219 Main St., Suite 2B, Santa Monica, CA 90405; (213) 452-2206.

AMERICAN RIVERS
801 Pennsylvania Ave. SE, #303
Washington, DC 20003
202-547-6900

This organization's mission is to preserve the nation's rivers and landscapes for fishing, boating, hiking, wildlife, and overall splendor. Results are measured by the number of river miles and streamside acres preserved. For more information and how you can get involved, write or call the above number.

CLEAN WATER FUND
317 Pennsylvania Ave. SE
Washington, DC 20003
202-457-1286

Water, water everywhere but maybe someday not a drop to drink. The purpose of this organization is to focus its efforts on research and education for safe drinking water, control of toxic chemicals and solid waste, and the protection of our natural resources. Write or call for more information.

EARTHWATCH
680 Mount Auburn Street
P.O. Box 403
Watertown, MA 02172
617-926-8200

Earthwatch to tower. Earthwatch to tower. Interested parties (ages 16 and older) may spend two weeks (plus transportation) preserving the Great Plains in Fort Collins, Colorado; humane trapping and monitoring of black bears in Asheville, North Carolina; or the humane capture and study of wild dolphins in Sarasota, Florida, as part of an ecologically sound vacation plan. Cost varies from $990 to $2,000.

ENVIRONMENTAL ACTION FOUNDATION
1525 New Hampshire Ave. NW
Washington, DC 20036
202-745-4870

Waste not, want not. This group engages in research, education, grass-roots organizing, and legal action in the promotion of a healthy environment. It focuses on issues relating to toxic pollution, energy efficiency, solid waste, recycling, and energy conservation. Write or call for more information.

NATIONAL AUDUBON SOCIETY
950 Third Ave.
New York, NY 10022
212-832-3200; 212-546-9100
Brochures

Ladybug, ladybug, fly away home—but will it be a safe haven? This group is dedicated to conducting scientific research, public education programs, and environmental action programs to preserve wildlife and important natural areas. The NAS office publishes numerous bulletins, reports, and journals. An education division produces manuals for teachers and information for students. NAS can be contacted at Rt. 1, Box 171, Sharon, CT 06069, (203) 364-0520.

**NATIONAL PARKS & CONSERVATION
  ASSOCIATION**
1015 18th St. NW
Washington, DC 20007
202-944-8530
Brochure

When you want to park it, let's hope there's a park left to enjoy. If you want to help, this association focuses on preserving, promoting, and improving our nation's park system. It offers educational information for students and teachers. Write or call for details.

NATIONAL WILDLIFE FEDERATION
1400 16th St. NW
Washington, DC 20036-2266
202-797-6800

This organization focuses its efforts on establishing strong, responsible conservation policies through educational activities and citizen action programs. It publishes reports, books, etc., sponsors workshops and activity programs, and prepares media presentations. Call or write for more information.

NATURE CONSERVANCY
1815 N. Lynn St.
Arlington, VA 22209
703-841-5300
703-841-1283 (fax)
Information packet

The Nature Conservancy engages in conservation activities in the United States, Canada, Latin America, and the Caribbean. They depend on donations to buy land where endangered plants and animals are living. Each preserve in turn provides a natural habitat for native plants and animals. Call or write for a free information packet for kids.

RAILS TO TRAILS CONSERVANCY
1400 16th St. NW, #300
Washington, DC 20036
202-797-5400

This organization is definitely on the right track. They are actively engaged in converting thousands of miles of abandoned railroad corridors to public trails for walking, bicycling, horseback riding, cross-country skiing, wildlife habitats, and nature appreciation. Write or call for more information.

RAINFOREST ALLIANCE
270 Lafayette St., Suite 512
New York, NY 10012
212-941-1900
Newsletter

Rain, rain, go away—but what if coming back another day may be in jeopardy? This organization supports informational programs that help educate the public about the effects of rain forest destruction. They operate by coordinating professional organizations, financial institutions, the business community, and concerned citizens on scientifically grounded programs to slow the destruction of rain forests. Publishes a quarterly newsletter. Call or write for more information.

SEVENTH GENERATION
800-456-1177

For anyone wishing to enter seventh heaven 100 percent pure, this is a catalog to send for. Being ecologically correct when it comes to shopping means that parents can no longer ignore the impact certain products make on the environment. The next generation is the Seventh Generation offering over 200 products that are environmentally sound. Recycling bins cost $48 (a set of three); recycled baby diapers (disposable and green cotton, which means they are organic), computer paper (1,000 sheets, $19.95), even Post-its on recycled paper ($13.95/12 pads).

SIERRA CLUB
730 Polk St.
San Francisco, CA 94109
415-776-2211
Brochures

If there's one club that fosters immediate recognition for the concept of conservation, it's the Sierra Club. Their primary objective is to protect and conserve the natural resources of the United States and the world, and to preserve and restore the quality of the environment and ecosystems. A variety of literature is available on environmental issues. Call or write for more information as well as how you can get involved.

UNION OF CONCERNED SCIENTISTS
26 Church St.
Cambridge, MA 02238
617-547-5552

Citizens of the '90s will be keeping a watchful eye on this scientific group, which conducts research and programs in the areas of nuclear power safety, energy policy, the greenhouse effect, nuclear arms control, and the impacts of science and technology on the environment. To learn of their activities and how you can get involved, call or write.

UNITED STATES FISH AND WILDLIFE SERVICE
18th and C Streets NW
Washington, DC 20240
208-343-5634

Fishing around for a good group to sink your teeth into? Well, throw a line to this agency, which operates a program of public affairs and environmental education on the status of America's fish and wildlife. Literature available through their Publications Department in Arlington, VA, 703-358-1711.

THE WILDERNESS SOCIETY
1400 I St. NW
Washington, DC 20036
202-833-2300

Return to the wild with this organization dedicated to preserving wilderness and wildlife and protecting forests, parks, rivers, and shorelands, as well as broadening awareness of our relationship with the natural environment. Write or call for more specific information.

WORLD WILDLIFE FUND
1250 24th Street NW
Washington, DC 20037
202-293-4800

"Without firing a shot, we may kill one-fifth of all species of life on this planet in the next 20 years." Do we have your attention yet? Rain forests that provide food and shelter to at least one-half the world's species of wildlife are being bulldozed and burned off at an alarming rate, but what can one person do? The World Wildlife Fund now directs more than 500 scientifically based projects, and contributions can help with gorilla conservation in Rwanda, panda research and habitat protection in China, and rescue of the Arabian oryx, the peregrine falcon, and the golden tamarin monkey in Brazil. Membership levels begin at $10, and for a contribution of $15, a special gift offer is being made to send a FREE, members-only tote bag.

FREEBIES
(AND ALMOST FREE)

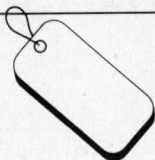

ANIMAL PROTECTION INSTITUTE
Free Animal Bookmark Offer
P.O. Box 22505
Sacramento, CA 95822
Free bookmarks

Want to find out everything "humane-ly" possible about cats, dogs, or birds? Send for these *free* bookmarks from the Animal Protection Institute and read about the eating, sleeping, and bathing habits of these three species of the animal kingdom. Enclose SASE along with your letter asking for "Free Animal Bookmarks."

ARM & HAMMER DIVISION—
 CHURCH & DWIGHT CO.
P.O. Box 7648
Princeton, NJ 08543-7648
Foldout ("How to Make Play Clay")

Summer boredom settin' in? Could be a great day for play with clay! Have hours of fun with clay you make yourself with baking soda and other common ingredients. This *free* foldout from Arm & Hammer shows you how to make jewelry, ornaments, and more. Enclose SASE along with your letter asking for "How to Make Play Clay" and mold some summer fun!

BASEBALL CARD NEWS—DEPT. BLW
700 E. State St.
Iola, WI 54990
Sample copy

Attention baseball fans! This biweekly newspaper is for people who collect baseball cards. In it you'll find the latest news, photos, and features. A sample copy is yours FREE, simply for the asking. Don't strike out and pass this one up!

THE CHILDREN'S MUSEUM—KID'S FUN PAK
533 Sixteenth St.
Bettendorf, IA 52722
Kid's Fun Pak

The "Kid's Fun Pak" is jam-packed full of fun including puzzles, facts, cartoons, recipes, mazes, games, crafts, and activity ideas . . . over 40 fun things in all! Write (enclose SASE) and ask for the FREE "Kid's Fun Pak."

COCA-COLA COMPANY
Consumer Information Center
P.O. Drawer 1734
Atlanta, GA 30301

Send for your *free* set of nine peel-off stickers, each with a Coke symbol in different languages, including Hebrew, Japanese, Arabic, Polish, and Chinese.

DUNCAN TOYS COMPANY
P.O. Box 5
Middlefield, OH 44062
Foldout

This one's for beginning yo-yo enthusiasts! Learn the "ups and downs" of this versatile toy with a *free* foldout from the Duncan Toys Company. Write a letter (enclose SASE) asking for "Duncan Yo-Yo Trick Sheet."

FREE STUFF FOR KIDS
Meadowbrook Press
Deephaven, MN 55391
800-338-2232

The number-one-selling kids' activity book now in its 15th edition with over 2.5 million in print is none other than *Free Stuff for Kids*, published by Meadowbrook Press. Who says you can't get something for nothing (or next to nothing) and keep the kids busy as bees down at the farm? Coloring books, comic books, posters, stories on cassette, magazines, maps . . . you're only a stamp away. Send check for $4.95 plus $1.25 for postage and handling to the above address and call for ordering information on the other terrific kids' books like *Learn While You Scrub* and *Rub-A-Dub-Dub Science in the Tub* books ($6.95 and $5.95, respectively); *Dino Dots* (connect-a-dot with dinosaur facts, $4.95); *It's My Party* ($5.95); and *Measure, Pour, and Mix Kitchen Science Tricks* ($5.95).

Many TV shows have live audiences. If you plan to be in New York or Los Angeles, write to the network's guest relations department for free tickets.

ABC
7 West 66th Street
New York, NY 10023
or
4151 Prospect Ave.
Hollywood, CA 90027

NBC
30 Rockefeller Plaza
New York, NY 10020
or
3000 W. Alameda Ave.
Burbank, CA 91523

CBS
524 W. 57th Street
New York, NY 10019
or
7800 Beverly Blvd.
Los Angeles, CA 90036

HOHNER, INC.
P.O. Box 9375, Dept. FD
Richmond, VA 23227-5035
Free instruction guide

Got a hankerin' to play the harmonica? This guide from Hohner teaches you how to play one of the world's smallest and most popular instruments, and it's yours FREE! Send SASE along with your letter asking for "How to Play the Hohner Harmonica" and start humming a different tune!

JUNIOR PHILATELISTS OF AMERICA
P.O. Box 1600
Trenton, NJ 08607

Help stamp out the high price of starting a stamp collection. Send for their FREE packet (enclose SASE) telling you how to start one, which includes 20 international stamps.

KIX KIDS PIX—GENERAL MILLS, INC.
Fulfillment Center
111 Third Ave. So., P.O. Box 112
Minneapolis, MN 55440
Brochure (full-color)

"Capture Your Cutest Kix Kid" is a free brochure from General Mills offered to parents as a guide to taking prize-winning mug shots. A checklist of helpful tips to focus on include ensuring that your camera is in good working order, entertaining your subject, and choosing your background. Helpful hints developed by award-winning photographer Patsy Hodge, an expert in child portraiture. Picture-taking buys wonderful memory insurance, so smile, and say cheese!

LITTLE PUBLICATIONS
2000 Rosini Dr.
Shamokin, PA 17872
717-648-2481

Coming from a town named Shamokin, it's gotta be good. Little Publications . . . little price . . . BIG offer! For only $5.95, you get the new directory of FREE items for parents and parents-to-be from the government and large corporations. FREE baby care books, baby shoes, rolls of film, games, 8″ × 10″ color newborn photos, baby photo albums, pamphlets, puzzles, newsletters, children's magazines, coloring books, and much more. Return if not satisfied for full refund.

MEADOWBROOK PRESS
Department PP/CYSM
18318 Minnetonka Blvd.
Deephaven, MN 55391
"Perplexing Puzzles Pamphlet"

Got a mind for mystery? Like the challenge of word games? All you junior Dick Tracys can take a crack at solving some of Professor Pinkerton's Most Perplexing Puzzles from Meadowbrook Press. You must enclose SASE and 25 cents with your letter asking for the "Perplexing Puzzles Pamphlet." (Oh, yeah . . . you get a "Can You Solve the Mystery?" sticker, too.)

Sports

Listen up, sports fans. Did you know that National Football League teams offer a fan-mail package that usually includes a team sticker, photos of the players, a schedule of the upcoming season, and more? For a FREE fan-club package, send your request to the following:

ATLANTA FALCONS
Suwanee Road @ I-85
Suwanee, GA 30174

BUFFALO BILLS
One Bills Drive
Orchard Park, NY 14127

CHICAGO BEARS
Halas Hall
250 N. Washington
Lake Forest, IL 60045

CINCINNATI BENGALS
200 Riverfront Stadium
Cincinnati, OH 45202

CLEVELAND BROWNS
Tower B
Cleveland Stadium
Cleveland, OH 44114

DALLAS COWBOYS
Cowboys Center
One Cowboys Parkway
Irving, TX 75063

DENVER BRONCOS
5700 Logan Street
Denver, CO 80216

DETROIT LIONS
Pontiac Silverdome
P.O. Box 4200
1200 Featherstone Road
Pontiac, MI 48057

GREEN BAY PACKERS
P.O. Box 10628
1265 Lombardi Avenue
Green Bay, WI 54307

HOUSTON OILERS
6900 Fannin Street
Houston, TX 77030

INDIANAPOLIS COLTS
P.O. Box 535000
7001 W. 56th Street
Indianapolis, IN 46253

KANSAS CITY CHIEFS
One Arrowhead Drive
Kansas City, MO 64129

LOS ANGELES RAIDERS
332 Center Street
El Segundo, CA 90245

LOS ANGELES RAMS
2327 W. Lincoln Avenue
Anaheim, CA 92801

MIAMI DOLPHINS
Joe Robbie Stadium
2269 NW 199th Street
Miami, FL 33056

MINNESOTA VIKINGS
9520 Viking Drive
Eden Prairie, MN 55344

**NEW ENGLAND
  PATRIOTS**
Sullivan Stadium, Route 1
Foxboro, MA 02035

NEW ORLEANS SAINTS
1500 Poydras Street
New Orleans, LA 70112

NEW YORK GIANTS
Giants Stadium
East Rutherford, NJ 07073

NEW YORK JETS
598 Madison Avenue
New York, NY 10022

PHILADELPHIA EAGLES
Veterans Stadium
Broad Street & Pattison
  Avenue
Philadelphia, PA 19148

PHOENIX CARDINALS
51 W. Third Street
Tempe, AZ 85281

PITTSBURGH STEELERS
Three Rivers Stadium
300 Stadium Circle
Pittsburgh, PA 15212

SAN DIEGO CHARGERS
San Diego Jack Murphy
  Stadium
P.O. Box 20666
9449 Friars Road
San Diego, CA 92120

SAN FRANCISCO 49ERS
4949 Centennial Blvd.
Santa Clara, CA 95054

SEATTLE SEAHAWKS
11220 NE 53rd Street
Kirkland, WA 98033

**TAMPA BAY
  BUCCANEERS**
One Buccaneer Place
Tampa, FL 33607

**WASHINGTON
  REDSKINS**
13832 Redskin Drive
Herndon, VA 22070

FURNITURE AND ACCESSORIES

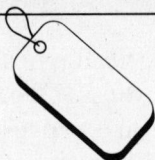

ANNEX FURNITURE GALLERIES
616 Greensboro Road
High Point, NC 27260
919-884-8088
Brochure, PQ

Annex-cellent choice for children's bedroom ensembles from bunk beds and beyond. Climb aboard a Stanley line and whistle "Dixie" at up to 45 percent off retail. Their brochure lists hundreds of manufacturers (hush, hush on certain ones for fear that that revelation would jeopardize their ability to discount). If you're visiting High Point, you can make a pit stop at their 45,000-square-foot showroom and see firsthand what we're talking about.

BARNES & BARNES
190 Commerce Ave.
P.O Box 1177
Southern Pines, NC 28387
800-334-8174; 919-692-3381 (NC)
Brochure, PQ

How are things down at the Barnes? And don't plan to stall around. The lines are endless. Over 200 of America's barn-storming manufacturers are represented, including several prominent lines for kids' furniture. Several groupings from Lexington for both boys (they get the rugged maritime varieties) and girls (French Provincial, bisque, and white-washed looks). There's also Stanley, Lea, and Bassett (cribs and other juvenile items) to choose from. Orders shipped nationwide; in-home setups available. This company will save you up to 50 percent.

CHERRY HILL FURNITURE
P.O. Box 7405
High Point, NC 27264
800-328-0933; 919-882-0933 (NC)
Brochure, PQ

Cherries can be handpicked from the orchard of juvenile furniture for less here. Both Lexington and Stanley lines are represented (up to 50 percent off) with darling white canopy groupings for little girls, and the whole gamut of wooden bunk beds, student desks, and bookcases for boys. A new line called Rooms to Grow includes several collections in both wood and painted groupings sure to delight any youngster. Also available for parents who work at home: complete home office furniture selections.

DECORETTE
1901 W. Parker, Suite 137
Plano, TX 75023
214-964-3580; 214-867-5874 (fax)
Brochure, PQ

Kids' rooms are often the last place to decorate. But when you want them to sleep cheap, and keep the sun out of their eyes so you can catch a few extra winks on the weekend, it's time for a mini-blind, or a vertical or pleated shade that's easy to open and shut. Then add a coordinated bedspread, dust ruffle, bed pillows or a big floor pillow, several window toppers, even a custom rocker seat, and plan on sitting on savings up to 80 percent. They've even done the decorating on a doll house complete with miniature draperies, matching fabric walls, and bedspreads. All fabrics used for kids' rooms including matching headboards are Scotchguard-ed or Teflon-coated for easy cleanup. Nationwide phone orders accepted. How-to-measure window brochure available upon request.

FRAN'S BASKET HOUSE
295 Route 10
Succasunna, NJ 07876
201-584-2230
Brochure

Rattan is dandy but wicker is quicker when it comes to redoing parlor to patio. And for baby's room, there's nothing more angelic than a wicker ensemble including dresser, cradle, and rocker. But don't stop there. The minimum order is $25 but with the considerable savings and the hefty selection, you won't find meeting the minimum difficult.

LOFTIN-BLACK FURNITURE COMPANY
111 Sedgehill Drive
Thomasville, NC 27360
800-334-7398; 919-472-6117
Brochure

A lofty idea became a reality in 1948 with the founding of the Loftin-Black Furniture Company. Lexington and Stanley are prominent players in children's furniture where bedding down in either the Locker Room line for boys or the Imagination line for little girls makes a fashion statement at up to 50 percent off. Then there's the Chez Michelle line of Country French Victorian reproductions, or the unisex Vail line of strictly contemporary. Offerings range from cradles and cribs in bedroom groupings to juvenile and youth lines that grow with the children. Expect to pay a 50 percent deposit (like most of the North Carolina discounters) before shipment is under way.

MARION TRAVIS
P.O. Box 292
Statesville, NC 28677
704-528-4424
Catalog $1

This 10-page catalog highlights, in black and white, country furniture at a fraction of what you'd expect to pay. Particularly noteworthy is the collection of ladder-back chairs with woven cord seat, armchair and rocker styles, and children's models beginning at under $25. Though the prices quoted are for "nude furniture," custom staining in natural, oak, or walnut is available.

PLEXI-CRAFT QUALITY PRODUCTS CORP.
514 W. 24th Street
New York, New York 10011-1179
800-24-PLEXI
Catalog $2; PQ

Plexi-craft sees the picture clearly. They manufacture their own line of furniture and accessories even in miniature for kids. Parents who foot the bill can save up to 50 percent over what is charged in retail boutiques down the street. Acrylic furnishings and accessories in Lucite and Plexiglas create a Pandora's box of possibilities: building blocks, pint-sized tables and chairs, doll houses and stands, doll cases, displays for toys, a trunk that serves as both table and toy box, notebook holders and clipboards—the only limit is your imagination. Send a sketch of what you want molded, and they'll send you a price quote.

SICO ROOM MAKERS
5000 Belt Line Road #250
Addison, TX 75240
214-960-1315 (call collect)
214-920-1320 (fax)
Brochure

Help put an end to the squeeze of tightening budgets! Make more room for enjoyment with the addition of one of Sico's wall bed and cabinet systems. Just imagine the space you could create for play in your little one's room. Or what about that spare guest/sewing room? Endless possibilities are open to you from this seemingly endless collection of wall beds and organized units for keeping *all* things in their proper places.

TOUCH OF CLASS CATALOG
Huntingburg, IN 47542
800-457-7456
812-683-5921 (fax)
Catalog

Enchanting Beatrix Potter's characters featured on a Cannon sheet ensemble would enhance any little girl's bedroom. Friends of Peter Rabbit also included a comforter, a dhurrie rug, bunny slippers, a vanity and stool set, prints, pillow cases, and shams. Hop to the next page for Cityscapes by Sumersault, a bold contribution to any child's room. Primary colors are the basis of a personalized statement for city (or country) kids' bedrooms. From sheets to wall hangings, monogrammed bedrests to zippered baggage, in skyscraper and airport motifs. Sesame Street and Minnie Mouse, too. Everything to coordinate a child's bedroom between the sheets of this catalog with a Touch of Class. A cute night's rest at a peaceful price.

TURNER-TOLSON, INC.
P.O. Drawer 1507
New Bern, NC 28560
919-638-2121
Brochure, PQ

Head for Highway 17 South to heaven for one of the oldest furniture discounters east of the Mississippi. Since 1887, the names are couched in secrecy until you get their brochure, but we'll spill the beans on a few goodies just for kids' rooms such as Lexington, Bassett, and Stanley. And for heaven's sake, don't overlook the brass possibilities by Wesley-Allen, including cribs and juvenile beds. A partial listing arrives with their brochure; the balance is available on a catalog-for-a-fee basis. Turner's prices are 40–50 percent lower than list, and shipping charges include in-home delivery and setup.

GARDENING

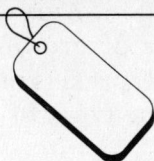

GARDENER'S SUPPLY
128 Intervale Road
Burlington, VT 05401
800-548-4784

Dig in and start tilling for tots. Even if you just give them
their very own dirt pile while you do the serious planting,
they will learn how to get their hands into the earth. Try
planting produce or a strawberry patch (without toxic pes-
ticides, of course). A 3-piece kids' tool set was only $24.95,
as was a children's wheelbarrow.

GARDENS FOR GROWING PEOPLE
P.O. Box 630
Point Reyes Station, CA 94956-0630
415-663-9433
Catalog

Kids interested in growing things can sink their rake and
hoe into this catalog's child-size gardening tools. A one-stop
shopping source for seeds, tools, and gardening books for
toddlers and children. Ask for their guide, "Gardens for
Growing People." A surefire way to plant the seed and
cultivate their green thumbs early.

KIDS' GARDEN SEEDS
P.O. Box 57053
Hayward, CA 94545

Send SASE for information. Kids can have the pleasure of learning the root-iments of growing their own flowers or vegetables with two FREE packets of seeds. Growing instructions included, though the types of seed vary.

LANGENBACK
P.O. Box 453
Blairstown, NJ 07825
800-362-1991

This beautiful catalog helps to make your garden grow with a little help from fine English stainless tools, hand-forged Yankee Craftsman tools, tools especially made for use in small gardens and window boxes. A children's tool set was $39.95. Not meant to be considered a toy, this 5-piece quality tool set can be used by kids 3-10. Includes bamboo leaf rake, hoe, shovel, cultivator, and rake.

PINETREE GARDEN SEEDS
New Gloucester, ME 04260
207-926-3400
Catalog

For green thumbs interested in saving some green (up to 30 percent off), this is the catalog to cull. Home gardeners love it because the seeds come in small-enough packets perfect for kids and beginners. Over 600 varieties of vegetable and flower seeds alone, including some epicurean delights like radicchio and snow peas. Plants and tubers for asparagus and shallots didn't appeal to a six-year-old, but the berries and potatoes did.

GIFTS AND GADGETS

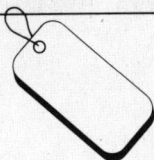

BAJA IMPORTS
P.O. Box 313
Hudson, NY 12534
$27.95 (includes UPS delivery)

If your Tarzan and Jane can't swing from the treetops, they might make do with swinging between the trees in this handwoven cotton hammock especially designed to fit a child's frame. Specify sky blue, pink, or natural color. If you don't have two trees conveniently planted, two walls will do.

BENNETT BROTHERS, INC.
30 E. Adams St.
Chicago, IL 60603
312-263-4800
312-621-1669 (fax)
Catalog (full-color)

From toy trains to board games, Bennett Brothers promises quality and blows the whistle on full retail prices. Radio-controlled cars and planes, Harvard Ping-Pong tables, boccie sets, and sporting goods from Wilson are just a few of the items offered by this company. Save 30 percent on most items, such as a desktop calculator from Canon for $46.49

(versus manufacturer's retail price of $64.95) or Playskool's
212-piece Lincoln Log set for $22.75 (versus $32.95 retail).
A new line of gifts from their "Bennett Brothers Blue Book"
and "Choose Your Gift" programs were specifically designed
for corporations, customers, and friends. Check in and check
it out!

BUDDY BUGGY
800-458-7400

When your plans call for traveling with two kids, this
lightweight, molded polyethylene stroller (either pull it or
push it) is the way to go. Shipped assembled for $149 (in
Alaska and Hawaii, $189), it seats children ages 1 to 6 and
comes with seat belts, reflectors, and fenders for safe riding.

CHINA CLOSET
1002 North Central Expressway
Richardson, TX 75201
214-238-7766
800-825-7766

Madam, dinner is served! How nice of you to bring out your
good dishes. Now, the best of china doesn't have to cost as
much as a trip to the Orient. China Closet claims not to have
any sales simply because their products are already marked
down 20–40 percent. What's in it for the kids? Oneida baby
cups and banks, Kirk-Steiff pewter picture frames, and the
Beatrix Potter collection of banks, plates, and figurines.

CURRENT FACTORY OUTLET
Corporate Office: 6200 SW Macadam #100
Portland, OR 97201
503-224-3944
Catalog (full-color)

Paper the town green with envy but don't tell them your secret. This paper goods, cards, and giftware catalog merchant finds itself with leftover merchandise that is not so current and sells it at closeout prices of 50–80 percent less than retail. Lucky kids live in Arvada, Aurora, Colorado Springs, or Englewood, CO, and Beaverton, Gresham, or Portland, OR. Call or write for catalog.

EXPOSURES
9180 LeSaint Dr.
Fairfield, OH 45014
800-222-4947; 513-874-9600
Catalog (full-color)

Feast your eyes on these fabulous finds for preserving family photos. A variety of ways to organize and display photos, mementos, stamp and coin collections, even wildflowers are featured in this catalog. Unique ways to preserve photos for generations at flea market prices.

GOLDS'
P.O. Box 448
Memphis, TN 38101-0448
800-284-7365 (credit card orders)
800-323-8077 (customer service)
Catalog (full-color)

How many times have you thought about buying your kids (or grandkids) a gumball machine and didn't know whom to call? Well, try the pages of this catalog. In fact, there are

pages devoted entirely to gumball machines, from $9.95 to
$34.90 (complete with antique-looking stand). Turn the
pages, and there's even a gumball machine lamp. Having a
snack attack? Munch out with plenty of Good and Plenty
gift boxes. Or stash the cash in lots of slot machine banks.
Chill out with a soda fountain music box ($26.95). Or try a
toy that'll teach you a lesson that it doesn't have to cost a lot
to mean a lot.

HARRIET CARTER
North Wales, PA 19455
215-361-5151 (orders); 215-361-5122 (information)
Catalog (full-color)

You'll cart off some fun as well as fabulous and useful little
gadgets and gifts from this catalog; you'll laugh and learn a
thing or two. Some favorites include a baby's first bib with
the date embroidered ($2.95), an Easter-egg tree to show off
decorated eggs ($11.98), a toy hammock to keep stuffed
animals and dolls neatly off the floor ($4.98), and a great
3-dimensional '50s malt shop clock for $34.98. All made the
top ten for a teen's bedroom.

HEIR AFFAIR
625 Russell Drive
Meridian, MS 39301
800-332-4347; 601-484-4323 (MS)
Catalog $2 (free to readers)

Parents (and grandparents) whose urge is to splurge will
delight in this collection, like a custom monogrammed chair,
a complete puppet theater for all of their performances, a
tricycle built for two, a beach cabana for an infant including
mosquito netting, a sterling dumbbell rattle, Wizard of Oz
hand puppets, a ski sled, or any other adorable, essential or
plain and simple loving gift that kids can't live without.

THE HERITAGE KEY, INC.
10116 Scoville Ave.
Sunland, CA 91040
818-951-1438
818-951-1010 (fax)
Catalog (full-color)

Variety is the spice of life and this catalog holds the key. An international potpourri of merchandising. Unlock jewelry from South America and Africa, bangles from India, books and toys from China, Korea, South America, and Africa, language tapes, multicultural heritage books, and much more. Soar to new heights with the Heritage Key International Children's Catalog—awarded the Parents' Choice Seal of Approval.

JOAN COOK HOUSEWARES
3200 S.E. 14th Avenue
P.O. Box 21628
Ft. Lauderdale, FL 33316-1628
800-327-3799; 305-761-1600 (Ft. Lauderdale)
305-522-0641 (fax)
Catalog (full-color)

Morning or night, through sleet or snow, your orders are filled seven days a week, without fail. Items that sure will get you cookin' include a 13″ × 16″ school picture frame for $28; a beanbag float for the pool, $65; a moving mouse watch for $44; a safety gate with a handy walk-through door for $55; and a wonderful piece of bathroom art showing a child wrapped head to toe in toilet paper.

LILLIAN VERNON CORPORATION
P.O. Box 69
Mt. Vernon, NY 10551
914-699-4131; 914-699-7698 (fax)
Catalog (full-color)

Lillian Vernon, the grande dame of catalogs, founded her empire humbly in 1951 but can now call herself the reigning Queen of Gifts. Over 30 million happy campers scamper to their mailboxes with glee for one of her catalogs. One of the highlights in our mailbox, too. Affordable, often personalized, great gifts and gadgets for kids and their families. Average price throughout is around $15, so you won't have to take out a second mortgage. Babies go goo-goo and kids go ya-hoo every time we send a surprise. The mini-bath wraps with their names on it still rate a surefire thank-you note. If you buy 15 or more of the same item, and spend at least $250, you will qualifty for discounts up to 50 percent. And that's not hard to do. Watch for sale catalogs for similar savings. Visit outlet stores in New Rochelle, NY; Potomac Mills at Prince William, Virginia Beach, and Williamsburg, VA.

LILLY'S KIDS
Lillian Vernon Corporation
Virginia Beach, VA 23479-0002
914-633-6300
Catalog (full-color)

Lillian Vernon is just Lilly to the 4 million readers of her Kid's Catalog. Her success story is legendary as she spreads her wings to things for kids. Practical and perfect, from puppet theaters to finger puppets, dress-up trunks for aspiring actresses, beads to string along your parents 'til the next holiday offering, bears, Kettcars, bath toys, toy helmets, crafts, and other creative sports that fit the bill in affordability and fun.

LITTLE KIDS, INC.
Wayland Square, P.O. Box 3192
Providence, RI 02906
800-545-5437; 401-435-4120 (RI)
401-438-0665 (fax)
Brochure (full-color)

No squeezes! No spills! No mess! Now juice boxes can be neat and easy to use. Just slide standard-size juice box into the durable, dishwasher-safe plastic Sipper Gripper and you've solved the problem of a sloppy slurper. Forget messy straws as the Sipper Gripper adapts for infant use with standard nipples, and includes holder, travel cap, trainer spout, and collar. The advanced sipper allows resealing of juice box to save leftover juices. Bold designs and neon colors make it "cool" for even older kids to sip a cold one. Also available, the "magic" Tumbler which eliminates spills even when turned upside down. Includes flexible, reusable straw. Perfect for squirt's lunchbox. Call for availability and a representative near you.

ONE STEP AHEAD
P.O. Box 46
Deerfield, IL 60015
800-274-8440; 800-950-5120 (consumer service)
708-272-8509 (fax)
Catalog (full-color)

One Step Ahead has taken one Giant Step for parentkind. This catalog offers innovative and practical solutions for the best in baby care. Created *by* mothers *for* mothers to make life with baby easier, more satisfying, and more fun. Such items as a variety of diaper choices, strollers, baby safety products, educational and interactive toys, health care products, clothing, and transitional beds designed to ease babies' growth stages and please parents' pocketbooks. Shop with the security of knowing your purchase is 100 percent guaranteed and shipped within 24 hours.

THE RIGHT START
5334 Sterling Center Dr.
Westlake Village, CA 91361
800-LITTLE 1
818-707-7132 (fax)
Catalog (full-color)

The right place to get the right stuff is Right Start! It's the world's largest infant and toddler catalog and the best anywhere. And it was awarded the prestigious Parents Choice Award for children's products for safety, quality, design, durability, and value. Innovative strollers, baby carriers, educational toys, vibrant colorful mobiles, health aids, Convert-a-cribs, and a sea of giggles for the bathtub. For baby diapers, wrap up "Drypers" (putting the "dry" back in diapers, and they do it with a conscience—they're recyclable). Ships within 24 hours using Federal Express; standard air delivery is available. Special wholesale discounts. Satisfaction guaranteed on every item or your money back!

SAB PRODUCTS, INC.
24 South Broadway St.
Akron, OH 44308
800-544-1705; 216-762-9952
216-762-9954 (fax)
Brochure

Keep little hands away from scalding pots with Shield-a-Burn from SAB Products. This rigid heat-resistant plastic shield easily attaches to the stove without the need of special tools; won't mar stovetop surfaces, either. Keep kitchen hazards to a minimum by eliminating the possibility of burns to infants or toddlers. Cleans with soap and water. Cost:

$19.95 plus $3 shipping and handling. One-year warranty. Call or write for order forms. (Also available through the Right Start Catalog.)

THE SAN FRANCISCO MUSIC BOX COMPANY
P.O. Box 7817
San Francisco, CA 94120-7817
800-227-2190
Catalog (full-color)

You'll leave your heart but it'll cost less to get it back at the San Francisco Music Box Company. Clean-sweep sales where every musical gift is 60 percent off are the best time to save, but if you want music in your child's life, this 72-page catalog couldn't be any more melodic. Bag a big bargain on a ballerina bag, $7.99 (was $19.95); or a ring bearer's pillow that plays Mendelssohn's Wedding March for $12.99 (was $24.95). This exclusively musical gifts catalog included wonderful terry-cloth cuddly rattles ($11.95) that are baby-safe and hand-washable, and with one squeeze, hear "Mary Had a Little Lamb." The Stanley Stork Gift Basket for $39.95 contains a nifty carrying case, huggable plush toy, and musical naptime soother. Includes baby's first safety comb and brush, formula bottle, rattles, and Tiny Teddy that plays "My Favorite Things."

SEALED WITH A KISS
6709 Tildenwood Lane
Rockville, MD 20852
800-888-7925
Brochure

Custom care packages, packed and Sealed With a Kiss are available when THEY leave home without YOU. A Super Camp Care Package, chock-full of surprises for when they hit the camp trail (suitable packages for handicapped campers, too); Super Travel Kits, filled with 10–20 toys and games appropriate to the child's age (3–16) and gender to keep kids entertained on a road trip; and the latest addition called Great Gifts For All Reasons, customized packages for year-round gift giving. A great way to say you care . . . and all you add is love.

SOUTHPAW SHOPPE
803 West Harbor Drive, Suite D
San Diego, CA 92101
Catalog (full-color)

Give this shoppe your paw and they'll send you a free catalog. The camaraderie among lefties is evident by the number of T-shirts, bumper stickers, buttons, and other paraphernalia having to do with being left-handed. Functional items such as scissors, cooking utensils, musical instruments, how-to books for calligraphy, embroidery, guitar, golf, writing, and even ego-boosting ("The National Superiority of Left Handers") won't leave you feeling "left out."

STORKS AND BONDS
#203, 10107—115th St.
Edmonton, Alberta T5K 1T3, Canada
403-482-3333
403-488-3966 (fax)
Flier (order form)

Got a flair for the "extraordinaire"? Sticks and stones may break your bones but Storks and Bonds won't break your budget. Custom-designed variations on two cherished themes—weddings and births (assuming these are two distinctive events and not one and the same). These happy occasions have been interpreted by designers for clients around the world. Here you will find an array of witty and ingenious designs to make for imaginative and one-of-a-kind announcements. The selected works explore the use of paper stock, including such mediums as three-dimensional treatments, flip-books, pop-ups, silk screens, hand-assembled books and cards, large posters, and even a music box. Their reference resource book (200 full-color pages) is also entertaining and idea provoking. An excellent gift for those preparing a wedding invitation or birth announcement.

TAYLOR GIFTS
355 E. Conestoga Road
P.O. Box 8700
Wayne, PA 19093-8700
215-789-7007 (orders)
215-293-3613 (customer service)
Catalog (full-color)

Since 1952, this fun-filled, 120-page gift and gadget catalog has been delivering the goods fast and furiously with unconditional guarantees of your complete satisfaction. Here's what our kids' panel of experts picked on a recent shopping expedition: a security beach blanket for $29.98, a University of Michigan official keep-warm blanket for $49.98, and a giraffe toy hammock for $5.98. Moms, on the other hand, voted for the Nintendo lockout device to monitor video games for $19.98, and a safety gate for pets and kids for $59.98. Sale edition catalogs save you up to 50 percent and include a FREE surprise gift with order.

UNI-USA, INC.
8025 SW 185th
Aloha, OR 97007
800-832-2376
Flier (full-color)

Fight flab with fitness fun and a little help from a Runabout Walking-Jogging Kart. In comparison with strollers, Runabout Karts have a lower center of gravity, better parking brakes, a better safety strap, a full restraining harness, better nighttime visibility, and better weight distribution . . . better not let this one pass you by! Some additional options: add-on Tandem Baby Kart Seats, baskets, and a Sun Bonnet (custom embroidered with baby's name). Uni-USA, Inc. has a variety of bikes for older children and adults as well, and also offers the opportunity for buyers to become reps and earn a 10 percent commission. Write or call for more information.

UNITED NATIONS CHILDREN'S FUND (UNICEF)
1 Children's Blvd., P.O. Box 182233
Chattanooga, TN 37422
800-553-1200
Catalog (full-color)

The UNICEF store (in Albuquerque) and their catalog offer a wonderful panorama of crowd-pleasing gifts besides their initial goal of providing children worldwide with a future. This grass-roots, people-to-people assistance program provides health care, safe water supply, sanitation, nutrition, education, and training. Taste the catalog for an international flavor of greeting cards, games, books, stationery, and collectibles. One highlighted item is *The Little Cook's Cookbook* that provides a cook's tour of different culinary cultures while teaching youngsters kitchen safety. Net proceeds from all sales are transferred to UNICEF.

WAVE
1103 Mission Ridge
Austin, TX 78704
512-443-7803
Brochure

Catch a Wave and create art for the bathroom! In the business for seven years, creator Debe Bentley takes your idea, color scheme, theme, and curtain size and transforms it into a one-of-a-kind shower curtain that's fully machine-washable, fun, and functional. Call for price range and specifics. Great fun for a kid's bathroom. Half of the purchase price required as down payment.

HEALTH, BEAUTY, AND FITNESS

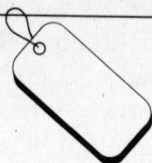

BERTSHERM PRODUCTS, INC.
1145 Galewood Dr.
Cleveland, OH 44110
216-791-1800
Flier (press release)

Oh, no, *B.O.*! Until recently, big-time firms turned their noses up at the idea of a deodorant for kids. Now those 7–12-year-old armpits can be protected from unseemly odor. Bertsherm Products of Cleveland developed its very own "Fun 'n' Fresh Deodorant." No, siree, there's no chemical irritants like those contained in "grown-up" deodorants and antiperspirants. Blended with natural ingredients, it's safe, effective, won't clog pores, and won't stain clothes. Fun 'n' Fresh is available at most Wal-Mart, K mart, and Toys 'Я' Us stores and comes in cool spice scent for him, rose petal for her.

FITNESSGRAM—INSTITUTE FOR AEROBICS RESEARCH
12330 Preston Rd.
Dallas, TX 75230
800-635-7050; 214-701-8001 (in TX)
Flier

Pump some enthusiasm into your child's physical fitness regime. This program uses a refreshing approach to fitness that adults as well as children can benefit from. A six-week report card rewards children for engaging in exercise over a sustained period of time instead of giving an award only to those who score well on fitness tests. Experts believe that by rewarding the process (the behavior), and not the product (fitness), the process will take care of the product. Program is designed to emphasize that regular exercise is the key to achieving a lifetime of healthy and fit citizens. Call for information on how to get a program started in your child's school.

KIDSPORTS INTERNATIONAL, INC.
257 Penn Ave.
Sinking Springs, PA 19608
215-678-8947
215-678-5248 (fax)
Brochure

The ultimate goal of Kidsports International is to network the talents and enthusiasm of thousands of people worldwide—people who are interested in working with children. By providing facilities, programs, and staff that help children feel good about themselves and the world around them, Kidsports International has become a leader in the youth fitness and recreation market with services across the United States. Besides the basic pint-sized gym equipment, this juvenile health club and its team of consultants encourage exercise through games and noncompetitive activities for kids ages 4 months to 17 years. Annual gym memberships range from $25 to $100. Kidsports-trained professional programs available worldwide, in the military, Jewish Community Centers, and YMCAs. Call your local recreational facility to see if they offer the Kidsports program.

MAMATOTO
c/o The Body Shop by Mail
45 Horsehill Road
Cedar Knolls, New Jersey 07927-2003
800-541-2535
Catalog

Since 1976, this English-born phenomenon in the skin and hair care business has kept us smelling like a rose, literally and figuratively, with their innovative products. The latest creation is an impressive lineup especially formulated for expectant mothers and newborns. The name Mamatoto is adapted from a Swahili word meaning "mother and child." Only naturally based ingredients are used, like wheat germ, cocoa butter, aloe vera, and chamomile, for example, which have long been known to have calming effects on the skin. From relaxing bath powder and soothing massage oil for moms, to bottom cream, shampoo, and wash wipes for babies, all products are beautifully packaged and developed with no animal testing.

PRESIDENT'S COUNCIL ON PHYSICAL
   FITNESS AND SPORTS
Dept. of Health and Human Services
Washington, DC 20001
Booklet

Teach your kids a lesson that'll pay them dividends the rest of their lives. Besides teaching the three R's, parents often skip the fourth R, Regular Physical Activity. Arnold is not the only one interested in terminating couch potatoes. The President's Council on Physical Fitness and Sports has information on starting personal exercise programs as well as fitness programs for schools. Your fitness package comes with the *Get Fit Handbook for Youth, Ages 6–17*, a physical education performance checklist, fitness fundamentals, and a Presidential Sports Award Challenge. Go for it! Make fitness a family affair. Write for your FREE fitness packet.

STAR PHARMACEUTICAL, INC.
1500 New Horizons Blvd.
Amityville, NY 11701
800-274-6400
Catalog

"A spoonful of sugar makes the medicine go down!" Not so in *My* house. That is, until these children's chewable animal-shaped vitamins from Star Pharmaceuticals came to the rescue. A new and improved formula that actually tastes *good* made for an easy dose of healthy living. There are chewables plus iron, multivitamin drops, and drops plus iron. Natural formula chewables, too. Star has multiformulas for all ages along with a vast array of health care products like the e-z-swallow pill crusher or splitter, for convenience or to reduce dosage. Taking the temp of a tiny tot is made quick and easy with their 15-second fever scan strips for tiny tots. Star is a shining light on the horizon, offering to save you a trip to the moon without out-of-this-world prices. Thirty-day money-back guarantee.

HEALTH AND MEDICAL

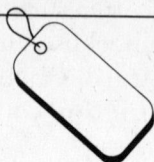

AMERICA'S PHARMACY SERVICE, INC.
P.O. Box 10490
Des Moines, IA 50306
800-247-1003; 515-287-6872
Catalog; PQ

Shop by phone at one of America's largest mail-order pharmacies offering name-brand trade and generic prescription drugs that represent savings of 25–60 percent off the cost of your Rx bill. (Generic equivalents are chemically indentical to brand-name products and are approved by the FDA.) Also available are vitamins and minerals, aspirin and cold capsules, creams and ointments. Refunds and exchanges are made within 30 days. There is no charge for shipping via UPS or parcel post, although there is a 75-cent handling fee. Check out their 32-page catalog for more information.

**AMERICAN ACADEMY OF ALLERGY AND
  IMMUNOLOGY**
800-822-ASMA (800-822-2752)

Call the toll-free Asthma and Allergy Information Line and request the helpful-hints brochure for the allergic patient. The Academy will send you a list of allergists best able to meet your needs as well as their credentials and the Academy's criteria for doctor acceptance. This way you'll know if their training is anything to sneeze at.

AMERICAN CANCER SOCIETY NATIONAL HEADQUARTERS
1599 Clifton Road NE
Atlanta, GA 30329
800-ACS-2345; 404-320-3333 (in GA)
Booklet

The national Cancer Society provides free information and publications such as *When Your Brother or Sister Has Cancer*, a booklet designed to explain the usual feelings of sadness, guilt, feeling left out or jealous, coping with hospitalization, communication between family members, and the importance of families trying to live as normally as possible.

AMERICAN COUNCIL OF THE BLIND
1010 Vermont Avenue NW
Suite 1100
Washington, DC 20005
202-393-3666

This is a clearinghouse listing of companies and organizations who, through catalogs, sell useful products for the blind and visually impaired. Write to the Council to learn of such companies as the LS&S Group, who sell talking watches, TVs, radios, and voice-activated telephones, and the Capability Collection Ways and Means, who sell over 1,000 products related to housekeeping, sewing, and yard and garden care.

AMERICAN DIABETES ASSOCIATION
National Service Center
1600 Duke Street
Alexandria, VA 22314
800-ADA-DISC

Published by the American Diabetes Association, *Diabetes '92*, the newsletter for people with diabetes, is brimming with information on managing diabetes, exercise, nutritious recipes, and the latest breakthroughs and newest technology.

AMERICAN FOUNDATION FOR THE BLIND
15 West 16th Street
New York, NY 10011
Brochure

Write for their brochure describing additional publication specifically related to the blind and visually impaired (single copy is free; bulk orders are processed with shipping and handling charges), from mobility issues to getting help for the disabled child.

ANATOMICAL CHART CO.
8221 N. Kimball
Skokie, IL 60076-2956
800-621-7500
708-674-0211 (fax)
Catalog (full-color)

This mail-order menagerie of modern medical miracles is guaranteed to tickle your funny bone! Products ranging from humorous to serious, and all related to the human anatomy. Videos on pregnancy and fitness, baby basics, diapers and delirium, diets, and emergency first aid, and a host of medical reference books. Hilarious posters are available, as well as calendars, puzzles, sweatshirts and T-shirts, skeleton and eyeball key chains, and even a pregnancy tummy cast kit—a unique memento that can be signed by your doctors, nurses, family, and friends, and treasured for years to come. Added features are educational toys like the Ear Bear Examination Kit, designed to help parents identify the signs and symptoms of middle-ear infections in young children. Gift wrapping and next-day delivery available. Guaranteed full refund or exchange within 30 days, "no bones about it"!

BETTER HEARING INSTITUTE/HEARING HELPLINE
P.O. Box 1840
Washington, DC 20013
800-EAR-WELL; 703-642-0580; 703-750-9302

For information about hearing impairment, causes of hearing loss, and how most people with this problem can be helped, contact the Better Hearing Institute. Included will be a two-minute self-hearing test, the results of which can indicate whether an actual hearing test is needed. A list of registered audiologists in your area will also be provided.

CHILD'S MEDICAL RECORD
P.O. Box 17718
Memphis, TN 38187

This sturdy, 16-page, pocket-sized booklet is just what the doctor ordered. A convenient way to record your child's medical information such as blood type, Rh factor, dates of immunization, allergies, childhood diseases, and other medically related data. Especially valuable in an emergency, where this information could conceivably be the difference between life and death ($1.75 each; two for $3).

COCAINE ANONYMOUS
World Services Offices
3740 Overland Ave., Suite G
Los Angeles, CA 90034
800-347-8998 (hotline); 213-559-5833 (office)
213-559-2554 (fax)
Brochures

Cocaine Anonymous (CA) is a fellowship of members who share experience, strength, and hope with one another to solve a common problem. The only requirement for membership is a desire to stop using cocaine or other mind-altering substances. There are no dues or fees. The national hotline offers a referral number in your area for dates, times, and locations of local meetings. Primary purpose of CA is to stay cocaine-free and help others to achieve the same freedom. If your kid's on coke, get help now!

CORPORATE ANGEL NETWORK (CAN)
914-328-1313

Longtime friends and recovered cancer patients Priscilla Blum and Jay Weinberg are the driving force behind this nonprofit organization that flies cancer patients of any age FREE to specialized medical treatment centers. (They will not fly to unacceptable or unorthodox treatment centers, however.) Over 400 companies participate by allowing patients to fill up the empty seats on their corporate jets and therefore avoid the hassle and strain of commercial travel.

COUNCIL ON FAMILY HEALTH
420 Lexington Ave.
New York, NY 10017
212-210-8836
Brochure

An ounce of prevention is worth it. As a public service by pharmaceutical companies in cooperation with the American Medical Association, the American Academy of Pediatrics, and the American Association of Poison Control Centers, the Council on Family Health offers a free Health Emergency Chart for first aid in the home, "Ten Guides to Proper Medicine Use," and emergency telephone stickers to keep handy numbers for the family doctor, pharmacy, and poison control centers. Send SASE for stickers and brochures.

EPILEPSY FOUNDATION OF AMERICA
4351 Garden City Drive, Suite 406
Landover, MD 20785
800-EFA-1000

The Epilepsy Foundation has a number of informative booklets at a very nominal cost ($.10 to $1.50). Some of their titles include *Epilepsy, Medicine and Dental Care, Answers to Your Questions about Epilepsy*, and *Seizure Recognition and First Aid*. Call the toll-free number for information. Their trained staff can answer your questions and direct you to local affiliates.

FAMILY COMMUNICATIONS, INC.
4802 Fifth Ave., Dept. A
Pittsburgh, PA 15213
412-687-2990
Brochure (free with SASE)

Family Communications produces audio, video, and print materials designed to help children cope by encouraging their communication with adults. Information is available on dealing with hospitalization, trips to the dentist, death, divorce, handicaps, imaginary friends, and starting school. Free brochure offered when you send SASE. Write or call for more information on the Let's Talk About It series.

IBM CORPORATION
P.O. Box 2150
Atlanta, GA 30055
800-IBM-2133; 404-238-4806 (GA)

IBM has designed a program to make selected IBM computer products available at special prices to persons with disabilities. For most people, technology makes things easier; for the disabled, technology makes things possible. IBM's National Support Center for Persons with Disabilities was created to inform disabled professionals and others on how computers can enhance their work- and life-style. The PC can be the window to the world for the blind and others who are visually impaired. It offers new hope, as well, to the deaf, voiceless, slow learners, mentally retarded, people with brain injuries, and perhaps most dramatically, to those with severe mobility restrictions. People who have control only of an eyelid or a toe, for example, can now communicate with little or no assistance using IBM's special equipment. Today, there are systems that talk, listen, teach, communicate, and translate. Equipment includes speech synthesizers, voice-recognition devices, keyboard emulators, "talking" terminals, and Braille computer printers and attachments. These tools are available for use in the workplace, at home, or in schools, where a modem can link its formerly isolated user to a whole new world. Request the list of participating national, regional, and community service organizations who will help in the selection, ordering, and installation of these devices.

JOHNSON & JOHNSON
Attn: Consumer Services
501 George Street
New Brunswick, NJ 08903

A FREE wall chart of first aid facts is yours for the asking. And what a lifesaver it can be.

METROPOLITAN LIFE INSURANCE COMPANY
One Madison Avenue
New York, NY 10010

Write for their FREE list of educational health and safety items, such as their wonderfully graphic First Aid Chart.

MIRACLE EAR CHILDREN'S FOUNDATION
P.O. Box 59261
Minneapolis, MN 55459-0261
800-234-5422
Brochure

Now hear this. This miracle-in-the-making program is designed for, and limited to, people whose incomes are significantly limited and are in need of a hearing aid or other such hearing services. Needy hearing-impaired children 16 years of age or younger are the recipients. The hearing aids that are donated through this program may be new or reconditioned, and style depends on the child's hearing loss. Literature available describes eligibility, responsibility of the client, and information on how the program works. Call or write for further information.

THE NATIONAL ALLERGY AND ASTHMA NETWORK
Mothers of Asthmatics, Inc.
10875 Main St., Suite 210
Fairfax, VA 22030
(800) 878-4403; (703) 385-4403 (VA)
(703) 352-4354 (fax)

The National Allergy and Asthma Network (NAAN) is an outgrowth of Mothers of Asthmatics, Inc., and is a non-profit, membership-supported organization founded in 1985. Known worldwide as an advocate for the family in the medical and educational community, its annual membership fee is $5 and includes a coupon packet worth $500 for discounts on asthma and allergy products. An eight-page newsletter, The MA Report, provides the latest update on treatments and medical research. Cost for 12 issues is $20.

NATIONAL CENTER FOR STUTTERING (NCS)
200 E. 33rd St.
New York, NY 10016
800-221-2483; 212-532-1460 (NY)
Flier

Get the current data on stuttering through this organization, which offers the latest research findings in a manual called *Stutter No More*. A compilation of current thinking based on clinical research, it includes chapters on possible treatment approaches, diagnostic tests, implications for the possibility of a permanent cure, and tips for parents, teachers, therapists, and family members. Hardcover book is 141 pages and priced at $18.95 (plus $1.80 shipping and handling). New York residents add sales tax. Call or write for more information and order form.

NATIONAL COUNCIL ON ALCOHOLISM
12 West 21st Street
New York, NY 10010
800-NCA-CALL; 212-206-6770 (NY)

Call toll-free for information if your child needs help with alcoholism or other drug addictions. Additionally, local resources are usually listed in the Yellow Pages under "Alcohol." Alcoholics Anonymous (AA) has chapters everywhere. Support groups for adults and adolescents affected by someone's drinking are Al-Anon and Alateen, respectively.

NATIONAL DOWN SYNDROME SOCIETY
666 Broadway
New York, NY 10012
800-221-4602; 212-460-9330 (NY)
212-979-2873 (fax)
Information packet

The National Down Syndrome Society was established to promote public awareness about Down's syndrome, to support research about this genetic disorder, and to provide vital services for families and individuals affected by this disease. Its mission is to help sufferers from Down's syndrome achieve their potential in community life as well as to find the scientific answers to this disorder. Referrals to community resources and a listing of reference books, periodicals, and audiovisuals are available.

NATIONAL DRUG ABUSE TREATMENT REFERRAL AND INFORMATION SERVICE
800-COCAINE
Brochure

This national service can refer callers to the nearest in- or out-patient treatment center, self-help program, or private practitioner, if your child or someone you know suffers from substance abuse. Though not a crisis hot-line, they will intervene in emergencies. Free brochure upon request.

NATIONAL INFORMATION CENTER ON DEAFNESS
Gallaudet University
800 Florida Avenue NE
Washington, DC 20002
201-651-5051 (voice); 202-651-5052 (TDD)

The National Information Center on Deafness is a centralized resource for information on all topics related to deafness and hearing loss. Their suggestion for *Great Buys* readers is a series of publications concerning communication tips, management strategies, commonly asked questions, hearing aids, and alerting and communication devices.

NATIONAL MARROW DONOR PROGRAM
3433 Broadway St. NE, Suite 400
Minneapolis, MN 55413
800-654-1247
Brochure

An estimated 16,000 children and adults are stricken with leukemia, aplastic anemia, and other blood-related diseases. For many, the only hope for survival is a marrow transplant. Of the thousands who could benefit from this process, nearly 70 percent cannot find a match within their families. As the pool of potential donors increases, so do the odds for survival.

The free brochure offered through the National Marrow Donor Program explains the program and answers the most often asked questions about the procedure. Give a gift for life. Write for information, which includes lists of local centers in your area.

PRISM OPTICAL, INC.
10992 N.W. 7th Ave.
North Miami, FL 33168
305-754-5894
Catalog $2 (refundable)

Since 1959, Prism Optical has been delivering eyewear for the entire family (yes, kids, too) including sunglasses. Save 30–50 percent on a wide variety of styles, from designer to studious, sport to functional. Choose from a number of lenses, color coatings, scratch-resistant features, and more. Their 16-page catalog tells all, including their guarantee of a perfect fit.

RITEWAY HEARING AID CO.
P.O. Box 597635
Chicago, IL 60659
312-539-6620
Brochure

Shop for hearing aids the Riteway and save up to 50 percent off dealer prices. Since 1959, this company has been turning up the sound for both adult and children's hearing aids (Royaltone and Danavox), including in-the-ear and over-the-ear models. Now hear this: They even offer a 30-day free trial period to ensure the perfect fit. Batteries are sold at 25 percent off list.

SIBLING INFORMATION NETWORK
**Connecticut's University Affiliated Program
on Developmental Disabilities
991 Main St.
East Hartford, CT 06108
203-282-7050
Brochure/sample copy of newsletter**

Sibling rivalry is not the operative word here. On the contrary, this network, composed of members from all states and several foreign countries, was established to assist individuals interested in the unique needs of families with disabilities. At present, network members include siblings, parents, special ed teachers, social workers, psychologists, physicians, nurses, journalists, and counselors. The network serves as a clearinghouse for information, ideas, projects, and literature regarding siblings and the needs of families with members who are handicapped. Membership dues are $7 for indviduals, $15 for organizations or institutions. A sample copy of the newsletter is available upon request.

SIGNATURE DENTAL PLAN
800-346-0310

Take the bite out of exorbitant and rising dental costs. This plan has got you covered for at least 30 precent less and even offers FREE select preventive services like X-rays and oral exams. Preexisting conditions are included, and there are no deductibles. Signature Dental Plan was conceived to help consumers save money on virtually all of their dental needs. The network includes dentists and specialists nationwide who participate because it helps expand their practices. All dentists are carefully screened for the highest standards of excellence in health care, facilities, and cleanliness. Individual memberships begin at $48 per year; $60 for husband and wife; $72 for a family, including all children and grandparents living within your home. Periodontal (gums), endodontics (root canals), prosthodontics (dentures), and oral surgery (extractions) are available, besides general restorative dentistry, i.e., fillings, crowns, bridges.

UNITED NETWORK OF ORGAN SHARING (UNOS)
1100 Boulders Pkwy., Suite 500
P.O. Box 13770, Dept. DB
Richmond, VA 23225
800-24-DONOR
Flier

Approximately every 30 minutes someone in the United States needs an organ transplant. Organ transplantation is one of the most remarkable medical success stories in the history of medicine. UNOS answers questions on obtaining donor cards, family and spousal permission, religious implications, donor recipient qualifications, and more. The UNOS National Computer System generates a list of patients ranked according to strict medical criteria and urgency of need. Donor and recipient indentities are confidential.

Additional Resources to Call

AMERICAN COUNCIL ON RURAL SPECIAL EDUCATION
NRDI-Miller Hall 359
Western Washington University
Bellingham, WA 98225

AMERICAN PRINTING HOUSE FOR THE BLIND
1839 Frankfort Ave.,
P.O. Box 6085
Louisville, KY 40206-0085
502-895-2405

CENTER FOR
  SLOWER LEARNERS
A.J. Pappanikou Center
4949 Westgrove, Suite 180
Dallas, TX 75248
214-407-9277

HELEN KELLER
  NATIONAL CENTER
  FOR DEAF/BLIND
  YOUTH AND ADULTS
111 Middle Neck Rd.
Sands Point, NY 11050
516-944-8900 (voice/TDD)

NATIONAL CENTER
  FOR LEARNING
  DISABILITIES
99 Park Ave.
New York, NY 10016
212-687-7211

NATIONAL CENTER
  FOR YOUTH WITH
  DISABILITIES
Adolescent Health Program
University of Minnesota
P.O. Box 721-UMHC
  Harvard Street at
  East River Rd.
Minneapolis, MN 55455
800-333-6293;
  612-626-2825

NATIONAL
  INFORMATION
  CENTER FOR
  CHILDREN AND
  YOUTH WITH
  HANDICAPS
7926 Jones Branch Dr.
Park Place Building,
  Suite 1100
McLean, VA 22101
800-999-5599;
  703-893-6061

NATIONAL
  REHABILITATION
  ASSOCIATION
633 South Washington St.
Alexandria, VA 22314
703-836-0850 (voice);
  703-836-0852 (TDD)

NATIONAL
  REHABILITATION
  INFORMATION
  CENTER
8455 Colesville Rd.,
  Suite 935
Silver Springs, MD
  20910-3319
800-346-2742 (voice/TDD);
  301-588-9284 (voice/TDD)

**NATIONAL SPINAL
  CORD INJURY
  ASSOCIATION**
600 W. Cummings Park,
  Suite 2000
Woburn, MA 01801
617-935-2722

**SPECIAL OLYMPICS,
  INC.**
International Office
1350 New York Ave. NW,
  Suite 500
Washington, DC 20005
202-628-3630

**UNITED CEREBRAL
PALSY ASSOCIATION**
7 Penn Plaza, Suite 804
New York, NY 10001
800-872-1827;
212-268-6655

Help-by-Phone Hotlines

Aids Information Hotline
800-551-2728

American Sudden Infant Death Syndrome Institute
800-847-7437

800 Cocaine Information
800-262-2463

Exceptional Children's Assistance Center
800-962-6817

Juvenile Diabetes Foundation
800-533-2873; 800-223-1138 (chapter information)
212-889-7575 (NY)

Kevin Collins Foundation for Missing Children
800-272-0012

Maternity Hotline
800-GLADNEY (452-3639)

Missing Children Help Center
800-USA-KIDS (872-5437)
813-623-5437 (Tampa area)

National Association for Parents
of the Visually Impaired
800-562-6265

National Center for Missing and
Exploited Children Hotline
800-843-5678

National Food Addiction Hotline
800-872-0088

National Runaway Switchboards
800-621-4000

Runaway Hotline
800-231-6946; 800-392-3352 (TX)

Sudden Infant Death Syndrome—
National Headquarters
800-221-7437

MAGAZINES AND NEWSPAPERS

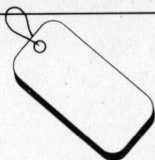

AMERICAN FAMILY PUBLISHERS
P.O. Box 62000
Tampa, FL 33662-2000
800-237-2400

Calling on a clearinghouse for magazine subscriptions often nets big dividends off the usual subscription price offered from the publisher, and even bigger savings off single copies. Kids might find a subscription to *Popular Science* appealing. Or what about *TV Guide* so you can monitor which shows have value to children? Popular books from these same publishers like Rodale's home-improvement series or *The Columbia University Complete Home Medical Guide* may prove an invaluable resource when health is the question. Call for more information.

BARBIE
300 Madison Ave.
New York, NY 10017
212-687-0680

What a doll! Now she's turned her attention to the business of publishing, giving Christy Hefner something to worry about. The quarterly *Barbie* magazine reflects on young girls' concerns and interests. Features on fitness, school, food, pets, decorating, crafts, good looks, and fashion. And don't worry, it's not all work. There's fun in the puzzles, entertainment updates, and celebrity interviews.

BOOMERANG
123 Townsend St., Suite 636
San Francisco, CA 94107
800-333-7858
Flier (free sample)

What a newsworthy idea! Like having *Newsweek*, *National Geographic*, *Highlights*, and *Mad Magazine* all rolled into one . . . except this is news that's not fit to print (it comes on an audiocassette). Developed for children 7–12 with dyslexia, visual impairment, or learning disabilities, Boomerang blurs the invisible line between "education" and "entertainment." This monthly "audiomagazine" talks big. Includes current events, geography, music, natural wonders, and a regular segment called "Weird Words," to help build a child's vocabulary. For the funny bone, even a few jokes are thrown in. Each issue is accompanied by a copy of the "Boomerang Flyer" featuring games and fun facts. A one-year subscription costs $39.95—just $3.32 per 70-minute cassette (which your child can listen to time and time again). A gift certificate will "boomerang" throughout the year.

BOYS' LIFE
1325 Walnut Hill Lane
Irving, TX 75038-3096
214-580-2366

This monthly magazine for Boy Scouts and their leaders across the country features stories on arts, crafts, nature, recreation, and animals. Membership is not required to subscribe.

CHILDREN'S SURPRISES, INC.
P.O. Box 236
Chanhassen, MN 55317
800-356-8899
Subscription $12.95 (4 issues)

You can count on your surprises coming four times a year. This magazine is published quarterly (fall, winter, spring, and summer) and geared for children 4-12. A magazine for kids and, surprisingly enough, parents enjoy it, too. It's filled to the margins with word-search activities, hidden-picture puzzles, jokes, riddles, sections on math, reading, and current affairs, and Kids' Corner, where young readers are encouraged to contribute art and poems.

COBBLESTONE
20 Grove St.
Peterborough, NH 03458
603-924-7209

Turn the pages of history by subscribing to this monthly magazine for young people ages 8-14. Covers historical nostalgia, how-to's, interviews, plays, biographies, recipes, and activities. Also includes historical, humorous, and biographical fiction.

CONSUMER INFORMATION CENTER
P.O. Box 100
Pueblo, CO 81002
Catalog

Yes, this it, the Pueblo, Colorado, "catalog" you keep hearing about. The ultimate consumers' source of information from child care to money management. It acts as a clearinghouse for federal agencies to dispense their vested information and publishes a FREE, 16-page quarterly catalog listing the pamphlets and brochures available (and many of those are FREE, too). A $1 handling fee is charged on all orders.

CRICKET MAGAZINE
315 5th St.
Peru, IL 61354
800-BUG PALS (subscription); 815-224-6643

Children curious about the world will be fascinated by this monthly publication geared toward children 6-12. Curious minds love to know. And if they love to read, they'll love to stimulate their adventurous minds and imaginations. Historical stories, biographies, fantasy, science fiction, sports, travel articles, and lively science experiments fill the pages. For added fun, there are also word and number games, riddles, and poetry. Also available: *Ladybug*, an equally entertaining magazine, especially for preschoolers.

FREEBIES
The Magazine with Something for Nothing
407 State Street
P.O. Box 20283
Santa Barbara, CA 93120
805-962-9135
805-962-1617 (fax)

A subscription to this magazine will cost $12.50 a year ($2.50 per issue). Expect to receive it 5 times a year packed with a bevy of bargains perfect for kids, parents, and grandparents. And best of all, the offers are FREE (save for the postage and handling involved in fulfilling each request). Recent highlights from just the Kids' Stuff section included a paper crafts kit, a yummy memo pad, a dinosaur stencil booklet, a multicolor neon surfer bracelet, a surfer key chain, an inflatable Tyrannosaurus rex, plus a set of four hologram decals—each for a small postage and handling charge.

HIGHLIGHTS FOR CHILDREN
803 Church St.
Honesdale, PA 18431

Talk about the highlight of most children's lives when the subject of magazines is discussed! *Highlights* is high on the list. This monthly magazine has unusual, meaningful stories appealing to both boys and girls ages 2–12, including creative thinking puzzles, brain teasers, games, and all-around just-plain-fun activities.

HUMPTY DUMPTY'S MAGAZINE
1100 Waterway Blvd., P.O. Box 567
Indianapolis, IN 46206

Published 8 times a year as combined issues, i.e., February/March, April/May, etc., this magazine stresses health, nutrition, hygiene, exercise, and safety for children ages 4–6. Lots of craft projects, puzzles, and a personal favorite, the dot-to-dot and hidden-pictures pages.

KID CITY
Children's Television Workshop
1 Lincoln Plaza
New York, NY 10023
212-595-3456

All's right in *Kid City*. Published 10 times a year for children 6–10, this magazine is right on target. Children are encouraged to play and experiment with words and are tickled with stories, crafts, puzzles, riddles, and jokes.

KID'S KORNER
P.O. Box 413
Joaquin, TX 75954

Little Jack Horner sat in the corner reading his monthly newsletter. *Kid's Korner*, written for kids, by kids, has the corner on kids' talk! While eating his Christmas pie, Jack enjoys the *Korner*'s short stories, fiction and nonfiction, pen-and-ink drawings, as well as poetry and general-interest stories. When he read the congratulatory and birthday notices, he declared, "What a good boy am I!"

LADYBUG
P.O. Box 58344
Boulder, CO 80322
800-BUG-PALS; 800-284-7257, Ext. 5L
Trial subscription 8 issues $14.95

This new magazine for children ages 2 to 7 is from the makers of *Cricket* magazine and is mostly for parents to read to their children (unless your child is reading almost from birth). A wonderful exchange takes place between parent and child when you're reading with a child on your lap or tucked in the crook of your armpit. The visuals are delightful.

NATIONAL GEOGRAPHIC WORLD
17th and M Streets NW, Suite 687
Washington, DC 20036

Write for your FREE copy of *World*, the National Geographic Society's children's magazine that rivals the grown-up version, complete with spectacular photographs and articles on geography, science, and nature. Special features include maps, posters, and more of interest just to kids.

NOAH'S ARK
7726 Portal
Houston, TX 77071
713-771-7143

This book should get a flood of new readers after they learn of its contents. The monthly tabloid is designed for Jewish children ages 6–12 and essentially reinforces learning about Jewish history, holidays, laws, and culture through stories, games, recipes, and craft projects.

ODYSSEY
800-446-5489
Subscription $21 (10 issues)

The stars shone brightly upon this new kid on the juvenile magazine block. This is a heaven-sent magazine on the subject of astronomy with down-to-earth contributors (lots of them are kids themselves). Lots of interesting new territory covered in a subject too often ignored. Geared to school-age children.

OWL MAGAZINE
56 The Esplanade, Suite 306
Toronto, Ontario M5E 1A7 Canada
416-868-6001
416-868-6009 (fax)

If you're wise, you'll find this magazine published 10 times a year food for thought. Includes how-to activities and crafts, personal-experience features, photo features on natural science, wildlife and the outdoors, and articles on science and environmental issues. Also publishes *Chickadee Magazine* with how-to arts and crafts, easy experiments, personal experiences, and wildlife photo features for children ages 4–9.

PENNYWHISTLE PRESS
P.O. Box 500-P
Washington, DC 20044
703-276-3796

The Pennywhistle Press, a weekly newspaper supplement, will blow you away with stories, poetry, and features for children 6–12. You'll find how-to's on sports and crafts and general information.

PURPLE COW
3423 Piedmont Rd. NE, Suite 320
Atlanta, GA 30305
404-239-0642
404-261-2214 (fax)
Also:
P.O. Box 64527
Dallas, TX 75206
214-824-5100

Reading this tabloid can be a moo-ing experience. Don't have a cow. Instead, just turn to the *Purple Cow*, a monthly tab circulated to area high schools and featuring general-interest stories, how-to articles, humor, and just about anything teen-related. It also includes college and work/career-oriented articles. It's written for teens, by teens, about teens. Who better to know about teen life than teens?

RANGER RICK
1412 16th St. NW
Washington, DC 20036
703-790-4274

A broad range of subjects is covered monthly in this publication for ages 6–12. Articles related to nature, conservation, the outdoors, environmental issues, and natural science are the major direction from this ranger. For added interest, photo features, fantasy, and science fiction are interspersed.

SASSY
230 Park Ave.
New York, NY 10169
800-274-2622 (subscription); 212-551-9500
Subscription $14.97 (12 issues)

For *the* magazine for a teen girl with an attitude, *Sassy* or not, this is the one to subscribe to. The focus is on fashion, fiction, health and beauty, politics, celebrities, and regular features like Diary, Sassy Club, Coming Attractions, etc. Geared to girls ages 12–19. A boys' version, called *Dirt*—all "guy stuff" headed by an all-guy staff—will soon be launched. A single issue will go out to subscribers of *Sassy* to give to their brothers or boyfriends.

SEVENTEEN
850 Third Ave.
New York, NY 10022

If you are a young woman between the ages of 12 and 20, you will revel in reading *Seventeen* magazine. This monthly publication goes back generations, it seems, and continues to dedicate itself to young women who are concerned with the development of their own lives and the world around them. Along with articles of general interest, you'll also find humorous fiction, mystery, romance, and tips on beauty, fashion, and health. Sixteen was sure sweet but *Seventeen* is sweeter.

SHOFAR MAGAZINE
43 Northcote Dr.
Melville, NY 11747
516-643-4598

Judas Maccabaeus would be proud of this monthly children's publication dedicated to the subject of being Jewish. *Oy!* We loved the stories, including historical nonfiction, nostalgia, humor, inspirational issues, interviews and profiles, personal experiences, photo features, and religious and travel features. Geared to 8–12-year-old readers.

SMART KIDS
Werner Media Corporation
12021 Wilshire Blvd., #509
Los Angeles, CA 90025

This quarterly magazine qualifies as the new kid on the block. Smart parents enjoy features that include child-rearing tips, education at home and school, sports, food, nutrition, and other pertinent parenting issues.

SPORTS ILLUSTRATED FOR KIDS
Time & Life Building
New York, NY 10020
212-522-5437
212-522-0120 (fax)

Sports Illustrated goes to bat for children 8 years and older with its monthly publication of hits featuring games, how-to spots, general-interest stories, interviews, photo features, and puzzles. That's a pretty good lineup, wouldn't you say?

TEEN MAGAZINE
8490 Sunset Blvd.
Hollywood, CA 90069

Get a subscription to this monthly magazine catering to teenage girls and contemporary young women. Fashion, beauty, suspense, humor, and, of course, romance fill the pages, cover-to-cover.

TEENAGE
2890 N. Monroe, P.O. Box 481
Loveland, CO 80539
303-669-3836
Subscription $18.95 (10 issues)

This magazine is published 10 times a year for members of high school–age Christian youth groups. Articles center on opinions, personal experiences, current fads, trends, and teen culture issues appropriate for Christian teenagers.

TOUCH
P.O. Box 7259
Grand Rapids, MI 49510

This is a monthly Christian publication for girls 7–14. Includes how-to crafts, information-packed articles, humor, inspirational themes, personal experience and testimony, and photo features.

TURTLE MAGAZINE
1100 Waterway Blvd., P.O. Box 567
Indianapolis, IN 46206
317-636-8881

Stop crawling into a shell and shell out a few dollars for this bimonthly publication geared toward children ages 2–5. Fun reading with an emphasis on good health, nutrition, and safety, plus stories, articles, crafts, games, poetry, and humor. Also, you'll fall in love with *Humpty Dumpty*, for ages 4–6; *Children's Playmate*, ages 6–8; *Child Life*, ages 9–11; and *Children's Digest*, for preteens.

VENTURE
P.O. Box 150
Wheaton, IL 60189
312-665-0630

Venture is an adventure produced bimonthly for Christian boys ages 10–15. Aimed at wholesome entertaining reading, with historical/nostalgic stories, humor, mystery, adventure, personal experiences, interviews and profiles, photo and religious features.

THE WORLD OF BUSINESS KIDS
301 Almeria Ave., Suite 330
Coral Gables, FL 33134
305-445-8869

If running a lemonade stand is your idea of fun, then this newsletter is for you. Designed especially for budding business owners, this quarterly publication includes the ins and outs of becoming a youthful and successful entrepreneur. Useful information on effective business operations and management such as how to invest and save money is valuable at any age. You'll also read about taxes, new products, and movie and book reviews. On the lighter side, poetry, cartoons, puzzles, and games.

YM MAGAZINE
Gruner & Jahr Publishing
685 Third Ave.
New York, NY 10164

Since 1953, this magazine has been targeted toward female teens whose passion for fashion is not the only issue addressed. Beauty tips, teen problems, music reviews, frank discussions of social issues, weight, parental concerns, and more.

YOUNG AMERICAN
P.O. Box 12409
Portland, OR 97212
503-230-1895
503-236-0440 (fax)

Extra! Extra! Read all about it! A newspaper for all *Young Americans* (older ones can read it, too) full of interesting tidbits like how-tos, crafts, fitness, humor, interviews, and profiles on the newsworthy accomplishments of kids. Adventure, fantasy, and mystery stories about many young Americans are hot off the press.

ZILLIONS
P.O. Box 51777
Boulder, CO 80321-1777
Subscription $16 (6 bimonthly issues)

Geared to the 8-14 reader whose disposable income comes from allowances, baby-sitting jobs, and mowing lawns. However, what monies are earned or given are spent wisely after a few issues of the kids' version of *Consumer Reports*. Published by Consumers Union, listen up to these departments: Tough Questions . . . answered by a child psychiatrist; Sneaky Sell, beyond the fine print of TV commercials and products on the shelf; U-Test-It, like, How long do the pencils write? Do you have to press hard? *Zillions* reviews books, videos, and movies. The Back Page is devoted to Commercial Breaks. A great read for the up and coming consumer.

MATERNITY

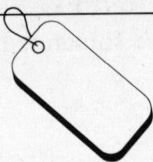

BOSOM BUDDIES
P.O. Box 6138
Kingston, NY 12401
914-338-2038
Catalog

Keeping abreast of the latest in discount shopping, this
company produces, as the name implies, fashions for the
nursing mother. In their 8-page catalog, choose from nursing
bras from a variety of manufacturers, including those that
make them in all-cotton. Sizes run to 46K, so every mother
is covered. Nightgowns and casual wear that make nursing
more convenient are available, too. They do not pretend to
be discounters; rather, they provide a one-stop shopping
experience for this category of merchandise, which is com-
mendable in itself. Sales are regular events, however.

CHEZ MERE
Corporate Office: 111 Cherry Street
Stamford, CT 06840

You don't expect expecting moms to pay retail for their
maternity trousseau, now do you? When the due date is
recorded, try shopping the next nine months for some of
Ma Mere's designer apparel along with Belle France, Precious

Cargo, Lady in Waiting, and you never know what else to expect . . . at Chez Mere.

DAN HOWARD MATERNITY
Corporate Office: 710 W. Jackson Blvd.
Chicago, IL 60606
312-263-6700

This nationwide chain of maternity clothes provides a direct link to the manufacturer, Dan Howard. He helps by delivering the goods straight to you, bypassing the middleman, while you maintain your middle. Nine months of clothes await you at 25–50 percent off comparable maternity apparel elsewhere. Check phone directory or call for location nearest you.

EXPECTATIONS
Corporate Office: 71-28 Main Street
Flushing, NY 11367
718-261-3006

If your expectations call for maternity apparel at 20–40 percent off, you will not be disappointed. This chain, though concentrated in the New York area, may be giving birth to additional stores soon. Now located in the Bronx, Brooklyn, Long Island, Nanuet, New York City, Paramus, Queens, Westchester, and Yonkers. Expect Cherokee, Jordache, and other popular brands.

FLO MOTION
800-472-7777; 212-366-6149

Jump off the bandwagon of high-impact aerobics if you're expecting and want to still be in shape for the blessed event. Moms-to-be can get fit with a tube of water called the Flo

Motion. This floppy, water-filled tube is swung from side to side and over the head in slow-motion moves guaranteed not to jar the little one from his/her nap. Its nonimpact rhythmic movement is a cross between yoga and aerobics. Combining the sounds of music and water makes you almost want to shout, it's so invigorating. Call toll-free for the Flo Bag and instructional video (and patch kit) for $39.95 plus $5 shipping and handling.

FORMAL EXPECTATIONS
341 W. 24th St.
New York, NY 10011
212-675-4859
Brochure

E-x-p-e-c-t nothing but convenience and affordability in formal wear for the mother-in-waiting. New York's only fashion rental wear for the expectant mother, Formal Expectations rents top-of-the-line garments for that formal affair at a fraction of the retail price. Expect similar rental stores to be birthing around the country this year. A one-on-one service offers personalized assistance with flexible hours by appointment only. Sizes petite to large, with 20 styles to choose from. Rental prices range from $40 for separates, to $215 for top-of-the-line dresses. Optional service charge for pick up and delivery (no, the dress, silly); refundable deposit required.

HOLLY NICOLAS NURSING COLLECTION
P.O. Box 7121
Orange, CA 92613-7121
714-639-5933
Brochure (enclose double-stamped SASE)

Holly and Nicolas are two lucky grandchildren to have an entire clothing line created in their honor. Choose from the feminine wiles inherent in all these nursing fashions . . . where's the opening? Concealed tastefully in all these garments designed so that there's never a hint of nursing. Samples of fabric selection are included with the brochure. Some transition garments, too, that take you beyond pregnancy. Affordable, fashionable, and usable.

MATERNITY WEARHOUSE
Corporate Office: 401 E. Hunting Park Ave.
Philadelphia, PA 19124
800-USA-MOMS

If you're with child, get with it. This chain is probably the largest discounter of the maternity wardrobe, from lingerie to slacks. Ma Mere, Puccini, Great Times, Sasson, and Belle France at 15 percent off and more. Save 15–20 percent on moderate dresses and apparel. Check phone directory for location nearest you, or call the toll-free number above.

MOTHER'S PLACE
P.O. Box 94512
Cleveland, OH 44101-4512
800-829-0080
Catalog

With your ever-expanding waistline, it will no longer be necessary to waist any more money not dressing to the nines. With this maternity catalog, you can dress in moderation without killing your budget. Save up to 60 percent on a full maternity wardrobe in plain vanilla styles that run from princess-line afternoon dresses to pleated jumpers, big shirts to big stretch pants. Minimum credit card order $10.

MOTHERS WORK
1309 Noble Street, 5th Floor
Philadelphia, PA 19123
215-625-9259
215-440-9845 (fax)
Catalog and swatches $3 (deductible)

A mother's work is never done and shouldn't be outdone when it comes to an executive decision in choosing maternity clothes. From the boardroom to the bedroom, mothers-to-be or not to be, that is the question. 'Tis nobler to spend a fortune for a 9-month wardrobe? No, says this company's annual report. A mix 'n' match expandable fashion concept puts items together as your waistline expands. Business and tailored separates are paired together to create a winning wardrobe for less. Savings compute to your bottom line in sizes 4–14 at 30 percent less. So "pay less for more"—their motto for a mother who works.

PRONET MEDICAL COMMUNICATIONS
600 Data Dr., Suite 100
Plano, TX 75075
214-964-9500

Attention, moms-to-be! The last thing you need to worry about is whether dad will arrive on time when *your* time arrives! ProNet Medical Communications offers the Baby Beeper Program so you can reach out and touch him even when *he's* out of reach. Keeps mom and dad synchronized during the final countdown to birth time. Comes complete with digital pager, instruction card, letter to dad, and a cute little teddy bear bag. Available through participating hospitals. Call for participating hospitals in your area.

THE TRIPLET CONNECTION
P.O. Box 99571, 800 Thornton Rd. #25
Stockton, CA 95209
209-474-0885
Brochure

Parents expecting a triple treat get the scoop at this organization. The Triplet Connection is a nonprofit, tax-exempt
support group that provides information and lends a helping
hand to parents of triplets, quads, and quints. Members
receive a multitude of information from how to promote a
healthy pregnancy and reduce risks, to the how-to's of home
care when there's more than one crying at the same time.
You'll feel better knowing you're not alone. Guided by a
scientific advisory board, the Triplet Connection offers a
quarterly newsletter with stories, helpful articles and letters,
and a hot-line in case questions or problems arise. Annual
dues $15. Make the connection—the network of caring and
sharing for multiple-birth families.

THE WIDGET FACTORY
Damonmill Square
Concord, MA 01742
800-366-9866; 508-371-9866 (MA)
508-369-6368 (fax)
Catalog (Widget guide)

Make 'em laugh, make 'em smile all the way to the post
office. These clever card ideas and the original artwork give
new meaning to being a card. The Widget Factory cards
give new meaning to your standard card-giving occasions
like birthdays, holidays, and graduations. Eccentric animals
and social comment inspire fresh lines and new designs. A
highlighted feature is Widget's "pregnancy advent calendar,"
an original tongue-in-cheek look at pregnancy. The mother-
to-be can open a different window labeled for each week of

gestation to find pertinent messages and (of course) a hidden baby for the last week. For all-occasion cards, birth announcements, shower invitations, and thank-you notes, whimsical inspiration from the Widget Factory will keep "sender" and "receiver" chuckling.

MUSEUMS

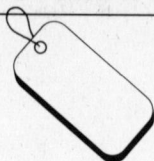

AMERICAN MUSEUM OF NATURAL HISTORY
Central Park West at 79th St.
New York, NY 10024-5192
212-769-5100 (museum); 212-769-5600 (membership)
Brochure (color)

Open the doors to history the minute you step into this museum and explore the natural wonders of the world and beyond. Explore 40 famed halls and numerous special exhibition areas. See nature's mysteries revealed in a vast array of objects drawn from the museum's collection that total more than 36 million artifacts and specimens. The largest museum of its kind, the American Museum of Natural History is a rich educational resource that will delight and fascinate. Don't miss the Naturemax Theater—4 stories high and 66 feet wide! Travel on fun-filled journeys without leaving your seat. Museum memberships available. Birthday party program for children 5–10 years available to children of members only. Choose from a menu of parties exhaustive enough to wear out Martha Stewart: Dinosaur, Safari, Leapin' Lizards, Aquanaut, or Plains Indian Party.

BOSTON CHILDREN'S MUSEUM
300 Congress St.
Boston, MA 02210
617-426-6500

Housed in an old refurbished warehouse on the waterfront, most exhibits emphasize cultural and social values, and others demonstrate scientific principles. The Kid's Bridge teaches how people can get along better with each other. "What if you couldn't . . . ?" helps children understand others' disabilities. "Bones" brings skeletons out of the closet, and "Raceways" shows the scientific principles of motion and momentum.

BROOKLYN CHILDREN'S MUSEUM
145 Brooklyn Ave.
Brooklyn, NY 11213
718-735-4400

With over 40,000 ethnological, historical, and technological artifacts, this museum is housed in a space-age geodesic dome. The tunnel-like entrance looks like a big drain pipe. Kids can operate the water wheels, turbines, gates, and steam controls—to see how water power and canal systems work. At press time, special exhibits included a live animal habitat showing what different creatures eat and "Night Journeys: Home Is Where I Sleep," expounding on what happens during sleep and dreams.

CHICAGO MUSEUM OF SCIENCE AND INDUSTRY
S. Lake Shore Drive at East 57th
Chicago, IL 60637
312-684-1414

With 75 display halls and over 2,000 displays, this is one of the premier technology museums in the country. Boasting a full-scale coal mine with elevator and animated miners, a working farm, and a World War II German submarine, it's housed in an old building from the 1893 Columbian Exposition. Also on display: a 16-foot walk-through model of the human heart!

CHILDREN'S MUSEUM OF MANHATTAN (CMOM)
212 W. 83rd St.
New York, NY 10024
212-721-1223
Flier

The Children's Museum of Manhattan features 4 floors of exciting spaces and places. There's the "Brainatarium" and "Brain Games," where kids learn about the wonder of the human brain and the five senses. In "Magical Patterns," kids explore patterns of art, science, and nature. In the Time Warner Media Center, kids get hands-on experience in a video and film studio. Kids have fun and learn by doing! The museum store has floor-to-ceiling shelves of books, toys, puzzles, and educational materials. (Museum is wheelchair-accessible.) Call for program details.

CHILDREN'S MUSEUM OF THE ARTS
95 Greene St.
New York, NY 10012
212-206-0812; 212-255-4401
212-255-4320 (fax)
Brochure (full-color)

When it comes to children's museums, this is one of the best bets. One unique offering entitled "A Child's World" exhibited paintings from 30 countries by artists ages 2 to 12. Exhibits are mounted at "child height," with a mission to build self-esteem and artistic competence. "A Child's World" exhibit allows children to speak to one another across oceans and language barriers. This is only one of the many inter-disciplinary programs and exhibitions offered through the Children's Museum of the Arts. Write or call for more information.

CINCINNATI CHILDREN'S DISCOVERY CENTER
Museum of Natural History
1301 Western Ave.
Cincinnati, OH 45203
513-287-7020

Go back in time and see how change affects the environment. At this center, help children learn about themselves. Exhibits focus on anatomy, the senses, and nutrition. The "Pathways to Change" exhibit explains how the various elements of nature—plants, animals, and humans—fit together in the environment.

THE DOG MUSEUM
1721 S. Mason Road
St. Louis, MO 63131
314-821-DOGS
Brochure

Have a hunger for more information on a canine companion? Well, "Bone Appetit"! The Dog Museum in St. Louis, Missouri is, dog-gone-it, the best source on how to train your dog. Turn your secondhand rover into a first-rate pet. This haven of "dog data" is dedicated to preserving the best of traditional dog art and artifacts, and also (dog)houses a fine collection of doggie books. A video theater in the museum offers a selection of over 80 videotapes useful in selecting purebred dogs or learning more about hunting or working dogs. An audio guided tour of the exhibits is offered as well. Become a museum member and receive *Sirius*, their quarterly newsletter. Too far to visit? A price list of novelty items and books that can be purchased is available along with a brochure (20 percent discount to members). Admission: $3 adults; $1.50 seniors; $1 children 5–14; under 5 free. Well-mannered dogs, on a leash, are welcome in the community room only!

THE EXPLORATORIUM, SAN FRANCISCO
3601 Lyon St.
San Francisco, CA 94123
415-561-0317

When visiting the Golden Gate Bridge, you won't want to miss this science, art, and human perception showcase. Part of the Palace of Fine Arts, it has pitch-black mazes of chambers lined with different textures that kids can crawl through, plus all kinds of displays that teach various physical principles.

FRONTIERS OF FLIGHT MUSEUM
Love Field Terminal, LB-38
Dallas, TX 75235
214-350-3600 (Office); 214-350-1651
Brochure

The Frontiers of Flight Museum is second in importance only to the aviation collection at the Smithsonian Institution. This collection covers and includes documents and memorabilia of aviation pioneers such as the Wright Brothers, Charles Lindbergh, Gen. Jimmy Doolittle, Amelia Earhart, and Chuck Yeager. The collection is one of the world's finest assemblages of artifacts, photographs, and documents of all facets of aviation and one of the few internationally recognized comprehensive aviation history research centers in the Western hemisphere. Museum and gift shop hours are 10:00 A.M.–5:00 P.M., Tues.–Sat.; 1:00 P.M.–5:00 P.M. Sun.; closed Mondays and holidays. Admission $2.

GUGGENHEIM MUSEUM CHILDREN'S PROGRAM
1071 Fifth Ave.
New York, NY 10128
212-360-3561
Complete information packet

No brush off the old palette here. Founded in 1970 to provide an educational opportunity for public school children in the metropolitan area, the Guggenheim Museum Children's Program brings a creative approach to elevating reading achievement. Art is the motivational strategy used by professional artists working in schools with teachers and students. Instruction takes place in workshops designed for children in need of an innovative, creative outlet to maintian their interest in school. "A Year with Children," an exhibition held annually at the museum, features children's artwork and writing from the workshops. Learning through art is made possible through generous support of individual contributors, foundations, and corporations, and should be a model for museum programs across the country. Pay attention to this space. Another Picasso may be in the making.

KIDSPACE
390 South El Molino Ave.
Pasadena, CA 91101
818-449-9144
Flier

One giant step for kidkind. Give these kids some space, some interactive and hands-on exhibits, and just watch them link up the concepts related to the arts and sciences. This "participatory" was designed and developed in scale and subject matter for children between the ages of 2 and 12. Included in the exhibits are a television studio and disk jockey booth exploring the world of media and communications. A wide variety of activities, special events, and drop-in workshops are available in addition to permanent exhibits.

A full summer program and memberships are available. Call or write for further details.

LAWRENCE HALL OF SCIENCE
University of California
Berkeley, CA 94620
415-642-5132

Children under 7 go free, 8–18 (and senior citizens) $1.50, adults $2.50 for one of the most spectacular science museums in the country. From a laser light show to interactive computer activities, an animal lab to roving robots, kids from 4 up will find this adjunct to the University of California a most hallowed hall for educational fun and games.

MAGIC HOUSE
ST. LOUIS CHILDREN'S MUSEUM
516 S. Kirkwood Road
St. Louis, MO 63122
314-822-8900

Don't you just hate to keep harping, "Hands off!"? This museum is the perfect hands-on solution. Children and parents love to reach out and touch the many exhibits, including a bubblemaker that blows giant bubbles, a TV camera that allows kids to make their own music videos, and a three-story slide. Admission $2.50; children under 2 free.

MUSEUM EDITIONS NEW YORK LTD.
12 Harrison Street, 3rd Floor
New York, NY 10013
212-431-1913
Catalog $5 (refundable)

This museum-quality catalog runs 32 pages of poster possibilities for your kid's room, at home or away from home. Posters by Klee, Rothko, O'Keeffe, Glaser, or Katz are popular at this home but in Josh's first apartment he picked the Avery series on James Dean. Mickey Mouse also brought down the house. Prices run from $15 to $25.

MUSEUM OF BROADCAST COMMUNICATIONS
800 South Wells St.
Chicago, IL 60607-4529
312-987-1500
Brochure (color)

AT MBC (not to be confused with NBC), kids are the stars of the show as they slide into the anchor chairs, report the news, give sports scores, read the TelePrompTers and interact with co-anchors just like their big-time real-life counterparts. Move over, Peter Jennings! Programs are taped for kids to take home and show their family and friends. This is a museum of memories containing lively exhibits and a library of vintage radio and television shows. Memberships available. Write or call for information on member privileges.

MUSEUM OF BROADCASTING
1 East 53rd St.
New York, NY 10022
212-752-4690
Brochure

What do Cher, Meryl Streep, Peter Ustinov, and Jack Nicholson have in common besides show business? The answer, my friend, is spoken in the wind. These stars narrate children's classics at the Museum of Broadcasting's Storybook Playhouse. This unique, nonprofit institution invites the public to experience its collection of 40,000 radio and television programs and commercials. Children 8 to 13 participate in hands-on workshops re-creating radio programs using scripts and sound effects to discover the excitement of early radio, while children 3 to 10 enjoy Children's Classics in the Museum Theater. Resident scholar programs and seminars are available for adults. Call for membership or information on upcoming events.

MUSEUM OF SCIENCE AND SPACE
  TRANSIT PLANETARIUM
3280 South Miami Avenue
Miami, FL 33129
305-854-4247

Miami's not just for beaches and palm trees. Breeze into this museum with one of the largest hands-on science exhibits for children in the country. From puzzles to muscle testing, killer whales to stargazing. Children under 3 go free; 3-12 and seniors $2.50; adults $4.

PLEASE TOUCH MUSEUM
210 North 21st St.
Philadelphia, PA 19103
215-963-0666; 215-963-0192 (mail order)
Flier

This is one museum where you won't see signs that say "Please don't touch," but rather a museum where learning is child's play. What you *will* find is lots of hands-on workshops, matinees of selected children's films, daily exploration programs, and programs exploring the arts, science, and dance. The *Please Touch Museum Cookbook* from the museum's Education Store has fun, easy recipes, stories, and riddles about food as well as projects and experiments to whip up in the kitchen. Too many books won't spoil the cook. The book costs $6.95 and makes a delicious gift. (Call mail order number when ordering book.)

SMITHSONIAN INSTITUTION
National Museum of American History
Visitors' Information Center
Constitution Avenue and 14th
Washington, DC 20560
202-357-2700; 202-357-1696 (hearing-impaired)
Brochure

Traveling across the U.S. this summer? Don't miss out on the Smithsonian's newest permanent exhibit that's perfect for kids: "Information Age: People, Information and Technology" located in the National Museum of American History. The exhibit features 1,400 artifacts and graphics illustrating the brief histories of everyday tools like the telephone, the computer, and robots. *Star Wars* characters such as R2-D2 are among the exhibits. Interactive exhibits allow you to create a record of your visit along with a printout of the experience before you leave. Tours also available for the hearing- and visually impaired. Call for further information on all of the museums within the Smithsonian.

DOING CHILDREN'S MUSEUMS
P.O. Box 185
Charlotte, VT 05445
800-234-8791

Over 225 hands-on museums from coast-to-coast including Canada are geographically and categorically inventoried for hungry day-trippers for $15.95. Kids are encouraged to touch. Age-appropriate guidelines are given by museum expert Joanne Cleaver, and nearby attractions are suggested for a full day (or weekend) excursion and diversion.

WORLD OF COCA-COLA
55 Martin Luther King, Jr. Drive
Atlanta, GA 30303-3505
404-676-5151
404-676-5432 (fax)
Flier (color)

Things go better with Coke. Put a little fizz in your summer agenda and check out the new $15 million World of Coca-Cola in Atlanta, Georgia. This three-story pavilion pays homage to the history of America's number-one soft drink —past, present, and future—told through fascinating exhibits, an eye-popping collection of memorabilia, classic radio and television advertisements, a fanciful presentation of the bottling process, and a futuristic soda fountain that you must see to believe (with complimentary servings of . . . you guessed it!). Can't beat the real thing! Admission: adults $2.50; seniors $2.00; children $1.50; under 6 free. Elevators available for handicapped visitors; special aids enhance the visit of the hearing-impaired.

MUSIC AND ENTERTAINMENT

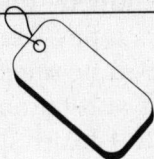

ALTENBURG PIANO HOUSE, INC.
1150 East Jersey Street
Elizabeth, NJ 07201
800-526-6979
Brochure

There are at least 88 reasons to shop the Altenburg Piano House. Since 1847, this house has been the keyboard of choice. Tickle the ivories on both pianos and organs for at least 35 percent below retail. Manufacturers such as Baldwin, Hammond, Kawai, Kimball, Mason, and Yamaha as well as Altenburg's house organ (they make their own line of pianos—uprights, consoles, and grands) are available for shipping to your music room anywhere in the continental U.S.

BEST BUY
Corporate Office: P.O. Box 9312
Minneapolis, MN 55440-9312
612-896-2300

It's all in the name. And indeed, some of the best buys in audio, video and videos, and computers are available through this nationwide chain of electronics showrooms. Making musical history, this chain's claim is "We won't be undersold!" They have both in-store and in-home service on products bought. CDs and cassettes from $3.29 to $8.89 were some of the lowest in town. The Nintendo Gameboy came with stereo headphones to ensure privacy and even included Game Link for $89.87. Gameboy software was also available. Wow, 4-pack TDK audio tapes were $7.47 and the movie *Ghost* on video was $13.99. The selection of Walt Disney and "Sesame Street" tapes was substantial. Many hours of entertainment pleasure with a 4-head special-effects Magnavox VCR for $239.93 is reason enough to shop one of the 60-plus Best Buy stores around the country.

BOSE EXPRESS MUSIC
50 W. 17th St.
New York, NY 10011
800-233-6357; 212-463-9300
212-627-2613 (fax)
Catalog $6 (refundable)

Music lovers of America, get on the Bose Express. Bose publishes the world's largest CD, tape, and video catalog, whose 240 pages include over 50,000 titles. Everybody loves to set records, and this catalog gets our vote. No kid would turn his nose up at a music gift certificate from Bose Express Music. (Don't even begin to pick out the tape yourself unless you *absolutely* know *for sure* what they like.) Choose from $35, $50, $75, and $100 gifts. Bose boasts every CD, tape, and video in print—all children's titles, too. Catalog $6; refundable with first order. Receive $50 in discounts in the front of the catalog. Monthly sales catalog mailed to subscribers only. Satisfaction guaranteed.

CARU
845 Third Ave., 17th Floor
New York, NY 10022

If those 900 numbers on your phone bill rankled your nerves, you can report any unethical ads for them to the Children's Advertising Review Unit (CARU) of the Council of Better Business Bureaus, or contact your phone company about their blockout service.

CMC MUSIC, INC.
1385 Deerfield Road
Highland Park, IL 60035
708-831-3252
PQ

Did you know that over 200,000 pianos were sold last year just in Korea? That means there's a lot of music being played in that country and *that* means they know a good piano when they build it. And they build some of the finest (at a lot less than a Baldwin or a Steinway). Some of the best brands around include Young Chang and Kawai, and if you want to save up to 50 percent on them, or any other keyboard instrument (organs, digital pianos, other electronic keyboards, etc.), just give CMC a call.

CARVIN
1155 Industrial Ave.
Escondido, CA 92025
800-854-2235
Catalog

When the boys of the band get together for a jam session, if they are serious about making music and saving money, they'd be fools not to consider a Carvin-made line of instruments and equipment. Comparable to other brands at up to 40 percent less, the exacting standards to which they adhere would make even the Van Halens fall to their knees. Choose from amps, mikes, mixers, and monitor systems, as well as the electric guitars. And listen to the sound of this: all items are sold with a ten-day free trial.

CHICAGO RECORDS
Corporate Office: 410 S. First Street
St. Charles, IL 60174

You never know what records will be broken at this record company's stores. All major labels are represented in records, tapes, CDs, and videos: Warner Bros., Capitol, CBS, Atlantic, and more at discounts of 10–40 percent. Stores currently in Hoffman Estates, Kankakee, St. Charles, and Schaumburg, IL; Birch Run, MI; Kenosha, WI.

CHILD'S PLAY TOURING THEATER
2650 W. Belden
Chicago, IL 60647
312-235-8911
Brochure

"To be, or not to be" is answered by the Child's Play Touring Theater. This unique theater company is committed exclusively to creating original plays and songs from stories and poems written entirely by children. Performances are filled with color, music, and rollicking audience participation. Past shows included *Animal Tales and Dinosaur Scales* and *One Monster After Another*. Although performing mostly for elementary, middle, and junior high students, they do keep

---

THE CHILDREN'S TELEVISION ACT OF 1990

In order for TV stations to use public air waves, stations must provide children's programs that are deemed educational. Futhermore, the act imposes a limit of 10½ minutes of commercials per hour during kids' programs on weekends and 12 minutes during weekdays.

---

handicapped and special audiences in mind. American sign language and bilingual pieces are important elements in their repertory. This touring troupe travels to schools around the country. For specific cost information and performance itineraries, contact June Podagrosi, Executive Director.

CIRCUIT CITY
Corporate Office: 2040 Thalbro Street
Richmond, VA 23230
804-527-4000

When kids scream for the latest in brand name audio and video gadgetry, plug into the circuitry at Circuit City. Their pulsating commercials beat to the tune of a different drummer, "where service is state-of-the-art." Sony Walkmans were as low as $27.97 and a Magnavox slimline AM/FM stereo cassette player was $39.97. This electronics and appliance chain is spreading nationwide. Check directory for location nearest you.

COCONUTS/RECORD TOWN
Corporate Office: 38 Corporate Circle
Albany, NY 12203
518-452-1242

You'll go bananas over the selection of records and tapes, albums, compact discs, and videos, including all the current releases. Then you'll go nuts over the prices . . . at up to 40 percent off. Almost 100 stores concentrated in the North, Southeast, Middle Atlantic, and Midwest so far.

CUSTOM VIDEO SERVICES
4500 Ratliff, #118
Dallas, TX 75248
214-380-8273
Flier

Lights. Camera. Action! "Roll 'em" into this imaginative way to celebrate a birthday, create a theme party, or capture creativity forever on celluloid. Custom Video Services in Dallas specializes in producing fantasy films or mini-movie productions. Scripts, musical scores, a cast and crew, locations, even special effects (no matter how weird) can be arranged anywhere in the country. Other unique services include "Laser Karaoke Sing-A-Long," the twenty-first century entertainment that allows any shower singer a chance to be a star. Recipe for an Oscar for best performance in a children's party role begins with a call to Custom Video Services. Add fantasy, a vivid imagination, put in a pinch of special production secrets from Custom Video Services, and Hollywood may be calling next. To readers of *Great Buys for Kids*, Custom Video Services offers a FREE duplicate tape of any finished video (a $27 value) that is produced. Satisfaction guaranteed.

DALLAS PIANO WAREHOUSE AND SHOWROOM
9292 LBJ Freeway
Dallas, TX 75243
214-231-4607

When the inevitable cries of "I want to take piano lessons" arise, find your best price and then call Dallas Piano. The reasons are here in black and white: First, of course, they have most of the top-ten brands of pianos. Second, they have some of the best prices around. Now that's music to *our* ears. Tickle the ivories of Kawai, Schimmel, Young Chang, Steinway, Roland, Technics, and more in pianos and keyboards. Even Beethoven would roll over at savings quite literally in the thousands on some. Shipped anywhere.

FRED BERNARDO'S MUSIC
212 W. Lancaster
Shillington, PA 19607
215-777-3733
Catalog $1

So you have a budding Holly on your hands, eh? Stop fretting about the prices of guitars and save up to 40 percent here. Strum to the tune of a steel guitar, brass or electric. Or try a mandolin, a banjo, an autoharp, or sitar. Choose from some of these brands: Aranjuez, Ernie Ball, Black Diamond, D'Addario, Darco, Fender, Gibson, Savarez, and Vega. Also available are mikes and other electronic accessories.

FREEPORT MUSIC, INC.
41 Shore Dr.
Huntington Bay, NY 11743
516-549-4108
Catalog $1 (refundable)

Not free, but almost. Shop to the tune of a different drummer here when the price of drums is eating your lunch. Since 1921, Freeport has been beating the sticks off the competition with their lowest-price guarantee as well as their complete selection. Ludwig, you bet, but also drum sets by Pearl, Slingerland, and Tama; strum on a guitar by Dobro, Gibson, Guild, Ibanez, Richenbacker, or Yamaha. Then amplify your sounds with Boss, Fender, Roland, Ross, or Simmons. And if your band is expanding, you'll be blown away with the selection of woodwinds and brass. Electronic keyboards, too. Disco lighting, cleaning supplies, piano-tuning kits, and more. If Lawrence Welk is in the picture, you can even buy a bubble machine. And a one, and a two . . .

GIARDINELLI BAND INSTRUMENT CO., INC.
7845 Maltlage Drive
Liverpool, NY 13090
800-288-2334; 212-575-5959
Catalog

Meet me at Giardinelli's catalog if you want to square off the prices of band instruments. When your children decide to toot their horns, shop for them either at pawn shops or discounters. This 24-page catalog has it all. Brass and woodwind instruments and accessories: trumpets, tubas, trombones, French horns, flutes, clarinets, saxophones, oboes, bassoons . . . at piccolo prices. All the best brands in the band are included. Also mouthpieces, metronomes, mutes, and music books at up to 50 percent off.

INTERSTATE MUSIC SUPPLY
P.O. Box 315
New Berlin, WI 53151
414-786-6210
Catalog; PQ

This 164-page catalog should be music to your ears. Savings up to 60 percent sound good to schools and music teachers, so why not you? Let Barry Manilow write the songs that the young folks sing. And you can sing the song all the way to the bank. The major sound groups are represented: woodwind, string, percussion, and brass. Top brass also shop here for stage lighting, sound systems, lab pianos, music stands, even risers for the orchestra or chorus. They manufacture their own brand of instruments under the IMS label, but also stock every major brand to call upon: Anvil, Bach, Buffet, Dynamic, Emerson, Engelhardt, Fender, Franz, Gibson, Holton, Korg, Ludwig, Mesa-Boogie, Orff, Pearl, Peavey, Roland, Vandoren, Yamaha, and Zildjian. And the catalog doesn't even tell the whole story. Call for additional price quotes or send SASE.

LONE STAR PERCUSSION
10611 Control Place
Dallas, TX 75238
214-340-0835
Catalog; PQ

"Drum on your drums, batter on your banjo, sob on your long, cool winding saxophone." This Carl Sandburg poem was only partially correct at Lone Star, for they only let you drum on *their* drums. Since 1978, this company has been selling drums, drumsticks, cymbals, castanets, gongs, triangles, tambourines . . . anything that goes bang in the night. Brands include American Drum, Bruno, Deschler, Tom Gauger, Grover, Holt, Hyer, Latin Percussion, Ludwig, Premier, Promarkk, Remo, Ross, Silverfox, Tama, Yamaha, and Zildjian. Prices were heard loud and clear at 40 percent off. Price quotes on items you don't see in the catalog by phone or letter.

MANDOLIN BROTHERS, LTD.
629 Forest Ave.
Staten Island, NY 10310-2576
718-981-3226
718-816-4416 (fax)

The Gatlin Brothers have nothing on the Mandolin Brothers, though they all make foot-stompin' music. The latter, though, have concentrated on selling guitars at up to 35 percent off in all shapes, sizes, and ages—from vintage guitars, banjos, and mandolins to new models in all the popular names like Alvarez-Yairi, Deering, Dobro, Epiphone, Flatiron, Gibson, Lowden, Martin, Ome, Jose Ramirez, Richenbacker, Santa Cruz, Sierra, Steinberger, Taylor, Washburn, Wildwood, and Yamaha. Add depth to the sound with amps, tuners, effects boxes by the Boss. And don't fret, there are straps, strings, cables, mutes, capos, books, and videos, too. Written appraisals and repairs available.

MUSIC 4 LESS
Corporate Office: 3730 Vulcan Drive
Nashville, TN 37211
615-833-5960

You'd expect a grand ole selection of top records and tapes from Nashville standards to include all the favorites alongside the country-western. Get into the groove with the top ten and beyond from Warner Bros., Columbia, RCA, and more. There are over 75 Music 4 Less stores in Alabama, Arkansas, Florida, Georgia, Illinois, Indiana, Kansas, Kentucky, Louisiana, Mississippi, New York, North Carolina, Oklahoma, South Carolina, Tennessee, Texas, and Virginia. More on the horizon.

NATIONAL EDUCATIONAL MUSIC CO., LTD.
1181 Route 22
P.O. Box 1130
Mountainside, NJ 07092
800-526-4593; 201-232-6700 (AK, HI, NJ)
201-789-3025 (fax)
Catalog

Shop where the band teachers shop and, even as a mere member of the band, you can save up to 50 percent off list prices. NEMC carries brass, percussion, and woodwind instruments without missing a beat. Their 32-page catalog also includes imported master violins and violas. And if you still are not wanting to bow out, they also carry cases, stands, music software, and other musical accompaniments. This company is also noted for the longest warranty in the industry for all their instruments (except fretted ones).

PATTI MUSIC CORP.
414 State St.
Madison, WI 53703
608-257-8820
608-257-5847 (fax)
Catalog

Okay, so the discounts are not that steep (only 15 percent), but where else can you find sheet music discounted, let alone by mail? Calling all piano teachers and students. This is it! Their 60-page catalog has been around since 1936. Note: Sheet music for both piano and organ is their mainstay but discounts were greater on metronomes and tuners (33 percent). Start playing patty-cake, chopsticks, Chopin, and Czerny and let's see how you can scale to even greater heights. Remember you read it here . . . in black and white.

PERFORMANCE MAGAZINE FANPOWER CLUB
1203 Lake St., Suite 200
Fort Worth, TX 76102-4504
817-338-9444; 900-446-1600 (Fanpower hotline)
817-877-4273 (fax)
Newsletter

Hot off the charts: Upcoming concert information at your fingertips! *Performance* magazine, along with interactive telephone technology, makes it possible to share private source information with you, the public, by way of Fanpower. As a member of the club, you are assigned a "PIN" number which gives you all the latest inside scoops, exclusive ticket request benefits, tour merchandise, etc. FREE 3-month trial subscription. Hotline information is 95 cents per minute (parents' permission requested). For further details write to Fanpower, c/o *Performance* Magazine.

RHYTHM BAND, INC.
1212 E. Lancaster
Ft. Worth, TX 76102
817-335-2561
Catalog

Though basically a mail-order source for musical instruments sold around the world, you can show up at their front door, browse through their catalog, and have merchandise retrieved from the warehouse behind. Then again, unless you happen to live in Ft. Worth, Texas, it may sound better to stay home and shop by phone. Their business was born out of selling rhythm instruments to preschool and elementary school music classes and bands. But they will sell to you at the same good prices such things as musical games, records and cassettes, folk and classical guitars (pint-sized versions sell for $82.50), rhythm sticks, triangles, and about 10 different kinds of tambourines.

SATURDAY MATINEE
Corporate Office: 38 Corporate Circle
Albany, NY 12203
518-452-1242

Okay, sports fans, take a seventh-inning stretch and tune in to some prerecorded videos sure to give hundreds of hours of viewing pleasure. Return to the days of old when you were able to sleep in on Saturdays. From new releases to classics, cartoons to music videos, and plenty of appropriate children's videos to choose from at up to 60 percent off. Concentrated in New England and the Southeast thus far with over 50 stores, but expansion planned for the Midwest and Southwest.

SHAR PRODUCTS COMPANY
P.O. Box 1411
Ann Arbor, MI 48106
313-665-7711
Catalog

Hail to the victors valiant, hail to the conquering musicians who have been playing this fight song from the University of Michigan since 1962. This company provides the string community with the academic option of paying up to 50 percent less for their instruments. And if that doesn't earn applause, what about their vast collection of classical recordings and sheet music? Even student violins by Glaesel, Schroetter, and Suzuki are available as well as fine instruments for the masters. Tons of accessories, including the

Suzuki books and records, videotapes of the masters (Heifetz and Segovia), classical cassettes, and more. A sheet music catalog is available at an additional charge ($3).

SILENT NIGHT AT THE SYMPHONY
500 N. Michigan Ave., Suite 200
Chicago, IL 60611
Brochure (SASE)

Do your kids balk at Beethoven or cringe at Chopin? Help them get the most out of Mozart and the symphony with a free brochure, "Harmony, Strings and Symphony Things," offered through Silent Night at the Symphony. Hey, even Billy Joel and Elton John studied classical music when they were young! This brochure offers insightful comments on minding manners, includes a musical glossary for better understanding of musical terminology, and touches on the instruments in the symphony orchestra. An ongoing effort to improve the symphony-going experience for patrons of all ages. Send SASE to above address.

SUZUKI ASSOCIATION OF THE AMERICAS, INC.
P.O. Box 354
Muscatine, IA 52761
319-263-3071
Flier

Formulated by the son of the first Japanese violin maker, this intensive approach to learning a musical instrument teaches a child as young as three the "language" of music, as one would teach him/her their native tongue. The Suzuki method differs from the traditional music lessons in the level of parental involvement: the parent learns the instrument along with the child. This method also utilizes creative and imaginative strategies like incorporating musical games and holding recitals for groups of stuffed animals (talk about a "captive audience") to help students and parents enjoy their musical studies even more. The Suzuki Association will send you a complete list of qualified teachers in your area. Call or write for details.

USA PRODUCTIONS
NEW YOUTH MUSICAL
4502 Ave. D, Suite B
Austin, TX 78751
512-326-2251
Review copy of book and sample tape available, $30; $25 refundable when materials are returned

Helping kids get their act together and taking it on the road is the tenor of *Ray's Café—The Musical*. This powerfully crafted and captivating original musical was especially written for young-adult performers to entertain high school kids and their families. Written by an adolescent psychologist, a professional stage and screen actress/playwright, and an Austin, Texas, songwriter, it's a zing-hummer complete with big production numbers, ballads, reggae, rap, pop, blues, and rock. Bring down the house with a message meant first to entertain, and second, to empower kids to change their own and each other's lives. Call to see how your high school can jump on the bandwagon with as few as 14 cast members and 11 stage band musicians (more if necessary). An accompaniment cassette tape is also available for schools or theaters who can't get a bank together. As one enthusiastic 16-year-old cast member said after its world premier in Temple, Texas, "This show is about us!"

PAPER AND PARTY ITEMS

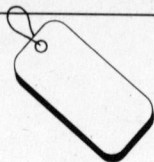

ACME PREMIUM SUPPLY CORPORATION
4100 Forest Park Blvd.
St. Louis, MO 63108-2899
800-325-7888, ext. 3
800-531-2106 (fax)
Catalog

Acme carries a brickload of tricks and treats for the party planner from balloons to stuffed animals. Carnival goers will recognize lots of prizes from their 136-page catalog. Even moms will delight in their zillions of doodads, paper and plastic products for entertaining, games for birthday parties, bingo supplies, and other familar premium items. Their catalog states that products are not intended for children under 5. Minimum order $50.

THE AMERICAN STATIONERY CO., INC.
100 Park Ave.
Peru, IN 46970
800-822-2577; 317-473-5901
Catalog

You don't have to climb the Andes to reach the pinnacle in custom-printed stationery. Save up to 35 percent for comparable customizing on everything from embossed sheets and notes to heavyweight Monarch sheets and matching envelopes. Kids will get a kick out of their own personalized memo pads, or bordered postcards to write Mom from camp.

BIG LEAGUE CARDS
265 Cedar Lane
Teaneck, NJ 07666-3444
201-907-0700
Flier

Join the Big League if you want to hit a home run. What a bonanza for children of all ages! The brainstorm of former Yankee pitcher Jim Bouton, Big League Cards are authentic baseball trading cards that feature the star of your choice. Pick a photo and have it printed on the front in full color with any data on the back such as the person's hobbies, newborn infant stats, nicknames, or special messages. Want a memorable business card, invitation, birth announcement, or really unique way to say congratulations or thank you? Well, you can't s-t-r-i-k-e out with a Big League Card! And the fun doesn't stop with just one. Collect, trade, share many of them, again and again. Not just for sports enthusiasts . . . amateur artists, good cooks, computer whizzes, and sales people should experience the thrill of a victory once in a while. Batter up! If not satisfied, return full set for prompt refund.

EVERYTHING BUT THE CAKE
607 Corona St., Suite 272-BH1
Denver, CO 80218
302-778-6228 (CO)
303-871-0640 (fax)
Catalog

This party paradise provides plenty of pickings for planning the perfect party. Pick a party plan theme that's perfect for your child's interests and age. You'll find all the paperware plus matching decorations—even party favors specifically coordinated to each party theme. Celebrate with Mickey Mouse, Sesame Street characters, Barbie, a Fairy Princess, a Dinosaur Kingdom, or the Rescue Rangers. If your mind's gone blank and you'd rather not just write a blank check, choose from hundreds of party planning books and games with countless party ideas (everything but the cake!). Party Express service delivers within three working days. FREE catalog to readers *plus* 10 percent off first order of $40 or more. Thirty-day guarantee with full refund if not completely satisfied.

GANTER FACTORY STORES
Corporate Office: RD #12, P.O. Box 251 A
York, PA 17406
717-252-1578

Set the stage for savings from this manufacturer of kids' costumes and recital wear (they also make women's swimwear and leisure wear). Where else can you find 50 percent savings on fabulous tutus complete with chiffon and netting for $10-$28? Shop for dance costumes, Halloween, etc. In York, PA (717-252-4075), and in Roanoke, VA, and all available by phone.

LA PIÑATA
#2 Old Town Patio Market
Albuquerque, NM 87104
505-242-2400
Brochure and price list $1 or SASE

These piñatas are perfect, amigo. *Hola* to these hollow papier-mâché traditional treats from Mexico. Hit the bull in the eye and watch the candy come tumblin' down. Custom-made piñatas, too, from an Idaho potato to a Dallas Cowboy. Lots from the animal kingdom, from kangaroos on down. Colorful paper flowers hanging from the rafters and growing from every inch of shelf space in this store in popular Old Town.

PALMER SALES
3510 E. Highway 80
Mesquite, TX 75185
214-288-1026
Catalog

Write for their free catalog if the carnival's just around the corner. You'll find trinkets, charms, and holiday decorations (Christmas, Halloween, Thankgiving). Birthday parties, clown supplies, balloons, baby showers, wedding decorations . . . it's your party and invite me if you want to. The catalog's a hoot and there are savings to boot!

THE PAPER WHOLESALER
795 NW 72nd St.
Miami, FL 33150
305-285-9229
Catalog $3

"Let us entertain you (and we'll have a real good time)" should be the opening song at the Paper Wholesaler. Their 32-page catalog is brimming with so many party supplies, so little time, so little money. Think about the year ahead and plan ahead—birthdays, showers, weddings, graduations. Shop for balloons, crepe-paper streamers, party hats, wrapping paper, paper plates, candles; you won't believe you bought the whole sale. Save up to 30 percent on institutional-size containers of Pepperidge Farm Goldfish or Planter's peanuts, giant-sized rolls of aluminum foil, cake-decorating supplies, and your hosts even throw in some tips on perfect party planning.

SAFETY TIPS FOR HALLOWEEN—
 GENERAL MILLS, INC.
P.O. Box 5001
Stacy, MN 55079
Brochure

Make this Halloween a treat rather than letting it end up in defeat. A little preplanning will help make this year's Halloween the best and safest ever. General Mills, along with the National Safety Council, put together a free brochure of invaluable safety tips for parents and kids before starting on the door-to-door trail. Included are Halloween stories to read and share with friends. Happy haunting!

PARADISE PRODUCTS, INC.
P.O. Box 568
El Cerrito, CA 94530-8300
415-524-8300
Catalog $2

Even if you don't like to gamble, this Paradise can sell you a pair-o'-dice at a discount. The game plan is simple. Collect everything you need under one catalog if you want to throw a theme party. From international events like Oktoberfest, to your class reunion from the '50s, you can paper the town with confetti or streamers. Say "Aloha!" to a Hawaiian luau and a packet of beach sand or say "And how!" to an Indian rain dance. You can even save a fortune on Chinese fortune cookies for your next chin-din. Though the minimum order is $30, it not hard to honor. All items are guaranteed to arrive on time (and not fashionably late) to the party and inperfect condition, or Paradise will cheerfully refund your money.

THAT'S A WRAP
1603 Orrington Ave., Suite 1005
Evanston, IL 60201
708-475-0324
708-475-0477 (fax)
Brochure

When the time comes to wrap it up, be sure you call on
That's a Wrap. Tie one on with their "Bow Magic" gift bows
by 3M if you want the perfect topping. Also, add a sticker
or two; they're quicker. For up to 30 percent off, you can
receive bows that are precut and looped, and can be molded
into different shapes and affixed to any package with their
own pre-sticking ribbon.

U.S. BOX CORP.
1296 McCarter Highway
Newark, NJ 07104
201-481-2000; 718-387-1510
718-384-3756
Catalog $3

You may have to hold a paper party to collect the minimum
order ($150) but it'll be worth it. Save up to 60 percent
through this giant 100-page catalog of packaging supplies
that'll keep you wrapped up for years. Help stamp out high
prices on boxes, bags, containers, canisters, wrapping paper,
tape, tissue paper, mailing envelopes, gift totes, baskets,
ribbons, gift ties, buttons, and bows. Oops! No buttons. Post
a note the next time your first-class taste calls for budget
mailings.

WILTON 1992 YEARBOOK OFFER
2240 West 75th Street
Woodridge, IL 60517-0754

For fussy five-year-olds, these birthday cakes are sure to please along with hundreds of cake, cookie, candy, and dessert ideas for the year-round. New designs and step-by-step instructions will help you meet any occasion—Sweet Sixteen, graduation, bridal showers, Halloween, or any other holiday that needs a cake baked to order. Make the next party or get-together more personalized with some help from Wilton. Order this $5.99 full-color, 196-page book and get a $6 certificate to use on any Yearbook mail-order purchase over $25.

SCHOOL SUPPLIES

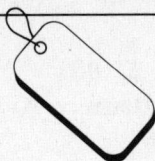

BIZMART
Corporate Office: 2000 E. Lamar Blvd., #310
Arlington, TX 76006
817-792-5200
Catalog

Arlington's home to the Texas Rangers, and this office and computer supply superpower packs a wallop in the savings biz. For home or office supplies, and school supplies as well, you can slash prices 40–60 percent off paper and pens, phones and fax machines. Stores in Arizona, Colorado, Kansas, Missouri, Nevada, New Mexico, Oregon, Texas, and Utah. More on the drawing boards (discounted, of course).

BUSINESS ENVELOPE MANUFACTURERS, INC.
900 Grand Blvd.
Deer Park, NY 11729
516-667-8500
516-586-5988 (fax)
Catalog

Make shopping for school supplies a study in savings. Save up to 75 percent on everything from A to Z when it comes to getting organized. Their 48-page catalog can help your child in many departments, from reams of paper, to grosses of pens and pencils, for starters. Add organizers, bulletin boards, even printed stationery so they can write grandma a letter or two.

DOLLAR TREE/ONLY $1.00
Corporate Office: 255 Ellsmere Ave.
Norfolk, VA 23501-2500
804-857-4600

Dollars don't grow on trees, but at this store, your dollar goes a long way toward establishing buying power. General merchandise like toiletries, home furnishings, toys, paper goods, car accessories, housewares, and tapes are all priced at $1. Over 150 stores and growing like weeds, concentrating on the East and West Coasts and in the Midwest.

FRANK EASTERN CO.
599 Broadway
New York, NY 10012
212-219-0007
Catalog $1

Setting up a study area in the den or a full-scale office in a spare bedroom shouldn't mean a home-improvement loan. From coast to coast, this Eastern-er has been Frank about the savings. Up to 50 percent off list or comparable retail throughout their 72-page shopping catalog. Reserve your seating early. Their selection of desk chairs (including the popular ergonomic models), desks, filing cabinets, storage units, book shelves, work stations, and wall units is staggering.

OFFICE DEPOT
Corporate Office: 851 Broken Sound Parkway NW
Boca Raton, FL 33487
407-994-2131
Catalog

Since their acquisition of Office Club, this is probably the largest discounting office and school supplies supercenter in the country. Back to school in brand-spankin' new notebooks, a red pencil case, a protractor, dividers, a new pocket dictionary, pens and pencils, and a 486 laptop. Fax and answering machines, and photocopying at 3 cents a sheet or $2.50 per 100. Check directory for location nearest you.

PHAR-MOR
Check directory for location nearest you.

Shop Phar-Mor where buying power gives you far more buying power when the subject is spelled k-i-d-s. This leader in the deep discount industry provides savings of 20–50 percent on an A-to-Z inventory of kids' shopping needs. From school supplies to no-membership lowest-price video rentals, you will spend less and get more bang for your buck. Disney classic videos are a must. Then on to baby needs from diapers to baby oil, children's books, magazines, baby announcements and birthday cards, gift wrap and bows, seasonal and holiday doodads, Halloween candy, cassettes, soft drinks, and snacks, prescriptions to children's vitamins, the full assortment of one-stop shopping and savings is available under one roof. When your little kiddy needs to go to market, shop Phar-Mor and save all the way home.

QUILL CORPORATION
100 Schelter Rd.
P.O. Box 4700
Lincolnshire, IL 60197-4700
708-634-4800
708-634-5708
Catalog

Their monthly 64-page catalogs come regularly and without pain. You will gain regularly, though in your bottom line. Your savings score a whopping 70 percent if you use their house brands. General office supplies and equipment including files and folders, ribbons and reams (all kinds of paper), computers and chairs, pens and pencils, and that's just for the *first* lesson. However, you must send your request for their catalog on letterhead. Ask Mom and Dad for help if you're a kid reading this book!

THE RELIABLE CORPORATION
1001 W. Van Buren
Chicago, IL 60607
800-869-6000
800-326-3233
Catalog

No fine, upstanding citizen kid should be caught dead paying full price for school supplies. This is a painless way to shop, toll-free on almost anything imaginable your teachers require to ace the course. Their catalogs are regular, like clockwork, and their prices are regularly discounted to 50 percent off. Their service rivals their selection. The selection rivals their prices. From notebooks to typewriter ribbons, pens and pencils to markers and highlighters, folders to file cabinets, reinforcements to most anything that is reliable.

STAPLES, INC.
P.O. Box 160
Newton, MA 02195
617-965-7030
Catalog

Staples has become a staple in the office and school supply business with their 160-page catalog crash course. Page after page of one-stop shopping in every department. From Cross pens to Hammermill paper, Texas Instruments calculators to Verbatim software, there isn't a subject that falls by the wayside. Get an A in Copiers 101 or an answering machine that answers all the questions instead. Save 20–50 percent. Add 5 percent of the total price to have it delivered, with a minimum order of $15. Check directory for location nearest you.

VIKING OFFICE PRODUCTS
13809 S. Figueroa St.
Los Angeles, CA 90061
800-421-1222
800-SNAPFAX (fax)

Isn't it a wonderful feeling to have everything new on the first day of school? Viking charges up to 67 percent less than retail, and the Viking brand as well as name brands are delivered with free shipping on order of $25 or more (in the continental U.S. only). The 208-page catalog has it all; the monthly mailings offer even greater savings.

VULCAN BINDER & COVER
P.O. Box 29
Vincent, AL 35178
800-633-4526; 205-672-2241
205-672-7159 (fax)
Catalog

Eagle eyes make a beeline to this Vulcanic source when the subject is 3-ring binders. Save up to 40 percent here. When you need to keep it all together, Vulcan's binders will blind-side you. Heavy-duty ring binders, catalog binders, 19-ring binders, magazine binders, zippered binders, pocket-sized binders, report covers, page protectors . . . perfect for an annual report or a book report. Minimum order $25.

SHOES AND SOCKS

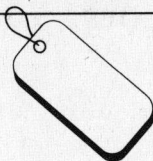

BABYBOTTE
P.O. Box 25715
Salt Lake City, UT 84125
800-533-1138
Catalog

Shake your bootie, baby, to your little heart's content. Infant footwear from Babybotte will stay put. Call for a list of retailers near you.

BOOT TOWN
10838 N. Central Expressway
Dallas, TX 75231
800-222-6687
Catalog (full-color)

One of Dallas's finest boot merchants mails its boots out of town and gives price quotes on over 30 top-quality brands. Boot Town stocks children's boots in size 4 to boys' size 6. Included in their inventory are play gun sets, chaps, vests, hats, and belts for younger cowboys and cowgirls. Call for customer assistance with brand and size, and before you can say "Round 'em up!" (if you're inclined to say such things), they'll ship a pair to arrive within a few days. (There's no

restocking charge on returns.) Open Mon.–Sat. 9:00 A.M.–
9:00 P.M.; Sun. noon–6:00 P.M. (CST).

CARLSEN IMPORT SHOES
524 Broadway
New York, NY 10012
212-431-5940
Catalog (full-color)

A lot of track shoes to keep track of here. This is where
athletes truly foot the bill for less . . . even peewee athletes.
For children's sizes 10½ and up, there's L.A. Gear for girls
and Reebok, Puma, and Etonic high-tops and low-cuffs for
boys. Discounts range from 15 to 30 percent off retail.
Unused items are returnable. All orders must be prepaid by
check or money order. No credit cards. Shipped within 48
hours.

DUNHAM FOOTWEAR
Corporate Office: P.O. Box 813
Brattleboro, VT 05301
802-254-2316

"Great Footwear for the Great Outdoors" and that means
shoes made for walkin' . . . , talkin' . . . , and workin'.
Dunham workboots are available in youth sizes 8½ to 3, and
boys' sizes 3½ to 6; waterproof youth boots in boys' sizes
only (3½ to 7). Also, footwear by Mitre and New Balance,
with Converse, L.A. Gear, and boat shoes for bigger boys.
Little girls feel pretty in patent leathers and sandals (infant
and youth sizes) . . . and all at a 15–20 percent savings.
Thirty stores; call or write for the one nearest you.

EL-BEE SHOE OUTLET
Corporate Office: 3155 El-Bee Road
Dayton, OH 45401-1448
513-223-4241

El Bee (short for Elder-Beeman, the department store chain that owns the outlets) takes the sting out of buying shoes. For kids, there's footwear by Eastland, Capezio, Hush Puppies, Calico, Nike, Reebok, and L.A. Gear in sizes 8½ through boys' size 6. There are 54 outlets (though almost 200 stores in the chain) carrying shoes for children with savings of 20 –25 percent. That's a honey of a deal.

FAMOUS FOOTWEAR/DIVISION OF
BROWN SHOE COMPANY
Corporate Office: 208 E. Olin Ave.
Madison, WI 53713
608-256-7007

In over 320 stores across the United States, Famous Footwear stocks millions of pairs of first-quality shoes, probably enough to cover every young foot in your town. Footwear for the whole family with a children's department offering name brands like L.A. Gear, Reebok, Buster Brown, Nike, Step 'N' Stride, and U.S. Sport in infant, youth, and children's sizes. They didn't become Famous for just standing still tapping their toes.

JUST JUSTIN BOOTS
1505 Wycliff
Dallas, TX 75207
800-292-2668; 214-630-2858
Catalog (full-color)

Do you feel pinched by high-priced cowboy boots? Get some relief with discounted boots from Just Justin. You won't find any labels here except Justin, but you *will* find boots for children in kids' sizes 8½ to boys' size 6. They also have Justin Western and Junior ropers: regular ropers, $49.95; lace-up ropers, $59.95. Belts and hats also available. Free catalog and exchanges or refunds if there's a problem.

LITTLE RED SHOE HOUSE—DIVISION OF WOLVERINE WORLD WIDE INC.
Corporate Office: 9341 Courtland Dr.
Rockford, MI 49351
(616) 866-5500

There's a lesson to be learned at this Little Red Shoe House: don't pay retail on quality name-brand footwear. Help keep the wolf from the door. Sh-h-h! This manufacturer's outlet offers body and sole in Hush Puppy, Town & Country, and Brooks. Infants' sizes 4-12, youth and children's sizes up to boys' size 6. Save 20–50 percent on dress, casual, and athletic shoes. Fashion feet-for-less in over 90 locations throughout the country.

MINNETONKA-BY-MAIL
P.O. Box 444
Bronx, NY 10458
Catalog $1 (full-color)

Minny-Ha-Ha if you don't know about Minnetonka moccasins and other casual booties produced by this old standby. Good buys, too. Save around 20 percent by shopping direct through their catalog where you can expect the real moccasin made famous by Minnetonka (not some cheap knock-off).

NIKE
Corporate Office: One Bowerman Dr.
Beaverton, OR 97005
800-344-NIKE; 503-671-6453
800-462-7363 (brochure request line)
Brochure

By 1992 this giant in the footwear and clothing business anticipates having 28 factory outlets across the country. For putting your foot down on high prices, these outlets are a showcase of discontinued items, closeouts, seconds, and overruns in infants, childrens, youth, and adult sizes in footwear and apparel. Surely it doesn't matter that you're wearing last season's Nikes in the scheme of things . . . especially when you're saving 50 percent. At the opposite end of the shoe spectrum is their state-of-the-art retail store in Portland, OR, called Nike Town (sort of a "Nike" Disneyland) in which all the new and innovative products they have to offer are available. For a peek, visit: Nike Town, 930 SW 6th St., Portland, OR 97204. Tentative openings of more Nike Towns are planned for New York, Chicago, and Japan.

REEBOK/ELLESSE/ROCKPORT FACTORY OUTLETS
Corporate Office: 100 Technology Center Drive
Stoughton, MA 02072
617-341-5000

Walk tall and carry a lighter load in a pair of Reeboks. Save wear and tear on your feet (and your budget) by visiting their outlet stores for athletic and fashion sport shoes and apparel for the entire family. Jog into their outlets or call Boaz and Foley, AL; Commerce, GA; Marlborough and Stoughton, MA; North Conway, NH; Lake George, NY; Lancaster, PA; Hilton Head, SC; Pigeon Forge, TN; Martinsburg, WV.

ROAD RUNNER SPORTS
6310 Nancy Ridge Rd., Suite 101
San Diego, CA 92121
800-551-5558 (Mon.–Fri. 5:00 A.M.–8:00 P.M.;
  Sat. 6:00 A.M.–6:00 P.M. PST)
619-455-6470 (fax)
Catalog (full-color)

Beep! Beep! This company can run circles around their nearest competition with guaranteed lowest prices on the best names in running shoes. Put your best foot forward for less in a pair of Adidas Phantom II Jr. high-tops, youth sizes 1–6 for $36.99, retail $55; Asics Tiger GT Intensity Jr., youth sizes 1–6 for $39.99, retail $50; and Etonic Stable Plus Jr., youth sizes 1–6 for $29.99, retail $60 . . . just to name a few. Also available as an accompaniment to their shoe selection is a full line of socks, clothing, and sports accessories for athletes. If you have a track team in need of shoes, call the Runner Hotline: (800) 662-8896 and ask for the Team Sales Supervisor. On your mark, get set, go!

SNEAKEE FEET
Corporate Office: 233 Broadway
New York: NY 10279-0099
212-720-3700

You don't have to "sneak" into the back door of this Kinney Shoe Corporation's discount division to sneak a peek at savings of 10–25 percent. The archenemy of high-priced footwear, SneaKee sells New Balance, Nike, Adidas, Puma, Converse, Tiger, and Fila in infant, children's, and youth sizes. Locations in Orlando and Tampa, FL; Gaithersburg and Towson, MD; Kansas City, MO; Colonie, Niagara Falls, and Rochester, NY; Burlington, NC; Philadelphia, PA; and Woodbridge, VA. Call for additional locations near you.

SOCKS GALORE & MORE/E.J. PLUM
Corporate Office: 220 Second Ave. South
Franklin, TN 37064
615-790-7625

Sock it to you in over 60,000 pairs of socks in every store throughout this outlet chain. Save 20–60 percent on family apparel and footwear by Socks Galore & More, Classic Sole, T.A. Cherry, Plum Toe, Plum Pac, T.G.I.F. (Toes Go in First), Giggles, and E.J. Plum. Call or write for location nearest you.

SPORTS AND EQUIPMENT

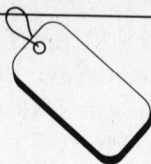

THE ATHLETE'S FOOT OUTLET
Corporate Office: 3735 Atlanta Industrial Parkway
Atlanta, GA 30311
404-699-8200

If you don't want to put the shoe on the other foot, call yourself by another name, instead. This chain of athletic shoes and clothing stores for the family has a host of aliases such as Heroes Outlet, Cheap Sneaks, and Athletic Attic depending on which state you're in. No matter what state, you can still choose from the same lineup of manufacturers: Avia, Adidas, British Knights, Keds, Converse, Everlast, Gitano, Reebok, Saucony, Vuranet, Head, and K-Swiss at 20–70 percent off. Stores thus far include: Boaz, AL; Sunrise, FL; Gurnee, IL; Dearborn, MI; Cincinnati, OH; Stillwater, OK; Pittsburgh, PA; Houston, TX; and Springfield, VA.

ATHLETIC X-PRESS
Corporate Office: 233 Broadway
New York, NY 10279
212-720-4104

This Kinney Shoe Corporate division is nearing 200 stores across the country sporting shoes and clothing as their major means of x-pression. Savings in the 20 percent game plan with names like Adidas, Nike, and Reebok for the entire family.

BART'S WATER SKI CENTER, INC.
P.O. Box 294
North Webster, IN 46555
800-348-5016; 800-552-2336 (IN)
Catalog (full-color)

Slalom on the waves and take the dips with the tide. Take a deep breath and save up to 40 percent on all your water skiing equipment and gear. Their 48-page catalog features skis for first-timers to professionals, boards, floats, tubes, and other toys for watered-down fun. Ride into the surf with wet suits (children are fully covered), swim suits, sunglasses, gloves, tow ropes, and videos on how to stay afloat.

BERRY SCUBA CO.
6674 N. Northwest Hwy.
Chicago, IL 60631
800-621-6019; 312-763-1626
312-775-1815 (fax)
Catalog (full-color)

This is a Berry-good source for scuba diving equipment and accessories. Deep, deep discounts down to as deep as 40 percent off the gear needed to get you in the swim of things. Save on masks, wet suits, fins, diving lights, strobes, diving watches, and tanks. Price quotes are available if you don't see clearly something to dive for in their 64-page catalog. Brands are all the best: Aquacraft, Chronosport, Dacor, Desco, Fuji, Nikon, Sea Suits, Tabata, Underwater Kinetics, U.S. Divers, Waterlung, and Wenoka.

BIKE NASHBAR
P.O. Box 3449
Youngstown, OH 44513-3449
800-NASHBAR
Catalog (full-color)

For both serious and semi-sedentary bikers, Nashbar is the place to dash for. Both racing and recreational bikes can be ridden off into the sunset, at prices up to 40 percent off retail. Their 64-page catalog tells all and all at the "guaranteed lowest prices." All major brands like Citadel, Shimano, Vitus, Colnago, Cinelli, and Guerciott as well as the Bike Nashbar brand with a listing of qualified installers across the country to hitch up to when assembly is called for. Accessories such as bike pumps, water bottles, shoulder holders, helmets, shoes, and mirrors are included in the bargains. Replacement parts like brake levers, cranksets, and flywheels, deluxe seats, tires, fenders, and tool kits are also available at discount prices. Sporty racing jerseys, caps, and sunglasses round out the gear. When you're in the Youngstown area, visit the stores listed in their catalog.

BILL LACKEY COMPANY
P.O. Box 35109
Dallas, TX 75235
214-526-5211

A washable peel-and-stick identification (called the Lackey Identification Tag) can be applied to your kids' walking or running shoes indicating their name and other pertinent information (like medical data, telephone number, who to call in an emergency). The size of a postage stamp, you'll get up to 4 lines and 20 letters per line. Four tags for $5.95.

BOWHUNTER'S WAREHOUSE, INC.
1045 Ziegler Rd., Box 158
Wellsville, PA 17365
717-432-8611
Catalog (full-color)

Cupid has known about this source for archery equipment since 1978. You can fall in love with it, too, for they have hit the bull's-eye on a complete range of archery and hunting supplies. The warehouse does not camouflage its clothing or its selection of feathers and bows, quivers, game calls, shooting equipment, and more. The prices are right on target, up to 40 percent off. Brand names to set your sites on include Browning, Bushnell, Golden Eagle, Indian, Jennings, PSE, and more. Minimum order $10.

BURLEY DESIGN COOPERATIVE
4080 Stewart Rd.
Eugene, OR 97402
503-687-1644 (in OR)
503-687-0436 (fax)
Catalog (full-color)

The best bicycles built for two are considered by industry standards to be the tandem bicycles developed by the Burley Design Cooperative in Eugene, Oregon. Since 1975, they have been supplying innovative products to the bicycling industry. For example, for bicycling parents, there's the "Burley d'lite," created especially for peewee passenger payloads. This folding bike trailer hinges to Mom's or Dad's bike and is the most versatile, safest, and easiest-to-use trailer. Available at leading bicycle stores nationwide. Call for the dealer in your area for a demonstration and/or for additional information.

CABELA'S
812 13th Ave.
Sidney, NE 69160
308-254-5505
Catalog (full-color)

Their catalog spawns accolades from serious hunters, fishermen, and outdoor buffs into swimming ahead of the stream at up to 40 percent off (but these discounts do not apply to everything throughout the catalog). For the best selection in overall sportsmanship, kids can hit the great outdoors with everything to keep them out, forever. Reel in the fishing rods, reels, and tackle from Berkley, Daiwa, Fenwick, Garcia, Mitchell, Shakespeare, or Shimano. We fell for Cabela's, hook, line, and sinker. Campers, too, have it their way with backpacks, sleeping bags, tents, flashlights, and knives.

CAMPMOR
P.O. Box 997
Paramus, NJ 07653-0997
201-445-5000
Catalog (full-color)

There isn't any camping or related gear that is not covered in Campmor's 120-page tome. Since 1946 they have been a camper's saving grace. Savings up to 50 percent are commonplace on everything you need to camp out. Clothing by Columbia Interchange System, Sierra Designs, and Woolrich; Timberland boots and Polypro underwear will keep you warm. What kid doesn't need a Swiss Army or a Buck knife? A canteen? A Coleman stove? A Coleman sleeping bag? And this is just the tip of the iceberg.

CRA-ZEE WEAR
737 L'Airport St.
El Segundo, CA 90245
800-933-WEAR
504-766-1885 (fax)
Catalog (full-color)

Where else but Los Angeles would you find the action? This sportswear manufacturer designs easy-on, easy off-ers that are hard to resist. Comfortable designs for active kids on the go. Skater and Muscle Man pants in solids, patterns and neons, featuring "Muscle Man," "Gym Rat," and "Crazee Cat" with solid and logo tops to match. Full-color catalog with children's sizes XS (2-3) to P (10-13). Be cool and add sunglasses for a pure, unadulterated Cra-Zee California look. Cra-Zee Wear comes in grown-up sizes, too.

CYCLE GOOD CORP.
2801 Hennepin Ave. South
Minneapolis, MN 55408
800-328-5213; 612-872-7600
Catalog $1

Bicycle enthusiasts get their Ph.D. in "cycl-ology" after their first purchase here. The 106-page catalog revolves around cycling gear, yes, but it also doesn't let you get away without a lecture about how to improve your performance and maintain your bike, as well as detailed product information. Both racing and touring bikes are up to 40 percent off retail and the names would impress any tour de force: Araya, Bendix, Bollé, Campagnolo, Cinelli, Citadel, Descente, Kingsbridge, Kirtland, Lemond, Maillard, Mavic, Messinger, Michelin, Nike, Rhode Gear, Sergal, Shimano, Sidi, and Weinmann.

THE FINALS, LTD.
21 Minisink Ave.
Port Jervis, NY 12771
914-856-4456
Catalog (full-color)

Swim with the sharks . . . and save up to 60 percent. Just make sure you're wearing a swimsuit from here. These form-fitting tank suits have been outfitting U.S. swim teams for years. Their specially designed fabric is a blend of Antron nylon and Lycra and is both fashion-forward and sleek, in and out of the water. Also unisex outfits for bicycling, working out, running, or warming up. Plus tote bags, duffel bags, goggles, fins, kickboards, the whole nine yards.

HERMAN'S WORLD OF SPORTING GOODS
Corporate Office: 2 Germak Drive
Carteret, NJ 07008
908-969-4544

This Herman comes on like a Sherman tank when orders come from the front line to hit the bunkers. The bargains in brand-name sporting goods could win the war single-handedly. There are almost 300 stores across the country selling sporting goods and apparel for the entire family. Names include Adidas, Nike, Reebok, Spalding, and Wilson.

HOLABIRD SPORTS DISCOUNTERS
9008 Yellow Brick Rd.
Baltimore, MD 21237
301-687-6400
Brochure

This ace has been serving up some of the best racquets this side of the net. If tennis is your game, you can save up to 40 percent on all the best in the world: Dunlop, Fox, Head,

Kneissl, Prince, Puma, Slazenger, Spalding, Wilson, Wimbledon, Yamaha, and Yonex are just a few to score. Tennis balls, ball machines, footwear in the latest styles by Adidas, Avia, Brooks, Converse, Ellesse, Etonic, Footjoy, Head, K-Swiss, Kaepa, Keds, L.A. Gear, Le Coq Sportif, New Balance, Nike, Pony . . . the list is as exhaustive as watching Martina. Gear for other sports including basketball, cross-training, aerobics, running and walking, golf shoes, and a full sporting line of clothing to wear on the courts, through the course, into the gym, or onto the streets.

L.L. BEAN
Freeport, ME 04033
800-221-4221 (orders); 800-341-4341 (customer service)
Catalog (full-color)

The source of all things sporty from this insomniac's shopping dream. Both economically and ecologically sound, L.L. Bean offers stress-free, toll-free, almost free-for-all fun sporting goods, exercise and camping gear, and apparel, from skis to the paraphernalia to keep you chic, sleek, and cozy on the slopes. There are also Swiss Army knives, tents, boots and treadmills, even pedometers, all fit to be tried. Specialty catalogs available upon request include Hunting, Home and Camp, Fall or Spring Women's Outdoors, Winter Sporting, Fly Fishing, and Spring Sporting. Gift certificates, too. No longer free shipping; you can still request Federal Express rush delivery for an additional charge. Their outlet stores are in Ellsworth and Freeport, ME, and North Conway, NH.

LAS VEGAS DISCOUNT GOLF & TENNIS
Corporate Office: 5325 S. Valley View Blvd., Suite 100
Las Vegas, NV 89118
702-798-7777

Stop putting around and paying full price for golf and tennis gear. Kids can get into the swing of things with a set of golf clubs, including the bag, for example, from Wilson (9–14-year-olds) or Bob Rossberg (5–9-year-olds) and only be out $114.95. If you are not near one of their 63 stores in the country, think sinking a hole-in-one and they will ship to you.

MACGREGOR FACTORY OUTLETS INC
Corporate Office: P.O. Box 297
East Rutherford, NJ 07073
201-935-6300

Listen up, sports fans. Even Tommy Lasorda could shop here for a week and save tons of money on his family's sporting goods and apparel. Donning the MacGregor label on most, it also hits a home run with Vitamaster exercise equipment, Roadmaster bicycles, and A.J. Sports at 50–60 percent off retail prices. Outlet locations include Palm Desert, CA; Silverthorne, CO; Kittery, ME; Monroe, MI; Keene, NH; and Reading, PA.

MEGA TENNIS PRODUCTS
800-228-2373
Catalog, PQ

Tighten those purse strings with savings on the strings here. Tennis racquets and racquet-stringing machines are their specialty, along with accessories for the court—grips, socks, wristbands, headbands, ball-hoppers, ball-machines, and most state-of-the-art tennis gear. Stringing your own racquet will save you even more. Service charge $3 on orders under $30.

MURRAY OHIO MANUFACTURING CO.
219 Franklin Rd., P.O. Box 268
Brentwood, TN 37027
800-251-8007; 615-373-6500
615-373-6771 (fax)
Catalog (full-color)

If you are looking to major in bikology, sign up for a course at Murray's. They're the folks to call when the subject is spokes. In business for over 35 years, they make top-quality, state-of-the-art bicycles and they haven't tired yet. They've got all-terrain bikes, cruisers, and touring bikes, all lightweight . . . sporting great graphics, exciting colors, and attractive features. Their 20″ boy's bike with full-line options even offers a 5-speed thumb shifter. And, for the very young, Murray starts 'em off right with quality bikes that are as durable as they are good-looking. The 16″ product line includes original styles as well as smaller versions of the popular 20″ models. Hurray for Murray! Call for nearest retailer.

NEVADA BOB'S DISCOUNT GOLF
Corporate Office: 3333 E. Flamingo
Las Vegas, NV 89121
702-451-3333

Little Arnie Palmers are not born every day, but if your kid's a swinger, you might start him or her off with a junior set of golf clubs for $60 (includes a driver, 2 woods, and a putter). Add a bag for $35 and you can get him/her on the green for less. Savings of 20 percent and more storewide for moms and dads, too, in over 300 locations nationwide. Check directory for one nearest you.

OVERTON'S SPORTS CENTER, INC.
P.O. Box 8228
Greenville, NC 27835
800-334-6541; 800-682-8263 (NC)
Catalog

Over the hills, and into the water, to the great white way of water sports. Overton's has the largest inventory of sports equipment in the world. For boating, water skiing, or snorkeling, you won't find a rope unturned in their 32-page catalog. Brands like Connelly, Kidder and O'Brien for the serious slalom skier for starters. And that's just the tip of the wave in their Water Sports Catalog. They also have a larger Marine Catalog which fuels your boating needs with the best buys in instruments, boat and seat covers, fishing equipment, and clothing. From Hummingbird to Shakespeare, to be or not to be paying full price is the question. Save up to 40 percent and sing "Anchors Away."

PERFORMANCE BICYCLE SHOP
P.O. Box 2741
Chapel Hill, NC 27514
919-933-9113
Catalog

When you are serious about biking, and you want to make a commitment to a high-end performance road bike, call on this mail-order bike specialist. For repairs and maintenance, Performance stocks whatever you need to do it yourself. From Campagnolo, Nitto, Shimano, Sugino, or Suntour components to the clothing to ride out of town with your kickstand up. Helmets, gloves, shoes, jerseys, and shorts to enhance *your* performance with their lowest-price guarantee part of *their* performance.

PRINCE MANUFACTURING, INC.
P.O. Box 2031
Princeton, NJ 08543-2031
800-2-TENNIS; 609-896-2500 (in NJ)
Brochure (full-color)

Now junior tennis players can get into the "swing" of things with Big Shot I and II rackets from the Prince of sports equipment manufacturers. Also in the area of sporting goods, you'll love the collection of apparel, sneakers, and accessories. Win at the net and at these price points. Ace your serve, too, with Big Shot rackets, available in two sizes for ages 3 to 7. Little rackets, big hits! Prices $35 and up. Call for the retailer nearest you.

RAWLINGS SPORTING GOODS
Corporate Office: P.O. Box 22000
St. Louis, MO 63126
314-349-3531

Score a touchdown in any one of the professional sports with MLB-and NFL-licensed apparel. Join the team and win a pennant with savings of 30–70 percent on team apparel and equipment with the Rawlings name. Bases located in San Diego, CA; Orlando, FL; Freeport, ME; Branson, MO; and Reading, PA.

RUSSELL FACTORY OUTLET STORE/JERZEES
Corporate Office: P.O. Box 272
Alexander City, AL 35010
205-329-4000

You don't have to be from Jersey to love Jerzees. This popular sporting line can cover your family from tops to bottoms. And in the process, you can save 30–50 percent by detouring to their outlet stores: Alexander City, Foley, and

Monroeville, AL; Ft. Pierce, Ft. Walton Beach, and Panama City, FL; Valdosta, GA; and New Braunfels, TX.

RUVEL & CO., INC.
4128-30 W. Belmont Ave.
Chicago, IL 60641
312-286-9494
Catalog $2

There's nobody that rivals Ruvel when you're ready to call out the duffel bags and the bug spray. Camping aficionados find this a source of real pleasure when savings (up to 70 percent) often rival their selection. Army-Navy surplus like rations and dummy grenades appealed to one army reservist while a mess kit and a first-aid kit seemed more practical to Mom.

SAILBOAT WAREHOUSE, INC.
300 S. Owasso Blvd.
St. Paul, MN 55117
800-992-SAIL
Catalog

This is the kind of sale that throws caution to the wind. If your kid has a hankering to windsurf or sailboat, there's no better place to get outfitted than here. Across the boards, you'll save 35 percent (more during clearance sales and closeouts). If you're a serious surfer, or someone just wanting to turn the tide, you can buy everything you need—from masts to wet suits, harnesses to how-to videos.

SAMUELS TENNISPORT
7796 Montgomery Road
Cincinnati, OH 45236
800-543-1152; 513-791-4636
Brochure

When the score is match point, you will want to ace your next serve. And Samuels Tennisport is the source you'll love. Everything to play by the book if your game's tennis, racquetball, squash, or badminton. Prices are up to 35 percent off (equipment only; clothing is full-price). Models that lined the runway included Dunlop, Fox, Head, Kneissl, MacGregor, Prince, Puma, Rossignol, Wilson, Yamaha, and Yonex. And that's just in the tennis department.

THE SKI LOFT
2203 N. Ballard
Wylie, TX 75098
800-899-LOFT (5638); 214-442-5842 (Dallas area)
PQ

Ski down the slopes and save 40–60 percent. Wonderful winter wear, skiwear, and accessories for the entire family (children, too) in a full size range available in names too famous to mention. Equipment, too: skis, boots, and poles for less. Call for price quote on everything you'll need to at least make the downhill journey an uplifting experience.

SPORTSWEAR CLEARINGHOUSE
P.O. Box 317746
Cincinnati, OH 45231-7746
513-522-3511
Brochure

Getting to the heart of the matter, this is a clearinghouse for the basics: T-shirts, sweatshirts, sweats, hats, and socks that for some reason made their way to this clearance center. Most of the items bear the name or logo of a corporate or institutional sponsor. But what kid wouldn't like a visor from Harvard or a T-shirt from a rock concert (even if they weren't old enough to attend or young enough to want to). Maybe they would like to make a political statement with a T-shirt from the American embassy in Beirut. Most items sold in bulk: three, six, or twelve at a time. The Texas Rangers baseball hat made a big hit with a few Nolan Ryan fans.

STUYVESANT BICYCLE, INC.
349 W. 14th St.
New York, NY 10014
212-254-5200; 212-675-2160
PQ (SASE)

Since 1939, Stuyvesant Bicycle has been a leading spokesman for the cycling industry. Soon after, they created a revolution when they started selling mainframes and top-of-the-line bikes through the mail. (Imagine the postman's frustration when he tried to stuff a Raleigh in your mailbox!) Children's bikes, racing bikes, tandem bikes, park bikes, plus all the parts needed to pedal your way to success (toe clips, water bottles, jerseys, bike shoes, and helmets, too). Wheel and deal with savings of up to 30 percent (more during specials and closeouts). Price quote either by phone or mail (SASE).

THE SWEATSHIRT COMPANY
Corporate Office: P.O. Box 5191
Martinsville, VA 34115
703-632-2961

Don't sweat the small stuff. This activewear suits the entire family to a tee, and at 30–40 percent less than retail, all you need to know is where to go. Outlet locations in Birch Run and Monroe, MI; Niagara Falls, NY; Durham and Gastonia, NC; and Milan, OH.

YAMAHA MOTER CORPORATION
6555 Katella Ave.
Cypress, CA 90630
714-761-7300
Catalog (full-color)

Yamaha's line of trail bikes mean low maintenance and really high times on the back roads tonight. This small-sized bike is fairly manageable (except for the terror it evokes in all mothers of little boys). Yamaha also sponsors a Dirt Smart Contingency Program worth $2 million in prizes for all amateur and professional riders. Get the "dirt" on these dirt bikes at your local Yamaha dealer. For additional information and upcoming dates, call the above number.

TOYS

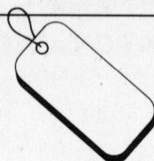

AMERICA'S HOBBY CENTER, INC.
146-K West 22nd Street
New York, NY 10011
212-675-8922
212-633-2754
Brochures $1 each: "Model Airplanes, Boats, and Cars"
and "Model Railroad-HO and H-Gauge"

Hop aboard the savings train for all your radio-controlled cars and planes and boats and trains. And if you want a helicopter ride, they've got those, too. Save up to 40 percent from this hobby center, which has been activating vehicular fun since 1931. Even if you have to build it yourself, these folks have the tools of the trade.

BABY'S MART
P.O. Box 13714
San Antonio, TX 78213-0714
512-493-MART
Flier

Talk about going to the head of the class! This infant stimulation toy store for babies features high-contrast toys. It's sponsored by the Infant Development Education Association, whose owner, Gina Morris, holds a master's degree in early childhood development. The new store offers about 350 toys from various manufacturers, including a line of toys put together by an associate professor of maternal child health at UCLA. Just in: a new line for the more mature babies—infants 8 months and older who will love the bold new chime balls, tactile toys, and Pat Mats. Baby's Mart even offers "Prega-phone," so parents can open communication channels with baby *before* it's born! ET doesn't even have to call-forward.

CEDAR WORKS
Route 1, Box 640
Rockport, ME 04856
800-233-7757; 207-236-3183 (in ME)
207-236-2574 (fax)
Catalog

Golly, gee . . . splinter-free! Wood-en it be lovely to sift through a detailed catalog of play sets designed with child safety in mind? Only chemical-free wood is used in the construction. Naturally rot-resistant cedar does not need to be pressure-treated with chemical compounds. The concept is simple. You choose the basic structure and then add the finishing touches. Cedar Works play sets stand on top of the ground and do not require digging or cement. Regardless of the options you might add, sets remain extremely rugged and stable. These adult-sized Legos require some assembly but come with clear, easy-to-follow instructions. Cedar Works is planet- as well as user-friendly. For every cedar tree used to make a play set, two seedlings are planted. Eco-nomically smart! Coast-to-coast delivery. Call for free catalog.

CHERRY TREE TOYS, INC.
P.O. Box 369-140
Belmont, OH 43718
614-484-4363
614-484-4388 (fax)
Catalog $1

The plum in the do-it-yourself toy business is Cherry Tree. Whirligigs—clever variations on the theme of weather vanes and wind toys—are one of the most popular items, sold at up to 50 percent off retail. Their 64-page catalog also showcases decorative clocks, wooden sleds and wagons, pull toys, vintage cars, dollhouses, and music boxes plus the parts to make them whole. All the tools and supplies needed to finish the job are included. The easiest kits to make are precut and predrilled and require only sandpaper and glue for assembly. If in the area, visit their factory outlet at 408 S. Jefferson in Belmont.

CHILD WORLD/CHILDREN'S PALACE
Corporate Office: 25 Littlefield
Avon, MA 02322
508-588-7300

Revamping retailing with the juvenile shopper in mind is the idea behind converting one of this chain's new stores in Torrance, California, to see if they are on target. One of 180-plus stores maybe in the wake of a mini-revolution. This mass-merchandiser has redesigned shelves for viewing at kids' eye level, and incorporated a snack area with a Peter Panda playground complete with a musical carousel and other outdoor activities to be tested by young shoppers. If it's toys (and children's apparel) you're toying with, write or call for a Child World/Children's Palace nearest you.

EARLY LEARNING CENTER STORE
40 Pepe's Farm Road
Milford, CT 06460
203-878-7999
203-878-7900

Forget the plea "Don't touch!" whispered (or screamed) by zillions of moms when shopping with kids. Early Learning Center Stores are a British import that are a whole lot less stuffy than the name indicates, and actually encourage kids to "try it . . . you'll like it!" Merchandise is organized by age and skill making it parent-friendly, and personnel are trained to give developmental play advice. Stores so far are located only in the eastern part of the United States, but watch for a mail-order catalog in 1992.

EDUCATIONAL INSIGHTS
19560 S. Rancho Way
Dominguez Hills, CA 90220
800-933-3277; 213-657-2131 (CA)
Catalog

Dominating the educational toy world is this wonderful, way-out catalog of teaching toys, games, aids, and tools. Educational Insights' full-color compendium is a treasure chest of fun and fascinating things for both kids and teachers: early learning games, beginning language arts, reading and literature, mathematics, critical thinking items ("Brain Booster," activity books and mind-stretching quiz games), science, social studies, and electronic teaching aids. *Adios*, Trivial Pursuit . . . *Buenos dias*, Educational Insights.

THE ENCHANTED FOREST
85 Mercer St.
New York, NY 10012
800-456-4449; 212-925-6677 (NY)
Catalog (full-color)

A bevy of beasts, books, and beautiful handmade toys celebrate the spirit of animals and old stories at this enchanted forest. See the light through the forest of treasures here. A selection of favorite things: an old-fashioned mohair teddy, Pooh's Library, *Tales of King Arthur*, toy tops, Pick-Up Sticks, hobby horses, wooden baby rattles, magic crystal gardens, kaleidoscopes, and puppets. A mystical journey through a wonderland of enchantment. Request a catalog for the child within. Satisfaction guaranteed with full refund, credit, or exchange. All orders shipped within 48 hours via UPS.

F.R.O.Y.D., INC.
300 E. 59th St.
New York, NY 10022
(212) 751-0809
(212) 371-5224 (fax)
Flier

Finally, a new toy that doesn't shoot bullets, need batteries, wet its pants, or grow hair! F.R.O.Y.D. (For Reality of Your Dreams) is a soft, huggable, 13″ friend who offers unconditional love, forever. He even wears a button to prove it! F.R.O.Y.D. arrives with a little book about making your dreams come true. Inside, there's a special place for children to pen their own dreams. The book can be stored in F.R.O.Y.D.'s pocket for safekeeping. A postcard is included for your child to mail in to receive a "Dreams Come True" poster and Official Yellow Dream stickers. Each time a dream comes true, a sticker can be placed on the poster to proclaim the achievement. F.R.O.Y.D. encourages children of all ages to dream, not making dreams their master, but rather to muster up enough confidence to make their dreams come true. F.R.O.Y.D.'s price is $24.95 plus $5 postage and handling.

FLEXIBLE FLYER COMPANY—DIVISION
   OF PAR INDUSTRY
100 Tubb Ave.
West Point, MS 39773
800-521-6233
Brochure (full-color)

In 1889, the Flexible Flyer Company, founded by Quaker businessman Sam Allen, pioneered the world's first steerable sled and it's still flying high making toys that borderline perfection. The company starts with imaginative designs, adds built-in extra-play value (like nooks and crawl-throughs where children love to make secret hiding places), and prices them right. Craftmanship leaves no doors locked. All open wide, edges are smooth, and colors stay bright. Flexible Flyer also offers outdoor gym sets, sandboxes, "Turbo Tot Trucks" and "Tot Rods," pools and playhouses. The steerable sled is featured in five sizes for ages 6 and up. Flexible Flyer stands behind their toys 100 percent because they're up front about kids having fun.

GOLDMANARTS
107 South St., Suite 403
Boston, MA 02111
617-423-6606
617-423-6601 (fax)
Brochure

It's fine art and fun art and lest we forget, GoldmanArts is expanding! This Boston business offers an inflatable nylon playhouse that is tot-sized and stands 4′ × 6′. It can be inflated in 60 seconds by a built-in, 6-inch fan (with built-in guards for safety). The company also offers artful inflatable furniture, accessories, and "Totally Tubular" display balloons. Totally fascinating! Write or call for details.

HOBBY SURPLUS SALES
287 Main Street
New Britain, CT 06050
203-223-0600
Catalog $3

Expect to pay up to 40 percent less if you buy your train at this hobby station. This family-owned business has been on the right track for three generations and offers the hobbyist radio-controlled planes, boats, cars, and other vehicles as well as one of the most extensive model train departments in the country (American Flyer, Lionel, and others), including all the spare parts in case yours has fallen off the track. Kits for dollhouses, mini-furniture, model cars, and the tools to make it happen (like X-Acto knives). Their outlet is next door at 283 Main St. in New Britain.

INTO THE WIND
1408 Pearl Street
Boulder, CO 80302
303-449-5356
Catalog

The next time your kid tells you to "Go fly a kite," go directly to this catalog. No string attached, either. This is probably the largest collection-by-mail of kites and wind socks in the world. From traditional Chinese silk birds and butterflies to high-tech space-age nylon airfoils, boomerangs, and wind chimes.

K & K TOYS
Corporate Office: 2555 Ellsmere Ave.
Norfolk, VA 23501

Toy, toys everywhere and they still cry out for more. There are over 140 stories in this chain that sell Fisher-Price, Mattel, Hasbro, and others at 20–25 percent off. Stores concentrated in the Northest, Southeast, mid-Atlantic region, and a few midwestern states. Check phone directory for store in your area or write to the address above.

LAKEMONT ROCKYHORSE COMPANY
Route One Box 2036
Lakemont, GA 30552
404-782-9928
Flier

Bye-bye, broomstick pony! At last, the classic rocking horse is all grown up. Had the series lasted, this sleek toy would have been stabled in Michael and Hope Steadman's "thirtysomething" home on TV. Available in seven sponge-painted colors (actual samples available with order form), each is produced by hand in the Lakemont Rockyhorse Company studio. Each horse measures 44″ × 26″ × 16″, and costs $95 plus $15 UPS shipping (allow 3 weeks for delivery). Order early to avoid the Christmas rush. Send a check or money order to the above address.

LIONEL KIDDIE WORLD/LIONEL PLAYWORLD/
   ## LIONEL TOY WAREHOUSE
Corporate Office: 2951 Grant Ave.
Philadelphia, PA 19114
215-671-3800

Guess who owns this choo-choo train outlet? Not just kits and cabooses here either. All the major manufacturers are included, like Fisher-Price, Hasbro, Mattel, and Playskool, at 20–25 percent off. Check directory for one of the more than 100 locations in Arizona, Colorado, Florida, Georgia, Louisiana, Maryland, New Jersey, New Mexico, New York, North Carolina, Ohio, Pennsylvania, South Carolina, Tennessee, Texas, Utah, and Virginia.

THE LITTLE TIKES COMPANY
2180 Barlow Rd.
Hudson, OH 44236
800-321-0183; 800-321-3291 (TDD)
Catalog (full-color)

Little Tikes is a toy company that believes "The best kind of research is simply watching children play." That's why the Little Tikes Company has an on-site child care center for employees' children. With product safety its first priority, all Little Tikes toys have rounded edges, eliminating any inherent dangers. Thick plastic walls ensure that toys last the test of time (and play). From mirrors to mowers, teeter-totters to treehouses, play pools to sandboxes, if it's for little tykes, it's from Little Tikes. Catalog available with a complete list of dealers in your area.

MI CASA: PLAYHOUSES FOR CHILDREN
4705 Chilton Dr.
Dallas, TX 75227
214-381-1523

Give children a place to call their own with Mi Casa Playhouses. Assembled easily on a frame of color-coded 1-inch PVC pipe, this tent of appliquéd fabric stands more than 4 feet tall, is stored in its own bag, is washable and dryable, and is interchangeable with all designs in the line. What versatility! Prices range from $79.95 to $225, depending on your design choice. All items are guaranteed (unless misused or mishandled). If defective, they may be returned for replacement or refund. A $20 deposit will initiate a layaway plan until paid in full. Mi Casa ships nationwide and pays postage on prepaid playhouses. For a down-to-earth alternative to the treehouse, try a Mi Casa Playhouse.

THE OPPENHEIM TOY PORTFOLIO, INC.
40 E. 9th St.
New York, NY 10003
1-800-544-TOYS; 212-598-0502

At last, intelligent help for parents who want to buy toys. Which ones? Well, don't always believe the copywriters' claims. *The Oppenheim Toy Portfolio* is a new quarterly written by noted child development specialist Joanne Oppenheim. Enthusiastically received by both regional and national press including CNN, CBS "Nightwatch", and *USA Today*, the Toy Portfolio is dedicated to helping busy parents pinpoint the most valuable toys, books, and videos for kids (birth to 8 years). There's even a thumbs-down, top-ten list of the dumbest toys that haven't even made the David Letterman show yet. One year (4 issues) $20; 2 years (8 issues) $38. Issues may also be purchased separately: holiday, spring, summer, and fall at $6 each. What a wonderful guide for new parents and grandparents on what to buy!

PUPPETS ON THE PIER
Pier 39—H4
San Francisco, CA 94133
800-443-4463; 415-781-4435
Catalog (full-color)

Furry Folk Puppets are hand-crafted in California and are all furry, fun, and fabulous. This magnificent collection of crafty puppet art is available in a full-color catalog from Puppets on the Pier. Parade out with puppets like Toads 'n'

Turtles, Bears 'n' Butterflies, Dogs 'n' Dragons, Witches 'n' Wizards, and others similarly inclined. These collectible creatures were voted the Parents' Choice award winners in 1989 and designed by Folkmanis. Puppets come in a variety of sizes and prices. Call for your catalog and cuddle up tomorrow.

RHYME AND REASON TOYS, LTD.
184 Kinsley Ave.
Providence, RI 02908
401-272-8369
401-272-8375 (fax)
Brochure

Give future little Einsteins a helping hand with toys that are pleasin' from Rhyme & Reason! Winner of the 1990 Parents' Choice honors, Rhyme & Reason offers a commitment to creating toys that make learning fun and also withstand the test of time. An unconditional guarantee to provide unparalleled play value is their promise. Detailed craftmanship and environmental sensitivity make these toys long-lasting and guilt-free. These "no frills" playthings challenge a child's inquisitive nature and keep the "play" in playtime. Add a little imagination and presto! A skyscraper or an entire village is created by your child. Call for your nearest representative.

ROSE'S DOLL HOUSE
5826 W. Bluemound Rd.
Milwaukee, WI 53213
800-926-9093; 414-259-9965 (WI)
Catalog $1 (free to readers)

With a Rose's Doll House, your child can blossom as a small-fry interior decorator and create her very own model dollhouse. Each kit comes complete with easy-to-follow instructions for assembly. Much like building and finishing a real house, a dollhouse encourages refinement of motor skills, an eye for detail, and a sense of color coordination and imagination. All furniture is handmade from select hardwood, crafted with great detail to replicate full-size counterparts. These miniature marvels include everything from turn-of-the-century bathroom reproductions, an upright piano that plays the theme from *Love Story*, and exquisitely crocheted curtains and intricate wallpaper to kitchens stocked with teeny-tiny gadgets that really work. Houses are made of thick wood (not plastic or substitute) to last for generations. Prompt replacement or full refund if not satisfied. For fastest service, call toll-free and place your order with a credit card.

T.C. TIMBER—THE BOOKIE BOOKS & TOYS
24 E. Genesee St.
Skaneateles, NY 13152
800-359-6144
401-521-3808 (fax)
Catalog (full-color)

Wood it matter if these toys were guaranteed for timeless quality and durability? Well, maple hardwood toys from T.C. Timber available (through catalog) from Bookie Books & Toys stand the test for life, knock on wood. Colored sorting cylinders that teach children to differentiate between geometric sizes, Touch Labyrinth for coordination and color recognition, plus activity blocks, beads, puzzles, train sets, and airplanes are all part of this catalog's choices. A wonderland of woodplay to stimulate reflexive action, coordination, and motor skills. Gift wrapping and second-day air or overnight delivery. Money-back guarantee.

TEXAS INSTRUMENTS
P.O. Box 53
Lubbock, TX 79408
800-TI-CARES
806-741-2146 (fax)
Flier (color)

Time to "tech" it out with a little help from your friends at TI. Texas Instruments' latest line of technical educational toys make for computer-literate tykes. Youngsters need all the help they can get even before they take their first byte in school. But first, here comes the fun stuff for little "techies." Some early-bird specials include Stack Around Clown, a first electronic stacker for infants and toddlers, and Discovery Learning toys like Touch & Discover, for ages 2–3, where children can learn the alphabet, numbers, and more. Older preschoolers can learn from toys like Words to Go, for ages 3–6, which helps develop prereading skills, and School Age Learning toys like Speak & Spell and Speak & Math, for ages 6–14, which help develop conceptual math skills, vocabulary, and spelling. Write or call for free color flier and product price list. Encourage imagination and provide fun through challenge by beginning with TI. Some units also available in Braille.

TOWER HOBBIES
P.O. Box 778
Champaign, IL 61820
800-637-4989
Catalog $3

A giant in the industry of radio-controlled vehicles, Tower sells them at up to 60 percent off. Hours of fun in both the building and driving processes. Leave the driving to the kids (you might have to help in the maintenance). Kits for every pocketbook; from Jeeps to 4WDs, sailboats to tugboats, plus all the tools needed to start the engines. Lots of information contained in their 300-page catalog adds to the shopping pleasure.

TOYS 'Я' US
Corporate Office: 461 From Road
Paramus, NJ 07652
201-262-7800

Grammar may not be their strong suit, but Toys are first-quality name brands stocked/stacked/stashed floor to ceiling for less cash. Furniture, games, the gamut. From Trivial Pursuit to Pictionary, Cabbage Patch to Nintendo, Barbie to books, save 20 percent and more. Almost 500 stores and still their Energizer batteries keep going, and going, and going!

TOYS TO GROW ON
2695 E. Dominguez St., P.O. Box 17
Long Beach, CA 90801-0017
800-542-8338; 213-603-8890 (in CA)
213-537-5403 (fax)
Catalog (full-color)

A catalog of fun and fascination for tots to 12-year-olds. From first playthings for infants to hands-on learning toys, you'll jump for joy when you find this one-stop-shop-by-mail for fun and games. Toys for travel, crayons, schooldays keepsake albums to remember those special moments, personalized stickers, and "Good for Me" goal charts (good for Mom, too). Not just toys for today, but Toys to Grow On! Free catalog.

The Toy Manufacturers of America reported percentages of toy sales in the following categories:

- 21% dolls and stuffed animals
- 18% action figures and vehicles
- 16% video games
- 15% miscellaneous
- 12% activity toys (like Lego, etc.)
- 11% infant and preschool
- 7% games and puzzles

TRAVEL

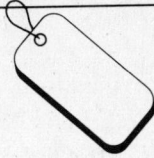

Making a list and checking it twice ensures a well-deserved rest from responsibilities when your plans call for a family vacation. Here's how to get in gear:

- Arrange for mail and newspapers to be picked up by a neighbor; or have your mail held at the post office and your newspaper delivery suspended while you're away.
- Call on a neighbor or a sitter to care for pets, plants, and lawns.
- Notify a neighbor of your itinerary and leave a house key.
- Notify the police of your absence and who to call in an emergency.
- Keep a few lights on and set security systems to automatic.
- Put valuables in safety deposit box; etch your Social Security number on all major appliances, computers, etc.
- Empty refrigerator and lower the thermostat.
- Secure all locks on doors and windows, including the garage door.

GUIDE TO BEST BUYS IN PACKAGE TOURS
Pilot Books
103 Cooper Street
Babylon, NY 11702
516-422-2225

This economical ($3.95) pocket-sized guide "lists and describes more than one hundred selected group tours that offer solid values for your travel dollar." This guide tells how to choose an agent and where to get accident, trip cancellation, or health insurance; gives a trip preparation checklist; and shows ways to create package variations. It even tells how to file travel complaints. Included are a list of countries that require entry visas and a set of fundamental health precautions. Packages offered have included a variety of tours for individual tastes—fly/drive packages, escorted and unescorted tours, cruise options, and adventure, luxury, economy, and special-interest tours.

Adventure

AMERICAN WILDERNESS EXPERIENCE
800-444-0099

What "babe in the woods" wouldn't like to see the light at the end of the forest! In the Sangre de Cristo Mountains in Colorado, rock climbing, trail riding, mountain biking, and rafting are all part of the American Wilderness Experience for six days/five nights. Adults $595; kids $570. Minimum age 10.

AMERICAN YOUTH HOSTEL BIKE TOURS (AYH)
Department 855
P.O. Box 37613
Washington, DC 20013-7613
202-783-6161

Bicycling today is fast becoming one of the most popular sports in America. People are finding great pleasure in riding more than just to the corner store and back. Biking is great for kids as well as a great family outing. Call or write for more information on bike tours and clubs in the U.S. and Canada.

GRAND CANYON DORIES
P.O. Box 216
Altaville, CA 95221
209-736-0805

Dories are the small, rigid boats that run the rivers and are the mainstay of this conservationist-turned-guide's business of keeping guests afloat. Float trips last from 5 to 19 days and include all the best the river has to offer. Recommended for kids over 7 (for short trips) and 12-plus (for longer trips). Packages include transportation to and from the Las Vegas airport.

IDAHO AFLOAT
208-983-2414

Stay afloat while you take a float trip on the Lower Salmon River in Idaho. Ho, ho, ho, what a way to go! Four days/three nights will cost adults $700 and children $665. Minimum age 5.

OUTDOOR ADVENTURE RIVER SPECIALISTS
800-346-6277

Tackle the rapids on the Snake River through Grand Teton National Park, Wyoming, for 5 days/4 nights. Adults $695, children $595. Minimum age 4.

OUTWARD BOUND USA
384 Field Point Road
Greenwich, CT 06830
800-243-8520

Ready, set, Outward Bound! Leave the comforts of home for the unfamiliar and adventurous in the most spectacular wilderness areas in the world, and discover your own capabilities under challenging conditions. Almost 20,000 people, ages 14 to 77, participated in over 600 course offerings last year alone, most of them with little or no experience in the wilderness. Special courses are offered for teens, women over 30, adults over 55, as well as for family members, couples, and parents with children. Recent catalog listings included backpacking, canoe expeditions, horse trailing, western alpine mountaineering, sailing and sea kayaking, cycling, whitewater rafting, and dog sledding.

SIERRA CLUB
415-923-5630

As a member of the Sierra Club, you can canoe in Florida's Everglades at Christmastime if you are at least 6 years old. Six days/five nights for adults $295, children $200, plus the Sierra membership (if you are not already a member).

SOUTHWEST ADVENTURE GROUP, INC.
P.O. Box 15759
500 Montezuma Sanbusco Mkt. Ctr.
Santa Fe, NM 87506-5759
800-766-5443; 505-983-0876 (NM)
Brochure

Yee-haw! A change of pace would confirm how the West was won. Rope a trip for your kids called Sante Fe Adventures. Nope, this is NO babysitting service! Children—the youngest age is 4 for some programs, 7 for others—can sign up to float the Rio Grande with a Native American storyteller, feast on tacos at a pueblo, or track animals in the desert. And if they're still bored, they can try sand painting or learn the techniques used by Native Americans to make clay pottery and sculpture. There's even river rafting, skiing, exploring cliff dwellings, and miniature golf. Forget about laying back. *You're part of the adventure!* And expect experienced, first-aid-trained staff supervision. Prices vary according to length of excursion or activity. Oh, yes, some of the activities are geared for grown-ups, too!

TRAIL BLAZER LLAMAS
Don Johnson
7819 N.E. 154th Street
Vancouver, WA 98662
206-573-1159

Trail Blazer Llamas make it easy for you to see the back country of the Pacific Northwest. Gentle, surefooted llamas carry your gear while you walk unburdened through alpine meadows and evergreen forests of southern Washington and northern Oregon. For 2, 3, or 4 days, you can camp amidst unrivaled scenery, fish in sparkling mountain streams, and enjoy the meals provided by Trail Blazers. What's not to like? Special consideration is given to the novice hiker, including easy trails with many rest breaks if needed. Groups of three to eight can be reserved exclusively and a 25 percent discount is offered on group custom trips, such as the Lewis River 3-day trip for $200, or the Indian Heaven 3-day trip for $210. They provide the tents, canteens, sleeping pads, rain gear, and all food and utensils.

WESTERN SPIRIT CYCLING
800-845-2453

Take a hike through the Colorado Rockies near Vail on the same routes once traveled by stagecoach. Five days and nights for adults is $725, for children under 14, $507.50. Minimum age 10

Agents

EASY CAMPING COMPANY
P.O. Box 20194
Jackson, WY 83001
415-283-1525 (September-May); 307-739-1120 (summer)
Brochure

"Summertime . . . and the camping is easy . . ." if you let these folks plan your trip to Yellowstone or the Grand Tetons. This family camping vacation service facilitates a visit to beautiful national parks by providing a handbook and a complete camping and equipment package—for example, to Jackson Hole, Wyoming. Call or write for a free brochure.

GRANDTRAVEL: THE TICKET COUNTER
6900 Wisconsin Avenue, Suite 706
Chevy Chase, MD 20815
800-247-7651; 301-986-0790 (MD)
PQ

Do you long to have a vacation with your grandparents or your grandchild/grandchildren all to yourself? To strengthen those ties and generate lifelong memories, take them along as GrandTravelers! What a delightful way to bridge the generation gap and to link a family's past with its future, preserving values for coming generations. These very special vacations provide itineraries that stimulate curiosity and encourage exploration and discovery as well as private time together; meals are well-balanced and delicious, and peer activities with other children and grandparents are planned. Exotic excursions to the castles of England and Scotland, to Viking Scandinavia, to Holland's waterways and canals, along with the popular domestic trips to the western national parks, our nation's capital, or to those perennial favorites, Sea World, Disneyland, and Hollywood—all part of Grand-Travel's modus operandi.

HIDEAWAYS INTERNATIONAL
800-486-8955 (MA)
508-486-8252 (fax)

Hideaways International, as its name implies, represents the little-known, out-of-the-ordinary secret escape where vacations are etched with indelible memories. This full-service travel resource specializes in premier villa and condo rentals, yacht charters, special cruises, intimate inns and resorts . . . even castles and ranches. A family that rents one of these hideaways over individual rooms in a hotel will probably come out ahead where money is concerned. Your membership entitles you to the quarterly newsletters giving the "inside scoop" on new places, a personal travel service for airfares, and money-saving discounts. From Antigua to Wyoming, Grenada to Quebec, this is the way to go, in style. The guide details handicap access, whether your pets are welcome, plus a myriad of details on every property.

JOURNEYS
4011 Jackson Rd.
Ann Arbor, MI 48103
800-255-8735
Catalog/itineraries

Eager to see elephants? Zany about zebras? Got a hankering to hike? Explore the world with your children through the worldwide nature and culture explorations offered by this family business for the past 15 years. Join other adventurous families for Himalayan trekking, camping safaris in Kenya, exploration of the Galapagos Islands, the Costa Rican rain forest, and the Australian outback. Write or call for a free color catalog and detailed intineraries.

RASCALS IN PARADISE
650 Fifth St., #505
San Francisco, CA 94107
800-U-RASCAL; 415-978-9800
Brochure

The Little Rascals never had it this good. Discover childhood dream vacations for the whole family with domestic and international travel.

TRAVEL AVENUE
800-333-3335; 312-876-1116 (IL)

All aboard this travel alternative. Instead of the traditional commission-based travel agency (with the exception of planning an in-depth vacation package or around-the-world-tour), this company charges an $8 service fee for domestic flights and rebates 8 percent off air fare with delivery of your ticket. International flights: $20 service fee and you'll get an 8–15 percent rebate. Receive an additional check (even after posted discounts) of 5 percent with proof of hotel stay or car rental. Tours and cruises: save 8 percent and a fee of $20 (for cruises less than $1,000) or $40 (for cruises over $1,000). Guaranteed lowest published fares and rates. Ask about specials, too, called "The Ultimate Deals."

TRAVELING WITH CHILDREN
2313 Valley St.
Berkeley, CA 94702
415-848-0929
Brochure

Planning a vacation? Let Traveling with Children family traveling specialists orchestrate your venture and you'll hear sweet harmonies as they sing of rentals and family resorts in Europe, Hawaii, California, and all across the U.S. They can even get you the best rates on air fare. Call for a free brochure.

Air, Train, and Sea

AIRHITCH
2790 Broadway, Suite 100
New York, NY 10025
212-864-2000
Brochure

Hitch a ride to Europe and back if you want to save plenty of money (a few domestic flights available, too) but you must fly standby. If your child's mature (some 15 year-old New Yorkers are pretty savvy when it comes to getting across town), you may want to have him/her use Airhitch, a low-cost service designed primarily for free-spirited, independent, and resourceful students. You know your kid . . . you be the judge whether they'd be okay laying over in Frankfort. Write for brochure and application.

EURAILPASS
800-544-5089; ask for J. Nurre

Before leaving the United States, be sure to buy your Eurailpass for unlimited first-class train travel in 16 European countries. Groups of 3 or more qualify for additional savings. Under 4 goes free (under 2 goes free on airlines); under 12 half-price; and a youth ticket is good until age 26, depending on the length of stay. Call toll-free for additional information.

REGENCY CRUISES
260 Madison Ave.
New York, NY 10016
212-972-4499

Regency Cruises' Regency Sun (northbound from New York or southbound from Montreal) offers some pretty mouth-watering passages for families with kids. This "Good Ship Lollipop" is full of activities under the watchful eyes of two youth counselors, disco and "coketail" parties, arts and crafts projects, and special views on the bridge. A private lounge area with games and supervision. Baby-sitting at additional cost.

Amusements

CLARK'S TRADING POSTS
Off Hwy 93 on Route 3
Lincoln, NH 03251
603-745-8913

In Lincoln, New Hampshire, there's lots to do for family fun in the White Mountains. An antique steam train ride is one. An American museum and black bear show is another. Adults $5, kids $3. Kids under 5 free.

CLIFF GRAY'S MINIATURE CIRCUS
120 W. Lafayette
Jefferson, TX 75657
903-665-8533
Flier

Lights! Music! Animation! Now children of any age can appreciate the Ringling Bros. and Barnum & Bailey Traveling Circus through a 5,000-piece miniature display on view in downtown Jefferson, Texas. This one-inch scale-perfect model was used by Cecil B. DeMille in filming *The Greatest Show on Earth*. Fifteen years in the making, each part is replicated in exacting detail—from the 4-inch-high ladders to the delicate teak elephants. Even some famous names and faces are represented in small ways like the Flying Wallendas, clown Emmett Kelly, and lion tamer Clyde Beatty. "Big top" entertainment at small-town prices. Adults $2, children $1.50. Call for more information.

DESOTO CAVERNS PARK
DeSoto Caverns Parkway
Shildresburg, AL 35044
800-933-2283

Just 35 miles east of Birmingham, Alabama, these colorful onyx caves include a main underground canyon that's larger than a football field, taller than a 12-story building, and more fun and fascination than money can buy. The tour takes about an hour and includes a laser light show, a bow-and-arrow shoot, and almost an acre of a fun maze. Adults $11.95, kids 5–11 $8.95. Kids 4 and under free.

KIDSPORT
2121 Crescent Drive
Denver, CO 80211
303-433-7444
Complete information packet

Kidsport is the first interactive family learning environment at a major U.S. airport. This planned discovery center was designed to provide positive experiences for youngsters and their parents waiting for flights at Stapleton International Airport in Denver, Colorado. The 3,500-square-foot space has five hands-on participatory exhibits along with nursing areas, changing tables, and a gift shop. Its main purpose is to educate, entertain, and provide some high-flying fun to traveling kids who need to blow off some steam! Admission $1.50 per person.

PARROT JUNGLE AND GARDENS
Southwest 57th Ave and US 1 (2½ miles)
11100 South 57th Ave.
Miami, FL 33156-4199
Mon.–Sun. 9:30 A.M.–6:00 P.M.; bird shows 10:30 A.M.–
   5:00 P.M.
305-666-7834

Miami has more than just dolphins. In this jungle paradise, you will hear the chatter of more than 1,200 birds and see the splendor of more than 12 acres of gardens. Birds of every species including parrots, flamingos, cranes, and macaws. Daily bird shows and a Florida wildlife show in which kids get to hold a raccoon or a flying squirrel. Adults $10.50, kids 3–12 $6, under 2 free.

QUARRY VISITOR CENTER
4545 Highway 40
Dinosaur, CO 84610
303-374-2216

See what has washed ashore on this river sandbar. Millions of years ago, dinosaurs roamed the area now known as Dinosaur National Monument, a 220,000-acre park on the Utah-Colorado border. The center is located 10 miles north of Jensen, Utah, and the dinosaur bones can be viewed in their natural habitat. Park admission is $5 per vehicle.

Books

BETWEEN YOU AND ME
3419 Tony Drive
San Diego, CA 92122
619-455-9370

Just between you and me, *A Vacation Adventure to Remember* is one journal and activity booklet a child is bound to keep forever. It's great for traveling when active little minds need diversion. For school-age children, it's only $3.50 plus postage.

DIRECTORY OF LOW-COST VACATIONS
WITH A DIFFERENCE
Pilot Books
103 Cooper Street
Babylon, NY 11702
516-422-2225

Farm vacations, bed-and-breakfast stays, home exchanges, people-to-people, senior programs, study groups, and vacation work programs . . . a selection of different ways are included in this directory to help you enjoy your leisure time. How do "Above the Cloud Trekking," "Arrow Adventure," "Bicycle Africa," "Meet the Aussies," "Off the Deep End," "Volunteer for Peace," or "Worldwide Yacht Charters" sound for starters? Choose your spot from the alphabetical listings and make good use of this thoroughly usable guide for only $5.95, postpaid.

THE FAMILY TRAVEL GUIDE CATALOG
P.O. Box 6061
Albany, CA 94706
415-527-5849
Catalog

Eureka! A gold mine of books on family travel. You'll find books on how to get the most out of your family vacations, sensational planning aids for hassle-free family trips, great games and activities for making car trips fun, and travel-related audio- and videotapes. Free travel game and toll-free travel directory included with every order. This is a one-stop travel resource guide that every travelin' man, woman, and child shouldn't leave home without!

GETTYSBURG TRAVEL COUNCIL
35 Carlisle Street
Gettysburg, PA 17325

Write for your FREE 56-page guide to Gettysburg if you're a history buff and bargain shopper rolled into one. Remember this famous Civil War battle by visiting this historic town, which offers over 1,000 sites and monuments commemorating the events.

Clubs

GREAT BUYS FOR KIDS TRAVEL CLUB
Sky Plus Travel
3509 Valley View Road
Blue Springs, MO 64015
$49 annual membership fee

Get off your high-flyin' horse and travel at the lowest prices, guaranteed. The Great Buys Travel Club is an exclusive membership program that allows your entire family (everybody that lives with you counts as family), to save thousands (millions if you're a Trump, a Sununu, or Sam Walton). As a member, you're guaranteed the lowest available fare *plus* you get back $25 for every $500 of air travel that you book. (Yes, there's an 800 number for members only.) Save up to 50 percent on hotels, condominiums, and last-minute airfares, and up to 40 percent on cruises. Also lowest rates for car rentals and any other travel needs (except finding you a bellman curbside). Now, fasten your seatbelts and leave the booking to Sky Plus.

METRO/PASSBOOK SAVERS
2252 Dixie Highway
Waterford, MI 48328
313-333-1000
313-333-3535 (fax)

Travelin' along with the tumblin' tumbleweeds is made as easy as saving 50 percent across-the-rack (that's hotel slang for retail) prices. This special program has been designed especially for VIPs of *Great Buys for Kids*. Very important persons traveling to over 400 hotels, motels, and tourist attractions all over the U.S., Canada, and the Caribbean can save 50 percent off the retail rate if they have their copy of *Passbook Savers Discover America at ½ Price*. Readers simply send in $4.95 for postage and handling to the above address to receive their copy. You'll also get up to 50 percent off at tourist attractions, cruises, and car rentals. Just one use will pay for your *Passbook* many times over. Similar programs sell for as much as $50.

Lodging and Resorts

AMERICAN YOUTH HOSTELS, INC.
P.O. Box 37613
Washington, DC 20013-7613
202-783-6161

You don't have to be a kid to enjoy the ultra-cheap accommodations of a hostel nationwide but it doesn't hurt, either. You'd be surprised at the convenient location of these hostels. No longer are they just in the boonies. In fact, sleep cheap in Washington, D.C., Boston, Chicago, San Francisco, New York City, and Los Angeles (the L.A. facility has 200 beds). Travel for cost-cutting students via the hostels is a way to cut costs, but not the fun or friendship along the way.

BALSAMS GRAND RESORT HOTEL
Dixville Notch, NH 03576
800-255-0800; 603-255-3400

This 118-year-old mountain retreat is a real treat on a grand scale of 1 to 118. Nestled in the White Mountains, it's a one-stop paradise vacation for you and your kids. Golf, swimming, downhill and cross-country skiing with daylong programs in the summer for the kids; ski school and free nursery for toddlers in the winter. All-inclusive family packages available exclusive of liquor.

CALLAWAY GARDENS RESORT
P.O. Box 2000
Pine Mountain, GA 31822
800-282-8181; 404-663-2281

Callaway the hours at any one of the inns, villas, or cottages within this 12,000-acre natural preserve and gardens. Rejuvenate in this magnificent natural setting with golf, tennis, bicycling, hiking, fishing, and hunting at your back door. Kids come along with their own set of outdoor activities (summer only), which include a full day of nature's best . . . fishing, rock collecting, even a circus performance thrown in.

CLUB MED
Corporate Office: 40 West 57th St.
New York, NY 10019
800-CLUB MED; 212-977-2100
Brochure (full-color)

Parents can get away from it all without leaving them all. A terrific option has been operating for the past 25 years and it's called Club Med. Over 125,000 children last year alone vacationed with Mom or Dad or both at one of Club Med's 44 family villages worldwide. At Club Med in Ixtapa, Mexico, for example, children ages 12 months to 12 years are tended to almost round-the-clock in a summer camp environment. But there's never a complaint of homesickness since Mom and Dad are always nearby. While Mom gets a tan and Dad chases golf balls, the younger set enjoys a swing on a trapeze, can bounce on a trampoline, paint their faces, or juggle in a circus workshop. They can also swim, snorkel, and play tennis, and always in a fully-supervised group. At Club Med's family villages in St. Lucia (West Indies), Punta Cana (Dominican Republic), Eleuthera (Bahamas), Ixtapa (Mexico), and Sandpiper (Florida), the whole gang can vacation together and "play" apart. The family that stays together doesn't necessarily play together. Mini Clubs are designed for children 2–11, and Baby Clubs are for children 4–23 months, both supervised by Gentil Organisateurs (G.Os for short). They love kids! For information on future events and a promotional brochure, write: Club Med Sales, Inc., 7975 N. Hayden Rd., Scottsdale, AZ 85258, Attention: Club Med Families. For "kids free" dates and accommodation rates, call toll-free (800) CLUB MED.

EMBASSY SUITES RESORT HOTEL
Palm Beach Shores
Singer Island, FL 33404
407-655-2229

Good grief, I think they've got it! The Embassy Suites offers some pretty sweet amenities when it comes to being family-friendly. A childproof suite includes plastic cups and protective covers for electrical outlets, a 24-hour hot line to baby sitters, diapers, even a pediatrician. The Fat Cat Beach Club, for kids 4-12, includes a day program from 9:00 A.M. to 4:00 P.M., including lunch; evening fare from 5:30 A.M. to 10:00 P.M. includes dinner. Such fun . . . from storytelling to snorkeling, treasure hunts, miniature golf, and windsurfing with a small ratio of staff to children (1 to 4). Cost: $15 daytime, $8 evenings. Kids under 14 stay free in parents' room.

FOUR SEASONS CLIFT HOTEL
495 Geary St.
San Francisco, CA 94102
415-775-4700
415-776-9238 (fax)
Brochure

This hotel heralds its V.I.K.—Very Important Kid—program. Children are greeted at check-in time and given helium balloons, a bag of toys, and sugar-free candy. There's a library of family movies available and even popcorn on the room service menu. If that's not enough, try Nintendo, board games, and books. And at bedtime, cookies and milk. Treating kids like royalty is their priority. For other participating Four Seasons hotels or accommodation rates, call toll-free (800) 332-3442.

HOLIDAY INN—MAIN GATE EAST
5678 Irlo Bronson Memorial Hwy. (US 192)
Kissimmee, FL 34746
407-396-4488
Brochure

Get set for "child's play" on a grand scale. Kids enjoy the Holiday Hound Club—a free, fully supervised children's activity program, 5:00 P.M. to 10:00 P.M. nightly. Young guests (ages 5–12) check in at the Candy House "registration" desk and receive a goodie bag filled with surprises. Admission is free to the Holiday Hounds Castle Clubhouse and Holly Hounds Movie Theater, with movies, magic shows, bingo, clowns, puppets, or arts and crafts. Free dinner in the "Gingerbread House" restaurant (when accompanied by an adult), where children order from their own menu, watch cartoons, and make their own ice cream desserts. Just 3 minutes from Walt Disney World. Call toll-free for room rates and other participating Holiday Inns (800) FON-KIDS.

THE HOMESTEAD
P.O. Box 99
Midway, UT 84049
800-327-7220; 801-654-1102

Carry us back to the ole Homestead for a resort that's right up nature's alley. This small, 105-year-old resort was built around hot springs and has a down-home, healthful approach to family lodging. Parents can golf, ride horseback, hot-air balloon, swim, ski, and sleigh-ride while daily programs for the kids include fishing excursions and swimming lessons. Package rates include a 2-hour horseback tour.

HYATT HOTELS CORPORATION— BROCHURE CENTER
5670 McDermott Dr.
Berkeley, IL 60163
800-233-1234
Brochure

Camp Hyatt is not for children only (parents love the idea, too!). Kids will love their very own frequent-traveler program, a welcoming check-in packet, while parents will love Camp Hyatt's special room rates. Family room rates, children's menu (featuring "Big Fat Wizard Waffles" and "Monster Mashed Potatoes"), and weekend supervised activities are available with crafts, game-a-thons, puppet shows, treasure hunts, kite flying, and sand castle building (at resorts only). Programs are for children 3-15. Activities vary from hotel to hotel. Cost is $5 per hour or $25 per day/per child. As always, kids under 18 stay free in existing bed space in parents' room. Available at Hyatt Hotels and Resorts in the U.S., Canada, and the Caribbean.

INN OF THE MOUNTAIN GODS
P.O. Box 269
Mescalero, NM 88340
800-545-9011; 505-257-5141

This is an all-inclusive family resort atop the Sacramento Mountains of New Mexico, owned and managed by the Mescalero Apache tribe. Overlooking a lake (that's obscured in wintertime), it offers a relaxed ski program in the winter;

golf, tennis, skeet shooting, trout fishing, and horseback riding usually year-round.

KAHALA HILTON
5000 Kahala Ave.
Honolulu, HI 96816
808-734-2211
Brochure

Say aloha to Kamp Kahala where children ages 6–12 learn to weave flowers, hunt for buried treasure, and take field trips to Sea Life Park and the Honolulu Zoo. This special kids' program is available mid-June through August. Contact Ms. Hashimoto for more information. For other Hilton Hotels participating in children's programs, call toll-free (800) HILTONS—but not before you and your chlidren have tried a little hula dancing.

LA CASA DEL ZORRO
3845 Yacqui Pass Rd.
Borrego Springs, CA 92004
800-325-8274; 800-824-1884 (CA); 619-767-5323

Bed down family-style in these 2- and 3-bedroom *casitas* nestled in the Anza Borrego Desert, the largest state park in the continental United States. Enjoy a world of no pollution, no traffic jams, and no blaring boomboxes. Recreation for the entire family plus lots of educational opportunities for the children.

MARRIOTT CAMELBACK INN
5402 E. Lincoln Dr.
Scottsdale, AZ 85253
602-948-1700
Brochure

Parents and kids don't have to walk a mile to Marriott's Camelback Inn resort, golf club, and spa in Scottsdale, Arizona, but they should take advantage of the Hopalong College on weekends from Memorial Day through Labor Day. Morning program is from 8:00 A.M. to noon and includes breakfast, pitch 'n' putt golf, scavenger hunts, and swimming ($12 per child). Evening program is from 5:30 P.M. to 9:00 P.M. with arts and crafts, games, movies, TV, and dinner for $13.50 per child. Available for children ages 5–12. (Children can enjoy either program or both.) Call for accommodation rates. For other Marriott Hotels participating in kids' programs, call toll-free (800) 228-9290.

RITZ-CARLTON HOTEL/BOSTON
15 Arlington St.
Boston, MA 02117
617-536-5700
Brochure

This luxury hotel boasts a "Junior Presidential Suite" with pampering (we're not talking diapers here!) and all the creature comforts of home—and then some. Decorated in bright primary colors and adjoining the parents' room, the kids' room comes with tot-sized furniture and bathroom fixtures (including a 2-foot-high sink), TV, VCR, closets with low garment bars, and special-sized robes for the evening. There are also side trips to a children's museum, a computer museum, aquarium and whale watching, as well as Teddy Bear Tea Time. Who could ask for anything more? Rates on this pint-sized penthouse: $395 for kids' suite sleeping 3 to 4 children. Call toll-free 800-241-3333 to find out about other programs and participating hotels.

ROYAL SONESTA HOTEL
5 Cambridge Parkway
Cambridge, MA 02142
617-491-3600

Enjoy a fun-filled program at this Boston hotel's weekend Summerfest available from June through September. Fri. noon–8:00 P.M.; Sat.–Sun. 10:00 A.M.–6:00 P.M. for children ages 5-12. As a special summer incentive, there is no extra cost for children as long as parents are registered guests. Activities include swimming classes and horseshoes, even free bikes for parents and kids to ride along the Commons. Just don't park them unattended in Harvard Yard.

SCHLITTERBAHN RESORTS & WATERPARK
400 N. Liberty
New Braunfels, Texas 78130
512-625-2351

There are two reasons kids like to go to New Braunfels. One is to shop at New Braunfels Mill Store Plaza (ha, ha), and the other is to go tubing. Yes, tubers head for the Hill Country of Texas to the first water theme park to offer natural river tubing. Though the tube chubes have been the park's most popular attraction, there are two new kinds of tubing to try: river tubing on the Comal River rapids next to the park, and tube surfing on the Boogie Bahn. Staying overnight with the kids is a cheap thrill. The Schlitterbahn Resort "at the Bahn" is a motel offering a night's sleep from $46 (2-person double bed) to one-bedroom cottages with kitchen for four for $100. Jacuzzi suites, two with fireplace from $110/day double occupancy to $1008/week for 6 people. No charge for children under 6. Write or call 305 W. Austin,

New Braunfels, TX 78130, 512-625-5510. The Schlitterbahn Resort "at the Rapids" motel costs $60 for 2; duplexes for 5, $100; two-bedroom suite for 5, $110. Write 370 W. Lincoln, New Braunfels, TX 78130, 512-620-9010.

ITT SHERATON INNS
Corporate Office: 60 State St.
Boston, MA 02109
617-367-3600
800-325-3525 (brochure and reservations)
Brochure (full-color)

At ITT Sheraton Inns, Fundays are a surefire way to enjoy the heat of the night. Keep it all in the family: kids under 18 stay free (including breakfast). Convert the long, hot summer into fundays with a stay at a Sheraton Inn. From sea to shining sea, Sheratons worldwide are a good bet to bed down with when traveling with kids. Some highlights of the chain include:

SHERATON CAVALIER INN
2620 - 32nd Ave. NE
Calgary, Alberta, Canada T1Y 6B8
403-291-0107
403-291-2834 (fax)
Brochure (full-color)

If you're planning a visit to Calgary, Canada, stampede your way to the Sheraton Cavalier. Whoa! Before you register, take a gander at the skyline view and the breathtaking Rocky Mountains. This hotel offers a swimming pool with two giant indoor waterslides, a kiddies' pool, and arcade games rolled into one child-centered complex. Food outlets cater to kids' tastes with special menus and coloring pages in the Coffee Garden, and a special Sunday brunch in Lily's Dining Room. Brunch bonanza includes: pizza, hot dogs, chocolate milk, cookies, and jelly beans. Call for accommodation rates and reservations (weekend family fates available upon request).

SHERATON LAKESIDE INN
7769 W. Irlo Bronson Memorial Hwy. (US 192)
Kissimmee, FL 34746-9408
407-239-7919; 407-828-8250
407-828-8250, Ext. 7888 (fax)
Brochure (full-color)

This little gem is parked right next door to Walt Disney World's main gate . . . talk about convenience! Sheraton Lakeside Inn offers Herbie's Kids Club (Herbie is an alligator), a fully supervised children's club program, and doesn't charge a dime for taking you for a ride. Children's activities from 3:00 P.M. to 9:00 P.M. Tues.-Fri., and 11:30 A.M. to 5:00 P.M. Sat. All children entering the clubroom must sign in and out. Games, movies, and arts and crafts are available with a special appearance by Herbie. (Free membership to Herbie's Birthday Club—birthday letter, membership card, and room discounts.) Program is for children 5-12 (4 and under are welcome with accompanying adult). In-room hotel baby-sitting service by "Fairy Godmother" (up to 3 children per single family—$6 per hour; 4-hour minimum, combined family—$5 per hour/per family). Call for accommodation rates and reservations.

SHERATON WAIKIKI
2255 Kala Kaua Ave.
Honolulu, HI 96815
808-922-4422
Brochure (full-color)

Do you know what "Keiki" means in Hawaiian? According to the people at the Sheraton Waikiki, it means "Kids Summer Program," and that means fun in the sun for children 5-12.

This Aloha program (available June 16–Aug. 31) includes beach activities, evening movies, daily excursions to the aquarium, and a museum (nominal charge for excursions) and even a candy lei on arrival. Rates and accommodations to suit every budget and taste. Call for specifics.

SUPERCLUBS
Boscobel Beach Resort
Ochio Rios, Jamaica
800-858-8009, Ext. 201 (reservations, or see your travel agent)

Take them. They're yours. And they're free! What could be better than this equal opportunity for kids and parents to have equal fun under the sun. Up to two children, under 14, may share your suite—including supervised sports, arts and crafts, computer science, and SuperNannies, for babies. Let them do their thing. You do yours. Golf, tennis, sailing, windsurfing, scuba diving, nightly entertainment, disco . . . it's all on the house. These all-inclusive vacations are beginning to rival traditional kids' camps or vacation destinations like Disneyland. Try it. You'll like it.

WESTIN LA PALOMA
3800 E. Sunrise Drive
Tucson, AZ 85718
602-742-6000

The Westin La Paloma in Tucson, Arizona, offers the Children's Lounge, a supervised area for kids 6 months–12 years, and is open Sun.–Thurs. 8:00 A.M.–5:00 P.M.; Fri.–Sat. 8:00 A.M.–9:00 P.M. Primarily a daycare facility, there are the basics: coloring books, toys, and puzzles for $3/hour. Summer months bring the Kactus Kids Klub, a Monday-through-Saturday camp program from 8:00 A.M. to 3:00 P.M. for children ages 5-12. Activities include sports like swimming and tennis, arts and crafts, and lunch for $15. One staff member for every eight kids.

Ranches

AVERILL'S FLATHEAD LAKE LODGE
P.O. Box 248
Bigfork, MT 59911
406-837-4391

This lodge has been in the Averill family since 1945 and offers families from far away a lodge facility and rustic cottages clustered around a crystal-clear lake in the northern Rockies. This 2,000-acre dude ranch could be just what the doctor ordered. Ride, swim, boat, waterski, fish, enjoy a rodeo, even get into the swing of things with a barn dance. Children enjoy similar activities plus nature walks, arts and crafts, and their own rodeo.

EL RANCHO STEVENS
P.O. Box 495
Gaylord, MI 49735
517-732-5090

For fifty years, Candy and "Doc" Stevens have operated this Michigan dude ranch, including a supervised summer program for kids 6 and older. Enjoy the countryside with a horseback ride, fishing, boating, square dancing, a hayride, and a cookout just like you did . . . how many years ago?

JJJ WILDERNESS RANCH
P.O. Box 310
Augusta, MT 59410
406-562-3653

Triple your pleasure at the JJJ Ranch, 5,500 feet up in the Rocky Mountains, where you can get in touch with the wilderness. Join in a fall hunt for elk and deer, enjoy horseback riding and pack trips, hike and fish 'til the sun sets. Kids are especially welcome.

ROCKING HORSE RANCH
Highland, NY 12528
800-647-2624; 914-691-2927

City slickers won't have to travel very far if they're from New York City. This Hudson Valley ranch and resort is just 90 minutes from Manhattan. Kids have their own day camp, activities, and special "night patrol" while their parents are busy with a million activities such as waterskiing, swimming, downhill skiing, horseback riding, or just relaxing.

WHITE STALLION RANCH
9251 W. Twin Peaks Road
Tucson, AZ 85743
800-782-5546; 602-297-0252

Neither the television show "Twin Peaks" nor the movie *The Black Stallion* bear any resemblance to the serenity of this Southwest ranch. No crowded spaces within the 3,000 acres of desert blooms. Spanish-style cottages are your retreat from a day filled with horseback riding, rodeos, nature walks, swimming, and cookouts.

Category Index

Magazines and Newspapers

Maternity

Museums

Company Index

FOR THE BEST IN PAPERBACKS, LOOK FOR THE (🐧)

In every corner of the world, on every subject under the sun, Penguin represents quality and variety—the very best in publishing today.

For complete information about books available from Penguin—including Pelicans, Puffins, Peregrines, and Penguin Classics—and how to order them, write to us at the appropriate address below. Please note that for copyright reasons the selection of books varies from country to country.

In the United Kingdom: For a complete list of books available from Penguin in the U.K., please write to *Dept E.P., Penguin Books Ltd, Harmondsworth, Middlesex, UB7 0DA*.

In the United States: For a complete list of books available from Penguin in the U.S., please write to *Dept BA, Penguin*, Box 120, Bergenfield, New Jersey 07621-0120.

In Canada: For a complete list of books available from Penguin in Canada, please write to *Penguin Books Canada Ltd, 10 Alcorn Avenue, Suite 300, Toronto, Ontario, Canada M4V 3B2*.

In Australia: For a complete list of books available from Penguin in Australia, please write to the *Marketing Department, Penguin Books Ltd, P.O. Box 257, Ringwood, Victoria 3134*.

In New Zealand: For a complete list of books available from Penguin in New Zealand, please write to the *Marketing Department, Penguin Books (NZ) Ltd, Private Bag, Takapuna, Auckland 9*.

In India: For a complete list of books available from Penguin, please write to *Penguin Overseas Ltd, 706 Eros Apartments, 56 Nehru Place, New Delhi, 110019*.

In Holland: For a complete list of books available from Penguin in Holland, please write to *Penguin Books Nederland B.V., Postbus 195, NL-1380AD Weesp, Netherlands*.

In Germany: For a complete list of books available from Penguin, please write to *Penguin Books Ltd, Friedrichstrasse 10-12, D-6000 Frankfurt Main 1, Federal Republic of Germany*.

In Spain: For a complete list of books available from Penguin in Spain, please write to *Longman, Penguin España, Calle San Nicolas 15, E-28013 Madrid, Spain*.

In Japan: For a complete list of books available from Penguin in Japan, please write to *Longman Penguin Japan Co Ltd, Yamaguchi Building, 2-12-9 Kanda Jimbocho, Chiyoda-Ku, Tokyo 101, Japan*.